To James.

Thank you for the
introduction to W.H. Smiths
"Keen low Move Fast"

Mad Marty.

ULTIMATE SURVIVOR

The Making of a Madman

Martin Edwards

Scratching Shed Publishing Ltd

Trecerus Industrial Estate, Padstow,
Cornwall PL28 8RW
www.tjbooks.co.uk

For Theresa, without whom I would not be here,
and Sophia, whose smile is my medication.
And for my lost comrades,
Dave Bruin, Jay and Graham Dyer.

All profits from the sale of this book will be donated to charities supporting military mental health and vulnerable children

ONE

Whenever I tell people that I was born in the town of Rhyl, which is situated on the north-east coast of Wales, my words are usually met with either a look of mild distaste – the kind you make when your dog lets one go – or an ill-advised comment such as, 'Rhyl? That's a right shithole.'

While I'm deciding what to do with the poor idiot who has unwisely decided to disrespect the town of my birth, and therefore my country, which I will not tolerate, I proceed to inform them that until the 1970s, which was some time after my childhood, Rhyl was one of the most prosperous seaside towns in Britain, and although it might have fallen on hard times recently it's still extremely dear to me.

All right, dickhead?

The look of panic that usually follows one of my educational tirades, which are invariably growled as opposed to spoken, is a picture, and is usually followed by a few hastily thought-up questions about what Rhyl was like when I was a child and why I thought it had gone downhill.

'Oh, *that* Rhyl! Oh yes, I've heard it's lovely!'

Now placated, and so less likely to attack, I then begin to engage with their pathetic attempts at backtracking; all the time staring at them menacingly, as if to say, 'Slag off my town or my country again and I'll rip off your head and shit down your neck.'

The thing is, what I always tell these nervous idiots about Rhyl is actually true. From the late 1940s onwards – when the British working classes began receiving, to quote the film title, *Holidays with Pay* – towns such as Rhyl, Scarborough and Blackpool went from being frequented by the generally well-to-do, for either a day trip or a long weekend, to being literally invaded by hundreds of thousands of factory workers who, for the first time ever, had been able to afford to take their families away with them for an entire week. Suddenly, these previously rather genteel seaside towns had become full-on, working-class holiday resorts. Residential homes were turned into boarding houses and before you knew it the annual population of these places had at least trebled.

When I was born, in 1955, Rhyl was arguably at its peak and so in that respect it was a great place to grow up. With so many people descending upon the town all throughout the summer, the local children, should they be arsed, would be almost guaranteed an income by carrying cases to and from the train and bus stations. Sixpence was the accepted tariff. How the hell we didn't end up developing diabetes or becoming toothless on account of the amount of sweets we bought each day, I'll never know.

Unfortunately, and I mean unfortunately, the happiness and prosperity that Rhyl enjoyed back then was completely at odds with my life at home. In fact, the unfortunate situation the town finds itself in today –

something a great many of these once proud seaside towns are experiencing, more's the pity – is far more akin to how things were in the Edwards household.

Home was a bog-standard pebble-dashed council house on the Gwalia Avenue estate, which is a mile from the beach and about half that from the train station. The houses on the estate hadn't long been built when I was born and consisted mainly of three-bedroom semis and terraces of six, which had alleys running between each of them. Our house, which was number 11, was a three-bedroom end-of-terrace abode and, in addition to a lawn and a few flowerbeds at the front, we had a large-ish garden at the back with a few trees at the end. These days you can buy a three-bedroom semi on the Gwalia Avenue Estate for less than a hundred grand, but back then they were about as sought after as a council house can be.

On paper, our family was dead ordinary: a husband who worked on the railways, a mother who was a home-maker and a dinner lady, and two children: me and my brother, Tony, who was three years my senior. When I say on paper, what I mean is that although we were a fairly stereotypical working-class family with regards to numbers, jobs and our social situation, when it came to things like behaviour, we broke the mould. Or at least one of us did.

My father, the son of a merchant seaman, was a control freak who, as well as micro-managing every facet of our lives, had a habit of practising extreme violence upon those he was supposed to love and protect, i.e. me and Tony.

My mother, who hailed from Borehamwood in Hertfordshire, wasn't allowed either to see or speak to anybody without my father's express permission. As is so often the way in these unfortunate situations, she gradually became complicit in his behaviour and, as well as weighing in occasionally, which was upsetting, she eventually seemed not to care. What's unfortunate here, although not nearly as unfortunate as the end result of my parents' actions, is that it could all have been so incredibly different.

Before meeting my father, my mother had been going out with an Italian immigrant who, at the time, went by the name of Carmine Forte. He had an ice-cream parlour on the front in Rhyl and was a bit of a man-about-town. Several years later Carmine changed his name to Charles. Anybody over the age of about forty will probably already have realised that the man I'm talking about is *the* Charles Forte, later Baron Forte of Ripley in the county of Surrey, who went on to become one the biggest hotel proprietors in the world. Unlike my father – at least, as far as I know – Charles Forte didn't take pleasure from beating the living shit out of his children or preventing his eventual wife from seeing her family and friends. In fact, according to a distant relative of his called Max who I go walking with and who will crop up later on, he was a very nice bloke.

God knows why but for some unknown reason my mother ended up ditching the aspiring billionaire baron in favour of a violent control freak who, as well as having a weak chest, didn't have a pot to piss in. As decisions go that was probably up there with Neville Chamberlain deciding that Adolf Hitler was actually quite a nice guy, or the prat from Decca turning down the Beatles.

Most people assumed that my father, who was about 5 foot 6 and, for want of a better description, looked like an Arab with a big nose, was some kind of erratic pisshead who had been drinking since he was six. In actual fact he very rarely touched the stuff. His own father was an alcoholic – and a depressive, so I'm told – which I suppose counts for something. But although my grandfather was also violent towards my father I refute anyone who tries to use that as an excuse. My father spent years beating the shit out of me, but did I follow suit? No, I did not. I hear it all the time, 'abusers abuse', but that's complete and utter bollocks. I became violent. Far more violent than anything my father was ever capable of. And it doesn't take a genius to work out that his behaviour towards me was more than likely a contributing factor. The difference, though, is that instead of me taking it out on children or people who couldn't defend themselves, which is typical bullying behaviour, I tended to take it out on thugs, bullies and terrorists. Sometimes all three.

On a slightly lighter note, my father's side of the family were related to a very famous boxing family from Rhyl called the Gizzis. I'm pretty sure the Gizzis have some Romany heritage somewhere along the line, which might explain my father's skin colour, and Carl Gizzi – a heavyweight who was once the Welsh champion and who fought for the British Heavyweight Championship more than once – went up against several big-name fighters during his career including Ray Patterson, Jack Bodell and Joe Bugner, although not at the same time. His fight against Bugner, which happened in 1971 for the vacant British Heavyweight Championship, took place at the Royal Albert Hall so he was definitely big-time.

My earliest memory as a child is watching my grandmother, as in my mother's mother, smoking a cigarette in the house. My mother, by the way, is short – about 5 foot 3 – and, in her day, was incredibly beautiful. A lot like Elizabeth Taylor. I must have been about four at the time and my grandmother must have been granted permission to visit from Borehamwood. She and my grandfather hated my father. Everyone did.

I think the reason the smoking stayed with me is

because the process of taking one out of the packet, lighting it up and then producing smoke fascinated me, and I'd sit and watch her for hours. The only people who didn't smoke in those days were either spinsters or vicars, and because I didn't know many of them, I was always around smokers. Suffice to say that by the time I was eleven I was on five Park Drive a day, which I bought from a shop using money I stole from my father. I've never looked back since. A cough and a funny walk. That's me.

It's probably fair to say that my father wasn't the only one breaking behavioural moulds on Gwalia Avenue in the late 1950s and early 1960s as my own conduct left a lot to be desired. I can't quite remember whether this started because of or in spite of the actions of my father, but there are three events from my early childhood that stick out in my mind. Suffice to say that if I were a betting man, which I'm not, I'd have at least a quid on them being catalysts for what eventually came to pass.

The first of these events was my fifth birthday party, which we had in the back garden. For some reason (I'm pretty sure it was because I sulked for not winning pass-the-parcel) I got sent upstairs to my room, but instead of just leaving me there to cool off for a while and then calling me back down again, like any normal parent would, my father made me watch the entire party from my window and I ended up staying there for the rest of the day. I remember thinking to myself, *What a horrible thing to do.* I mean, why on earth would you do that?

A few weeks later I was swinging on the washing line in the back garden, as boys do, and without warning my mother came running out and broke a tennis racket over my back. Again, I remember thinking, *Why?* Parents didn't do that to their kids. Or at least, I didn't think they did.

The last of these events happened during the summer holidays that year while we were visiting my grandparents in Borehamwood. My father, the micro-managing control freak, obviously had to come with us and while we were out walking one day I fell into a lake. I forget how it happened, but I must have been arseing around – again, like boys do. After pulling me out of the lake my father dragged me into a public toilet and told me to strip off. While I was doing as I was told he started taking off his trousers and underpants and when he was done he threw his Y-fronts on the floor in front of me.

'Put them on, now,' he growled.

Stupidly, I decided to suggest an alternative course of action. After all, I was only wearing shorts, underpants and a T-shirt and it was boiling outside.

'But Dad,' I began, 'can't I just keep my pants on and dry my shorts and T-shirt in the sun? It won't take long.'

He didn't say anything but the way he looked at me suggested that if I didn't do exactly what he'd asked within ten seconds flat he was going to make me wish I'd never been born. Funnily enough, he used to succeed at that quite a lot.

After handing him my wet clothes I put on his Y-fronts (which were obviously far too big and had to be held up constantly) and followed him out of the toilet. For the rest of the day I was pointed at and laughed at by probably hundreds of people and by the time we got off the bus I was completely demoralised, which was probably the idea. What I remember most about that episode is feeling my faith in him as a parent beginning to deteriorate. I was losing all feeling for him.

Looking back, I think the issue that welded these events together and gradually began to alter my behaviour was the fact that my brother, Tony, who was academically gifted, was openly venerated by my parents. Although he would later suffer at their hands too, while I was having tennis rackets broken across my back and being made to wear nothing but underpants in public, he was being sent on school trips. If you start treating a child of five or six in such a way, what little amount of self-confidence they might have built up during their short life is going to disappear very quickly; that's to say nothing of their sense of self-worth.

I was made to feel like I didn't really exist. Not all the time, but enough to make me react by behaving like a twat at school. Unfortunately, this switched my father's behaviour from being cruel to being violent and once he'd started, there was no stopping him. There are obviously ways of dealing with badly behaved children, but when the parents themselves are ultimately the ones to blame, I'm afraid you're fucked.

The biggest shame here, apart from the violence itself, is the fact that I actually enjoyed school and showed quite a bit of promise right from day one. I perhaps wasn't quite as academically gifted as Tony (art was more my thing), but had I been educated without a monkey on my back (or in this case, the end of my father's belt) I could have done really well. More importantly, though, I might have had a more normal, and even perhaps enjoyable, childhood.

What drew even more attention to my behaviour at school was the fact that my mum was a dinner lady there, and so she got to hear all the gory details first hand. Also, because we lived in quite a tight little community, I quickly became an embarrassment to her, and subsequently to my father. On the few occasions that my mother wasn't at school when the shit hit the fan, a letter would be sent home. Posted, usually, although sometimes they were daft enough to hand them to me to deliver by hand. Oh aye, of course, I will. You leave it to me! Unfortunately, that only happened once or twice so they must have cottoned on. The bastards.

I don't remember the first couple of beatings my father gave me for the simple reason I wasn't expecting them. They just happened. What changed and made them memorable was the element of expectation, which generated fear. A lot of fear. It was my dear mother who first came up with the idea. A flash of inspiration. I remember the first time as clear as day. A letter had arrived in the post from school – wishing me well, obviously – and by the time I arrived home at about 3.45 p.m. she'd read the contents and was ready for me.

'Right you,' she shouted, waving the letter in my face. 'Go and stand in the parlour facing the wall. And you can stay there until your father gets home. He'll deal with you.'

To some, that may seem like a standard parental response to their child's misbehaviour, but my father would come home any time from about 8 p.m. until midnight, which meant I'd have to stand there for anything up to eight hours. On this occasion he turned up about half past ten so I was there for over six. There was no food or drink, by the way. Nothing. Nor was I allowed to visit the bog. There was also no heating in the parlour, as the only fire we had was in the lounge. In the end, I pissed myself and when my mother spotted the pool on the floor she warned me that not only would it be added to my list of crimes but that I would be punished accordingly.

What always signalled my father's return was the sound of his motorbike pulling into the avenue.

'Right, get upstairs to your room,' said my mother. 'Your father's home.'

As I sat on the end of my bed I remember wondering, and worrying, what he was going to do. I'd been belted before, just as I imagine every kid in the land had, but the atmosphere now was different. It was serious. Shortly after the back door had been opened my parents started talking and as the conversation went on my father's voice became louder. This amplified the worry, but it was his ascent up the stairs that put the fear of God into me.

Because my father had a bad chest he used to wheeze a lot and in that particular situation it sounded quite unnerving, like something out of a horror film. Then, when he was about halfway up I heard him take his belt off. On future occasions this was my cue for praying that he'd use the strap end of the belt as opposed to the buckle, but this time I just felt very scared. When he finally reached my room he was clutching the strap end of the belt and the buckle was swinging from side to side by his knees.

'Right you. Take your shirt off,' he said.

After doing as I was told he went straight for me, but as opposed to just standing there I instinctively ran into the corner of the room, turned around and then faced him. He had me cornered now and as he walked forward and swung the belt over his shoulder I bent forwards and put my hands over my head. This too was done by instinct, but it was just as futile. A second later I felt a piercing pain right in the middle of my back and before I could try and move out of the way I felt another. The second strike brought me down to my knees and I knew, once again, instinctively, that the sensible thing to do was to just let him get on with it. I'd just turned six when this happened, which was about a year after the worm had started to turn. In that time things had been deteriorating but I never thought for a moment it would turn into this. I knew he was a bastard. I just didn't realise how big.

The beating, which lasted about two or three minutes,

was mainly confined to my back (something that I later realised was intentional as it meant nobody could see the injuries) and each blow was punctuated with a verbal warning about what would happen if I did it again. By the time he'd finished I was in agony, but I didn't cry. Funnily enough, despite being very young I think I already had an inkling as to why he was doing this. I can only now put it into words but I think my father wanted to humiliate me, just as he had in Borehamwood and at my birthday party. Me crying, in any situation, merely accentuated that humiliation and so not doing so was my only means of attack. Or defence, for that matter.

When my father had finally had enough – or, should I say, when he hadn't the breath to hit me any more – he told me to take off the rest of my clothes. 'Run a bath for him,' he shouted down to my mother. It was getting on for 11 p.m. by now and it was only when I was in the bath that I realised why he wanted me to have one. Although it wasn't terribly hot, the moment the water touched my back I felt an overwhelming stinging pain, as though I was being stabbed. By the time my father had finished beating me the pain had begun to subside because my back had become numb. Now, as the feeling came back again, so did the pain, and the water, although eventually soothing, was at first like a conductor. Almost sixty years on, I can count on the fingers of one hand the amount of times I've felt pain like that and the same applies when it comes to having a bath. And this is from a man who has been knifed, shot, gored, trampled and has had more bones broken than an accident-prone jockey. I still didn't cry though. I was desperate to, but I didn't. I wasn't going to give that bastard the satisfaction.

After being in the bath for about a minute, I suddenly noticed that the water was starting to turn pink. I had no idea what it was at first, which was probably down to my age. Blood's dark red and it just didn't occur to me. It was only when I looked behind, where the water was a lot darker, that I realised I was bleeding.

By the time I got out of the bath the bleeding had stopped, thank God, as if I'd bloodied one of the towels I'd have no doubt been in for round two. I was absolutely starving when I got into bed, but I didn't dare ask for anything to eat. I also couldn't sleep, which is hardly surprising, and had to lie on my front for about two weeks afterwards.

The following morning nothing at all was said. As with my father, my relationship with my mother had changed and her maternal instincts, such as they were, only ever appeared when my father was out of both sight and mind. When he wasn't there, she'd occasionally become maternal. Warm, even. Then, after a few minutes, she'd remember who she'd become – and who she was married to – and would suddenly revert to type. At first, I used to build my hopes up when she became warm again, but after a while I knew exactly what was going to happen so I stopped responding. This would bring her around even quicker and as time went on these maternal moments eventually stopped. In that respect, my father had won the day as he'd finally deprived me of my mother. Or, at least the mother I originally had. Don't get me wrong. My mother wasn't always horrible to me. She just wasn't at all motherly. It's also fair to say that the person she had become since marrying my father was, in part, down to him. Or at least that's my theory.

What I find difficult to come to terms with is the fact that despite her knowing what would happen when she informed my father what I'd been up to, she almost delighted in doing so. It was like a victory, almost. She was also the one who started the whole *Wait in the corner for eight hours* bollocks. She didn't have to do that, nor did she have to stand around while he beat me till I bled. There are obviously scores of women in abusive relationships who do horrible things out of fear, but this was different. My mother was complicit right from the word go and had she been given the opportunity to bring it all to an end – my behaviour included – I'm honestly not sure she would. As sad as it undoubtedly is, cruelty can be strangely addictive.

When I arrived at school on the day after the beating my head was all over the place. I was on the road to becoming pretty fucked up, both physically and mentally. Because of the pain, I found it difficult to walk normally and spent the entire day trying to protect my back from any kind of contact. Well, not the entire day. I did find time to write 'FUCK OFF JAMPOT' all over the toilet walls. Jampot was the nickname of the headmaster and when he saw it he went apeshit, as well he might. Unfortunately, my mother was still at work so as opposed to receiving a letter from Jampot she heard about it first-hand. As ideas go this was bordering on being foolish, even for me, and I couldn't even begin to tell you why I did it. Junior masochism, perhaps? I expect a psychiatrist could give you an explanation, but I'm afraid I'm at a loss. Needless to say, the evening that awaited me was a carbon copy of the previous one and after arriving home I was sent to stand in the parlour facing the wall. After managing not to piss myself this time I was eventually sent to my room. Then, once the wheezing old bastard had made it home and up the stairs he beat the shit out of me, careful to avoid striking any previous injuries, which was kind of him.

The reason I'm being slightly flippant is because I don't want to be too maudlin. I often switch from being angry and upset about what happened in my childhood to being angry and philosophical; the catalyst being my grandchildren. Seeing them, which I do most days, makes me realise how lucky I am and for as long as they are there the sadness will go away. The anger's still there, though. It would take a stadium full of psychiatrists and a canyon full of pills to sort that out. Still, it's better than being completely fucked up full time.

TWO

When I was about ten years old I decided to run away from home. I don't think there was a specific catalyst. A culmination of long-term abuse and misery, I suppose.

What was it I just said about not being maudlin?

In order to fund my adventure I decided to nick my brother's Post Office book and the first thing I did after wiping out his account was to buy myself a flick knife. As you do. Even now, I'm not sure what I was going to do with it. It would be very easy for me to say that I was going to use it on my father, but I can't say that for sure. It was probably an act of defiance and self-preservation mixed in with an underlying yearning to damage the person who'd abused me. That sounds plausible. I have to say it looked great though!

After a few hours, like most kids who run away from home, my rumbling stomach got the better of me and I decided that, as hideous as it was there, that was where I should be. I felt quite bad about pinching Tony's Post Office book because despite the fact that he was my parent's favourite and hadn't been abused – yet – I liked him. When my father saw the flick knife he went ballistic and asked me where I'd got it.

'I found it,' I told him.

'No you didn't. Get upstairs, now'.

The beating I received was biblical. Worse than anything he'd dished out previously.

The following morning Tony found his Post Office book (I'd put it back after returning home) and when he realised that it had been emptied he naturally told my parents. Now, for some unknown reason their suspicions turned immediately to me. I denied it, of course, and even tried to tell them that it must have been Tony as the signatures in the withdrawals column were all the same. You see, I told you I was good at art! I'm a demon forger.

Instead of just beating the living shit out of me my father decided to call the Post Office fraud department and the following day two men appeared. After examining Tony's Post Office book they questioned me and the interview lasted about a minute. A decent forger I may have been, but unfortunately I was a shit liar and so I just confessed. From my father's point of view, this course of action wasn't about finding out the truth. It was about humiliation. He knew I'd done it. He also knew I'd own up to it.

Once the Post Office police had left I was told to get upstairs and you don't have to be a genius to work out what happened next. This was double bubble for the old man. Humiliation *and* a beating. It's a wonder he didn't send me a thank-you letter.

That Post Office book wasn't the first thing I'd pinched. I think I've always been a bit of a kleptomaniac and even today if I go and stay at a house somewhere I'll always nick something from it. I've got to have something. One of the last things I nicked was a Church's shoehorn, as in the footwear manufacturer, from a house that was on sale close to ours in Yorkshire. We were looking at buying the place and when I went into the utility room I saw it hanging there on a hook. *You're mine now*, I thought, and I slipped it into my pocket.

My time away from home and school when I was young was mainly spent working at the Marine Lake Fun Fair. We used to get two sets of clothes a year, which were bought with a Provident cheque and always from the same shop. So, if I wanted anything else I always had to buy it myself. I used to work twelve hours a day at the fair but instead of doing anything glamorous like working on the dodgems or dishing out the candy floss, one of my main jobs was doing laundry for some old bastard who lived on site. In terms of personal hygiene he left a lot to be desired and, apart from cleaning out the bogs, it was probably one of the worst jobs going. Even so, because I worked there seven days a week I got a good whack – £3 every Saturday – and because I was pinching at least another £10 – at a conservative estimate – I was minted.

The extra tenner used to come from working the hoops, as in payment for me cleaning his undies the old man used to let me run the stall and take the money. Well, I never let him down. I ran the stall *and* I took the money – home! I had to give some to my mother for extra clothes but neither she nor the old bastard I called my father had an inkling I was on the rob. It was a rare victory.

I think that what people now call the consumerist throw-away society actually started with me because once I'd gorged myself on sweets I used to buy a load of shit I didn't need and then just throw it away. I couldn't take it home, for obvious reasons, so I used to just chuck it. I remember buying a red jumper once and when I was about a hundred yards from home I threw it over a fence. It was like sticking two fingers up to my parents.

One of the unluckiest experiences I ever had in my early childhood happened on a Friday night when I was sent out to get the crisps and shandy. Having a packet of cheese and onion crisps and a bottle of Corona shandy on a Friday night was the highlight of my domestic week and however hard or however much the old man hit me I always derived enough pleasure and excitement from this to get me through the week. Well, that and a few cigarettes. One day, as I was walking to the shop to make the purchase I dropped the money I'd been given down a drain. Knowing what would probably happen I just sat there for about two hours wondering what the hell to do. In the end, the old man came looking for me and when he found me he asked me what I was doing. I was sitting right next to where I'd dropped it and pointed towards the drain.

'The money you gave me fell in there, Dad,' I said. 'It was an accident. Honest.'

After being called a liar and one or two other things he dragged me home and, yes, you guessed it, told me to get upstairs. At least he was consistent.

I should point out that despite the above we led quite a normal family life, in that we went on holiday and did things that normal families did, like having crisps and shandy on a Friday night. We just had a very dark secret. Heroin addicts and alcoholics often go on for years without anyone knowing about their addiction, and in that respect we were exactly the same. People knew that my old man was a control freak and an arsehole, but they had no idea about how this manifested itself.

We had a holiday on a narrowboat once and my father, who was a keen fisherman, had been told by my mother that he wasn't allowed to bring his maggots on the boat. On the first evening, while I was in bed, I suddenly started itching like fuck. When I got up and turned the light on I realised that I was covered in maggots!

After screaming my head off for a few seconds my mother ran in and on witnessing the scene she told me to put on my wellies and go to the galley. It turned out my father had smuggled his maggots onto the boat in – wait for it – my fucking wellies, so when I began to slide my feet in I got the surprise of my life. I will never, ever forget that for as long as I live.

Because of the way things usually went I assumed I was in for a hiding but fortunately it was my father who got it in the neck. Not literally, more's the pity, but she bawled him out for about half an hour.

It was about this time that I took the eleven-plus and believe it or not I pissed it and won a place at Rhyl Grammar School. I definitely got my brains from my mother's side of the family. Her mother, Dorothy, the woman who taught me to smoke, was very bright and her husband, my grandpa, had been a headmaster. Their daughter, Barbara, was a librarian when I was young and their eldest son, David, was an insurance broker and a playwright who worked for the BBC. At the very top of the pile, though, at least from my point of view, was their youngest son Peter, who was an artist and graphic designer. Peter and I got on well together and he eventually became my saviour.

Incidentally, Carol Vorderman's brother, Anton, was in my class at school. They lived just around the corner from us and as far as I know they also had it rough.

It was my dream at school to become an art teacher. To be honest, I was good at most of the subjects at school but because I found the work quite easy I didn't have to try and so never really had much interest. It was the same with art, in that it came naturally, but the results both excited and fascinated me. They also made me feel like I'd achieved something, which was a rarity. My art teacher at the grammar school was called Miss Watson. We used to call her UHU because whenever the opportunity arose where something needed sticking she'd bring out the UHU glue. She was mad on the stuff. The woman who'd introduced me to art in the first place was a teacher at primary school called Mrs Mallalieu. Believe it or not she was addicted to the old fashioned throat lozenges. I know it sounds daft but her teeth were all brown and she reeked of them. Eat a packet of those and you're flying!

Miss Watson was also my form teacher at Rhyl Grammar and about once a week, after she'd taken registration, I'd wait until the classroom had cleared and then hide in the book cupboard. This was situated behind UHU's desk and as well as running the entire width of the classroom it was at least 4-foot deep. It was full of medical books for some reason and as well as building myself a fort with these books I'd also rip the pages out and write lewd comments all over them. Nobody ever found me and I was as happy as a pig in shit.

Another teacher at the grammar school, called Mr Williams, had a glass eye and whenever he had to leave the classroom he'd take it out, put it in a glass of water on his desk and say, 'I'm just popping out for a second, but remember, I'm keeping my eye on you!' Funny fucker.

After being there about a year, Rhyl Grammar School was turned into a normal comprehensive. I think it was because the local comprehensive school was oversubscribed and so instead of building another comp they decided to expand the grammar school and downgrade it. Academically,

I'd fired on all cylinders in that first year and despite spending about a fifth of my time in the book cupboard I'd still managed to attain about 98 per cent in every subject. From year two onwards, however, everything started to go downhill because I was far more at home among the rough arses than I was among the scholarly types and the school was now full of them. All of a sudden, instead of having my ear clipped for being cheeky every so often, I was being caned four or five times a week for smoking. The teachers must have hated me. My language too left a lot to be desired and I followed up writing 'Fuck off Jampot' on my exercise book and the toilet walls at primary school with a succession of artistic expressions that were written anywhere there was a space: classroom walls, textbooks, pupils' foreheads. I didn't give a fuck.

I don't think my parents even noticed that my school had been turned into a comp. By this time they'd had another child, a daughter called Joanna, and with Tony flying through his O levels my own academic situation simply didn't register. I also started being bullied around this time and, in hindsight, I'm not surprised as regardless of my behaviour I probably screamed 'victim'. Don't get me wrong, I didn't just lie down and let them walk all over me. Fuck no. I was a scrapper. It was always four or five against one though, so I nearly always came off worst. And, because of my reputation, I'd often get the blame. It wasn't just the pupils. In fact, the teachers were the biggest bullies of the lot. Let me give you an example. Sometime during that second year some stuff started going missing in the changing rooms and I knew who was doing it. It was a nasty little bandy-legged wanker called Mikey Brown and another dickhead called Stuart Cardone. The games teacher, a horrible man called Berwyn Evans, called me in one day and started accusing me.

'You know who did this, Edwards,' he said, 'and you're going to tell me.'

'I am not,' I said. 'I'm saying nothing.'

Evans then said that if I didn't tell him who had nicked the stuff he'd blame me and call the police, which was nice of him. The consequences of this course of action – in that I'd be absolutely fucked if he called the police – obviously wasn't lost on me, but before I gave him the information he wanted I needed some assurances.

'How do I know that you won't tell them I grassed?' I enquired.

'You'll just have to trust me,' he said. 'It'll be completely confidential though.'

To cut a long story short the culprits went to court and my name was read out – that's right, *read out* – as the person who'd offered the information. Subsequently, I must have received a battering from every scrote within a 20-mile radius. I couldn't go anywhere. Seriously, if I walked out of our house I would be accosted within five minutes, regardless of what time of day it was.

'You're a fucking grass, Edwards. We're going to kick your head in.'

Sometimes I managed to avoid getting a hammering by either running away, or, if they were just gobshites, kicking the shit out of them.

In desperation – I was only twelve – I tried to talk to my father but he was on their side. In fact, his exact words to me were, 'You grassed on them. You deal with it.' Tony tried helping me once or twice when I was being set upon but he wasn't happy with me either. In the eyes of everyone, I was a grass. This went on for about two years in all, although the fights did become less frequent after a year or so.

Whether this was a contributing factor or not I

couldn't say, but around this time – it was about six months after it happened – the shit at home started going up a level. In actual fact, it went down a level in terms of location as instead of sending me to my room for a thrashing I started being sent to the parlour. I don't think my father could be arsed going up the stairs any more as it almost killed him.

Unfortunately for me and my back, he kept his fishing rod in the parlour and during one particularly intense beating he dropped his belt after a couple of minutes and reached for the rod. The parlour was a lot bigger than my bedroom and by now I'd started dodging the blows. This meant I was a lot harder to strike and so the fishing rod made it easier for him to hit me and it inflicted more pain.

The first time he used the rod wasn't too bad, in that he was already knackered and didn't really catch me. The second time it happened, however, was a very different kettle of fish, if you'll pardon the pun. A letter had come home about my language in class and for some reason my mother had taken particular exception to this. Subsequently, when my father returned from work she all but encouraged him to go in there and teach me a lesson I'd never forget. Not that he ever needed encouraging. Beating me was almost a hobby.

When he came into the parlour I was standing facing the wall as usual and as soon as he'd closed the door he told me to get undressed. I did as I was told, leaving just my pants on.

'Right then,' he said, already breathing heavily. 'Stand in the corner and face the wall.'

Stupidly, I again did as I was told and about five seconds later I felt an incredible pain on the top of my back, just above my right shoulder blade. He must have stood to one side of me so that he could hit me diagonally and one of the eyes where the fishing line passes through, which are made of metal, pierced my skin. That wasn't the worst of it though. The rod itself hit the full width of my back a millisecond afterwards and the pain was indescribable. This was the first time I ever screamed when he hit me, and I genuinely prayed to God that he might leave it there. He didn't, and I turned around just in time to see him swing the rod back again. Unfortunately, it was too late to dodge, but at least I didn't get a metal eye this time. After that I spent the next three or four minutes running around the parlour like Gollum trying to dodge the rod, and, in particular, those metal eyes. About a year later he caught me with two eyes in one blow and it's the only time it ever made him stop, at least momentarily.

When I was thirteen I ran away from home again, except this time I got as far as Liverpool. Between this and the first time I ran away I must have done it about seven or eight times but I always ended up going back home, except for on one occasion. I had two friends at school, Ashley Francis Jones and Stephen Campini, and after running away one day I ended up at Ashley's auntie's house where Ashley, Stephen and I drank about an inch off all the spirit bottles in the house, and there were loads of them! We got absolutely shitfaced. That's why I can't drink spirits. If I smell whisky I throw up immediately.

Anyway, after that I went to sleep in his auntie's garden shed and to keep warm I collected some carpet remnants that were lying around and tried to make a fire with them – in the shed. You should have seen it go up. It was like a firework. And the smoke! With my digs now ablaze I made my way, quite quickly, as it goes, out of the shed and as far away as possible. Then I had an idea. About a year earlier I'd worked at some stables which were situated quite close to the house of Ashley's auntie and so I made my way there. The horses were still out and when I scrambled through the hedge into the paddock where they were kept the bastard things attacked me. I had never been as scared in my entire life. They'd always been very placid when I'd worked with them but now for some reason they were rabid. I now own a share in a racehorse and, bearing in mind my history with them, I must be daft.

The thing that gave me the confidence to make a proper stab of running away and venture as far as Liverpool was that I'd reached puberty. Well, that and the fact that I was ever so slightly pissed off with my home life. It's amazing what a fishing rod across your back, your balls dropping and a few strands of pubic hair can do.

The reason I chose Liverpool is that I often hung around with Scousers and tended to get on with them. They were my brother's friends mainly and would come down to Rhyl on scooters. The catalyst for me buggering off is comical, yet rather painful. I'd been caught smoking at school one day and subsequently a letter had been sent home to my parents. In an attempt to prevent a beating I got somebody to push the cricket roller over my hand; the idea being that if my hand was broken he'd let me off. This wasn't the first time I'd tried to injure myself – in the past I'd given myself black eyes in the hope that they would lead to somebody discovering the bruises and scars on my body. It didn't work.

In terms of logic the roller idea was pretty twisted, and it backfired spectacularly. You see, one thing I hadn't considered was that my father was now working as a school caretaker and so when I went home and told him that the cricket roller had gone over my hand (it only dislocated my fingers) he just looked at me and said, 'Bollocks. You did that deliberately.' The moment he said that I realised what a fucking idiot I'd been. First of all, how on earth does a cricket roller – something that is like a steamroller but without an engine – accidentally roll over somebody's hand? Being a caretaker in a school – a school with a cricket pitch – meant that he would be acutely aware that, unless the roller had been placed at the top of a hill and my hand glued to it halfway down, there was no way in the world that this could happen. Well, the best-laid plans of mice and men often go awry.

'When that bandage comes off,' he said, 'you're going to get the hiding of your life.'

To be honest that didn't resonate with me too much. What did resonate was when the bandages were removed. That's when I decided to scarper!

One of Tony's mates had said that he'd give me a lift to Liverpool on his scooter and so I chucked some things into a bag while my parents were out and away I went. The only thing I remember about the journey from Rhyl to Liverpool is passing an RAF base somewhere and he eventually dropped me outside a house.

'Go and see her,' he said. 'She'll look after you.'

When I knocked on the door this huge fat lady answered and she seemed to be expecting me. After showing me upstairs I dumped my stuff, went down to the kitchen and she gave me a plate of belly pork. Fuck me! That was almost as bad as the cocktail of alcohol I'd had at the house of Ashley's aunt. It had more hairs on it than there are on my arse and I can still taste the fat. Jesus!

I slept under a bed while I was there as I was shit scared of being found by my old man. This woman had kids of her own who were a bit older than me and I was put in their care. The eldest one was about seventeen and he used to like playing knuckles. Sorry, I meant he used to like playing knuckles with me. Talk about painful! This lad was a big bastard and within about two days my hands were black and blue.

The following morning they got me a job on the local Corona wagon passing pop bottles down to the bloke who was selling them and then once I'd finished that we went on the rob to Woolworths. Even at that age I could have given Raffles a run for his money. Once we'd nicked what they deemed to be a good haul we went to a school in Huyton to sell it. What a life! I was literally on the run at thirteen and being treated like some kind of useful fugitive.

Because I could fight, the kids of the family also started putting me up against some of their mates as – wait for it – the cock of Rhyl! I was more like a bantam than a cock. I think I was there for about two weeks in all and during that time nobody bullied me and nobody beat me up. Unless, of course, it was the result of a scrap, which I didn't mind. I was fed, watered and treated like a human being. It was fantastic.

My undoing was underwear, believe it or not. I'd run out and so decided to go and nick some from Woolworths. This was at a place called Pierhead and unfortunately the police did a swoop just as I was – in effect – changing my undies.

At first the police thought I was an absconder from a youth detention centre and they took me to the local police station. I was shoved in a cell in what resembled a dungeon and was in there with five or six proper hardcases. Luckily, because I'd been missing for so long a photograph had been circulated to all the stations and before any of these hardcases could get their hands on me one of the policemen recognised me, thank fuck, dragged me out and then called my parents. I think it's the only time I was ever pleased to see them. And I mean, the only time.

I still had to go to court because of the theft and

during the hearing the magistrate held up a 50-inch pair of Y-fronts that had been found in my possession when I'd been collared.

'Young man,' he said, 'do you honestly think that these would have fitted you? You could camp out in these.'

Unfortunately, an outsized pair of underpants weren't the only things I had on me and I ended up getting two years' probation. Afterwards, my parents took me for an apple pie and I can still remember my father's face. He was absolutely incandescent and I could tell that all he wanted to do was give me a hiding. I'd had a few weeks' grace, and a bit of fun, and I think he hated that. Strangely enough, the hiding I was expecting didn't materialise. I still can't work out why.

THREE

One thing I haven't touched on yet is drugs. Back then we used to take anything we could get our hands on but, in particular, we used to have something far more original than either acid or dope.

We had Benzedrex and sherry!

Benzedrex – or propylhexedrine to give it its unbranded name – is basically what's inside a congestion inhaler. We used to take out the propylhexedrine from the inhaler, swallow it, and then drink a load of sherry. I did this on the beach once and I swam a quarter of a mile out to sea and back again, in the middle of October. That's a very vivid memory. I was invisible. For about half an hour.

One thing I have to mention about secondary school is my lunch, as to this day I still believe it to be the lunch of champions. Each day – and I never once deviated – I used to get half a crown and I'd have a packet of cheese and onion crisps, two ounces of cheese and a packet of five Park Drive cigarettes, which I'd buy from a machine for one shilling.

Even today one of my big pleasures in life is a packet of cheese and onion crisps and a slab of cheddar. You can keep the Park Drive though. My lungs must be as black as coal as it is, so I'll have twenty Royals instead.

One of the most outrageous things I did in my early teens was to buy a half share in a Norton single cylinder ES2 motorcycle with a 500 cc engine. The lad who was doing it up was a friend of Ashley's and his mum was one of the dinner ladies at school. These days it would be worth thousands but me and the lad I bought it with, who was also a friend of Ashley's, paid fifteen quid for it. Fifteen quid for a newly refurbished Norton! The thing I remember most about it was the brass parts. It seemed to be covered in them. I got the money from my father, mainly. Only he never knew about it. Or the motorbike. Had he known about either he'd have gone off his rocker so we kept the bike at the house of the lad we'd bought it from.

My co-owner and I used to turn up whenever we liked and we'd take this thing out for a spin. I was about six stone wet through back then and me and this lad used to have to push the bike up against the wall just so we could get on. I remember going over a bridge close to our school once. I was driving and this lad was on the back and, when I looked down at the speedo, I saw we were just touching 80 mph. The fact that I was only thirteen and weighed the same amount as a few bags of sugar obviously didn't bother me then, but it does now. Even so, I still almost shat myself when I saw the speed we were going. We were literally clinging on for dear life. What a buzz!

A few days later, obviously believing I was the bastard son of John Surtees, I decided to take the Norton up to the Bee Hotel in St Asaph, about 7 miles away. That's where all the rockers used to go and I wanted to show off the bike.

After getting there and driving around the car park for a while looking incredibly cool I decided to ride home, and when I was about 4 miles outside Rhyl I passed a police car – very quickly. Not surprisingly the blue lights came on straight away and I remember thinking, *Oh fucking hell!*

I hadn't even considered what might happen if I got caught but now my mind was full of consequences. What's more, all of them hurt!

Without even thinking I skidded the bike into a farm and then hid behind a hedge. The noise I'd made had woken the farmer and within seconds he was standing over me.

'How the hell can you drive that?' he asked – quite understandably – pointing at the bike. 'Have you stolen it?'

'No!' I replied indignantly. 'I bought it. It's mine. Well, half of it is.'

Just then the police car pulled into the farm and so that was that. I was fucked.

Because I wasn't old enough to own a motorbike the police didn't believe me when I told them it was mine (although that wouldn't have made much difference given my age). I asked them to speak to the lad we'd bought it from, only he denied ever selling it to us and said we'd stolen it.

I got fifteen charges read against me in court. Fifteen! Apparently the police had been meaning to speak to me about some goods I'd purloined earlier and I was fined £15, which is what I'd paid for the bike. I think most people had found the underpants charge quite funny, which is perhaps why I didn't get a hiding. This was very different, though, not least because I could easily have killed somebody.

Not my finest moment.

*****

Ultimate Survivor

By this time we'd moved into a farmhouse situated on the grounds of the school where my father was caretaker. Life here became even more harrowing than the last place, both physically and psychologically. My brother, Tony, was fighting all kinds of personal issues and I know it sounds selfish but I found this very difficult. He was the only person I looked up to at home and seeing him suffer was like losing a limb. He too had become a bugger for the drugs and booze, and he was also struggling with his sexuality. Being gay or even bisexual was obviously a big issue in those days and the chances of you having an understanding ear at home were, in most cases, less than zero. Tony was bisexual, which in many ways made it worse as he was left in limbo. Imagine the confusion?

About the only good thing that ever happened at this place was when my father got a dog – a beautiful Dobermann pinscher named Zelda. I am a dog man through and through, and she and I were as thick as thieves. I think he'd bought her partly as a guard dog but whenever she showed the slightest bit of defiance he'd take her out into one of the stables and give her the same treatment as me. That broke my heart. By then I couldn't give two shits what he did to me but hearing that dog yelp was awful. It's funny, but if I ever tried to get Zelda off my bed she'd let out a growl and then look at me, as if to say, *If you try that again sunshine I'll take your fucking hand off!* Yet when my father got hold of her she would just submit. She could have killed him if she'd wanted to. If only.

Even as a teenager I used to wet the bed quite a lot. Whether due to embarrassment or an attack of pyromania, one day, after a particularly wet night, I decided to try and dry the mattress using a cigarette lighter. God knows how (perhaps it was something I'd drunk?) but while I was gently blowing down on the flame to get it as close to the mattress as possible the material suddenly caught alight. The mattress was soon in flames. Luckily for me there was nobody else in the house and I spent the next ten minutes running up and down the stairs fetching jugs of water. The smell was absolutely rancorous and afterwards not even Zelda would come in the room. In the end, my parents had to get me a new mattress but as it was the first new one I'd had in about ten years they couldn't really complain.

On another occasion I fell asleep while reading under my covers and the reading lamp, which had a plastic shade, suddenly set alight. The only things that got burnt were my pyjamas, but I don't mind admitting that I very nearly shat myself.

Incidentally, the only time I ever scrapped with my father was when I was about fourteen years old. I forget what the argument was about – him being a twat, probably – but after coming at me with his fists flying I pushed him back and he fell into the ironing board. The iron, which unfortunately wasn't turned on, fell on top of him and cut open his head. The next thing I knew my mother had pushed me into a corner and was trying to smother me with a cushion.

'I'll kill you, you bastard,' she said. It was fucking chaos.

By then I'd become numb to all the drama, just as I had the pain. Regular beatings tend to do that to you and in my case I was also left with an increasing amount of anger and an unhealthy lack of fear. There was no pain, no consideration for the consequences – nothing. Even now, in my sixties, if a load of blokes came through my door mob-handed I'd have a go at them without a care in the world. And, I wouldn't stop until either them or I had been killed. That's not blether. None of that bollocks interests me and I've got nothing to prove to anybody. I'm merely trying to explain – for myself, as much as anyone – what years and years of physical and mental abuse can do to a human being.

You see, I've got two voices in my head: one wants to be nice to people and have a good life, and the other one hates everybody and wants to be left alone. Sometimes the latter will take over and run amok, and regardless of who I'm speaking to at the time I'll just fuck them off. Later on, I'll be reminded of what's gone on and unless it was somebody I didn't like in the first place I'll experience a certain amount of contrition. Not much, but enough to make me apologise, if I really have to.

I have vocalised these conversations that go on in my head once or twice and the last time I did it the people who were with me, who were members of my family, started laughing. Despite this, I just carried on. After all, it's been happening in my head for the last fifty years.

A question people often ask me, when they're trying to get all Sigmund Freud, is whether my father had it in him to be pleasant, and the answer I always give them is, yes. But only when people were watching.

To be fair, he used to raise quite a lot of money for the Royal Air Force on what is now Armed Forces Day (he'd been a conscript in the RAF) and as part of that fundraising he and I would dress up as Batman and Robin. Tony always refused to join in on account of not wanting to look like a daft twat so I was always Robin. It was all for show, of course, but it was still preferable to what went on behind closed doors. He also took me fishing once, which I quite enjoyed.

When I think about the few times we had together when he wasn't being a complete arsehole I'm tempted to think well of him, but it never lasts more than a second or so. It's human nature to try and forgive people, but it's also human nature to be wary of those who do you harm, and I'm afraid that particular set of memories is always going to prevail.

My father used to dish out emotional abuse, which was in some ways far worse than his physical abuse. The worst thing he used to do was threaten to put me into care and then tell me what would happen to me once I was in there. He made it sound horrific and once he'd finished with me I'd be a nervous wreck. Unfortunately, because it had the desired effect he would do it again and again and it's the only thing he ever did that gave me nightmares.

His other speciality was running me down. It didn't matter what I did, as far as my father was concerned, I was shit at it. I must have been only five or six when it started, which was also when he started threatening to put me into care.

The only thing he didn't belittle me at was rugby, which I was good at, although he still managed to bugger things up for me. I used to play flanker for Powys, and I was a damn good player. That old bastard Berwyn Evans once said that I had more guts than any player he'd ever seen before but that I didn't know when to stop.

'You have no fear, Edwards,' he used to say. 'That's not a good thing!'

One day when I was about thirteen I lost my kit but, as opposed to giving me a beating and buying a new one, my old man stopped my career there and then.

'That's it,' he said. 'No more.'

When I was fourteen I was driven towards a more serious solution to the abuse, rather than just than running away. This would have been shortly after I'd had a go at my father and he had hit his head on the iron. I remember being at my wit's end. One day I went into school armed with a little tub of twenty-five paracetamol and a half bottle of cherry brandy. Halfway through one of the lessons I asked to go to the toilet and, after emptying the paracetamol into my mouth, I downed the cheery brandy.

Did I do it at school so I'd be found? I honestly couldn't tell you for certain. Probably.

The next thing I remember I was being rushed to hospital and shortly after I arrived there they started force feeding me sour milk. Had I known that was going to happen beforehand, I'd have jumped off a bridge.

The question you're probably asking yourselves now is, *Did you get a beating for trying to take you own life?* and the answer is, yes, of course I did. I'd embarrassed my father and he couldn't handle it.

I was sent to a psychiatrist but that must have just been a box-ticking exercise as they sent a letter saying that I was completely sane. Me, sane!

The psychiatrist was based on Brighton Road, which is near the seafront, and the first thing he asked me to do when I walked in was to sit down, pick up a pen and paper, and draw exactly what I saw outside the window. The first thing I saw was a Tudor-style building so I drew that. It was a masterpiece, even though I do say so myself. The next thing he did was show me some pictures that were supposed to depict either butterflies or demons.

I said, 'Which one do you want then – the nice one or the horrible one?'

'Just tell me which one you see,' said the shrink.

'Well, if I show you the nasty one you'll send me to a nuthouse, and if I show you the nice one you won't, so look,' I said pointing at the picture, 'here's a nice one.'

I don't think he thought I was sane. I think he just wanted me out of his office.

By the time I was fifteen Tony had become a full-on depressive. He was never diagnosed while he was at home but my son Bryn has suffered from bouts of depression in the past, especially after serving in Afghanistan, and the symptoms are exactly the same. He used to spend all day in bed and had no energy to do anything. He was dead, basically. What hadn't helped matters was the fact that he'd been smoking dope since he was about twelve, which might well have exacerbated everything.

The difference between Tony and me, from my parents' point of view, was that he, being the golden child, had had an almighty fall from grace, whereas I had never raised their expectations beyond having a letter sent home for smoking. Or swearing. Or fighting. Or vandalising.

Because of his lethargy, when Tony wanted to go to the toilet he'd drag himself out of bed and piss out of the window. He did this for a while until one day the old man caught him and he threw him out of the house there and then. It was a hell of a racket and I stayed well out of the way. I think Tony went to Scunthorpe initially to stay with a mate and dossed around there for a bit. Given the state he was in, it was an awful thing for my parents to do, but then I suppose they had no idea.

Luckily for me, as well as not having quite as many demons as Tony, I also had Uncle Peter. When I say he became my saviour, that's not an understatement. In fact, if it hadn't been for him I genuinely don't know what I'd have done. Exploded, probably. Or killed somebody.

My mother's side of the family were actually all OK and some of the times I spent at Borehamwood during the holidays were fantastic. My father couldn't always go if he was working and that was when it came into its own. For everybody.

Ultimate Survivor

I got on famously with my grandparents, especially my grandmother, and we'd often see Peter there. He was an artist and he was also gay. I didn't know that until later and I think the family were in denial about it. He later told me that he'd known he was gay since his early teens when he'd started getting a hard-on while watching the wrestling. Big Daddy never had that effect on me.

How the hell we got this past my father I'll never know, but in September 1968 when I was thirteen Peter took me up to London to see the opening night of the musical *Hair*. Tim Curry, Elaine Paige, Paul Nicholas and Oliver Tobias were in the cast and there were tits and bollocks flying absolutely everywhere. They all went under this big sheet during the show and then appeared naked a few seconds later. I had never been as shocked in my life. Despite being a hairy little bastard I was a late starter with things like that and I didn't know where to look. Actually, I did know where to look, but it took me a minute or two to get the confidence to do so. After that, there was no stopping me and my eyes were out on stalks! I think they call it ogling. Well, that's where I cut my teeth.

The following day Peter had some friends around for lunch. He had a flat just off Kensington Square, which is as posh as hell, and I remember it was a very flash affair. Most of the guests were either actors or artists and had it been a few years later it would have been a who's who of British television. The first person to arrive was an actor called Peter Wyngarde who lived around the corner. Although I didn't recognise him, he was appearing in a television programme called *Department S* at the time but would become best known for playing the author and detective, *Jason King*. Next to appear was Millicent Martin, who was already well known, and her boyfriend Norman Eshley, who had just starred in an Orson Welles film, but they were both unknown to me. Next up was an actress called Yootha Joyce who, unbeknownst to everybody at the time, would go on to appear with Norman in *George & Mildred*. She would play Mildred, of course, and Norman would play Jeffrey Fourmile, the snobby next-door neighbour. What I actually remember most about that lunch is it was the first time I ever ate pitta bread and taramasalata. What a life changer that was!

After that, I started going up to see Peter every three months or so. I'd stay at his flat either for a weekend or for a few days during the holidays. I never once spoke about what was going on at home. If I had it would have been like bringing it with me: it was a sanctuary more than anything and a very welcome one at that. Also, because Peter was scared of my father – everybody was – he might not have invited me again and that would have been a huge bombshell. It was best to keep quiet and just enjoy the time away, which is what happened. I did mention the violence to Peter about three or four years ago, which was shortly before he died. He broke down when I told him and the first thing he asked was, 'But why didn't you tell me?' That was to be expected, I suppose, but when I told him how much the visits meant to me and how I didn't want them to be clouded by it all, he understood.

FOUR

One of the most surprising things about me, apart from the fact that I'm apparently still alive, is that I managed to leave school with five O levels to my name. I certainly didn't revise for anything so it was all down to aptitude, I suppose. And maybe some luck. This merely highlights the fact that there might actually be some brains in that funny old head of mine, and, had my home life been slightly less fucked up, I could have become – well, anything really. I definitely got an A for Art and as far as I can remember I got the same for Maths and English. I used to love writing essays and I still insist on writing letters by hand. That's got fuck all to do with English, I suppose.

As it was, the last thing I wanted to do when I left school was carry on my education as that would have meant staying at home for at least another two years while I did my A levels. No thank you very much. I wanted to get as far away from my parents as was humanly possible.

A few months before I was due to leave school I

started putting the wheels in motion on a plan that would hopefully be my ticket out of Rhyl.

Since the age of about eleven I'd been a member of the Sea Cadets, which, in addition to my visits to see Peter, had given me something to look forward to. I'd even been on a two-week trip to HMS *Raleigh*, which isn't a ship, but a 200-acre Navy training centre in the south-west. The trip had been brilliant and they'd even managed to instil a little bit of discipline in me. I said a bit. I was still a bastard.

I did the *Raleigh* thing with a view to joining the Navy and so when I left school I applied to become an artificer – a mechanic – with them. In those days joining the armed forces was viewed as being something you did as a last resort so my father wouldn't sign the forms. Fuck knows what he thought I was going to do. Become a priest, perhaps? Had my mother not signed the forms instead I honestly think I'd have killed the old bastard. That's how desperate I was to get out.

Because I had English and Maths O levels I got to bypass the exams and so went straight to the recruitment office for an interview. While I was sitting there waiting to go in, a colour sergeant from the Royal Marine Commandos suddenly came out holding my application form. This bloke had the green beret on his head and he was absolutely enormous.

'Edwards?' he said.

'That's right, sir.'

'Never mind sir. You can call me sergeant.'

'Yes, sergeant.'

I'd have called him God if he'd asked me to.

'I've got your application here,' he said tapping his clipboard with a pen. 'It says here you like a bit of rugby. And I see you're a bit of a rebel too, eh?'

I didn't know what to say to that so I just smiled and

kept quiet. What he said next flabbergasted me. 'How would you like to become a Royal Marine Commando, Edwards?'

'What?' I said, finding my voice again. 'I thought you had to be picked.'

'You do, and I'm picking you. Now, would you like to become a Royal Marine Commando or would you like to join the namby-pamby Navy?'

'I'd like to become a Royal Marine, sergeant.'

'Right then. You see that?' He pointed to a metal bar that was fixed to one of the walls. 'Give me five pull-ups.'

Within about five seconds I'd given him ten.

'Shall I do any more, sergeant?' I said looking at him expectantly while hanging off the bar.

'No, that's enough. You can get down now, Edwards. Stringy bugger, you are.'

Once you'd finished your exams at our school you had an interview with the deputy headmaster. In modern parlance, you'd probably call it an exit interview. The gentleman who had the pleasure of interviewing me was one Ronald Edwards (no relation, thank God). It's safe to say that Mr Edwards and I did not get on, and when I walked into his office and saw his ugly mug I could tell that he was itching to have a pop at me.

'I hear you're going to be joining the Royal Marines,' he said before pretending to laugh.

'That's right,' I replied indignantly.

He walked around to the front of his desk where I was standing and started poking me in the chest with his finger.

'You will not take the discipline in the Royal Marines, Edwards,' he hissed. 'You couldn't take it here, and you sure as hell won't take it there.'

Now, if there's one thing I don't like people doing to me (actually there are about fifty) it's poking me in the chest and because he was, in effect, also belittling my future, I took offence. The moment he'd said his piece I took a step backwards and I hit him as hard as I could. I think I got him just below his left eye and he went flying back over his desk. Before he could say anything or even stand up I decided to have my say.

'The reason I didn't respond to discipline here is because I don't respect you,' I began. 'Any of you.'

That wasn't strictly true as quite a few of the teachers were OK. I was just trying to be dramatic.

'Consider yourself expelled, Edwards,' said the deputy head as he picked himself up. 'Now get out!'

Had I done this before I'd been picked for the Marines – or the Junior Marines, as I was first attached to – I would have been fucked. As it was, I was leaving school with five O levels, my dream job, and the indescribable pleasure of having dropped the twat that was Mr Ronald fucking Edwards.

Perhaps my luck was changing.

The Junior Marines were based down in Deal, Kent. The sergeant in charge of us, who was supposed to be a kind of father figure, was called Alec MacMillan. He was at least six-and-a-half feet tall and right from the start I thought he was a bit of a weirdo. In fact, I thought most of the people in charge were. Nothing ever happened – to me, at least – but there were always rumours about Junior Marines being interfered with so I was always quite wary. The strangest rumour I heard involved the aforementioned Sergeant MacMillan and was relayed to me during the first week.

Charles Hawtrey, who appeared in the *Carry On* films, lived in Deal. He also liked men in uniform. Apparently, after becoming friendly with Sergeant MacMillan, he invited him back to his house and, after running a bath, he handed the giant soldier a large bag of sticky buns.

'What do you want me to do with these?' he asked Hawtrey.

'Give me a minute and I'll tell you,' replied the actor.

After getting undressed Hawtrey got into the bath.

'Right then,' he said. 'I want you to throw the buns at me one by one and as hard as you can.'

Well, at least nobody got hurt. As fetishes go that has to be one of the most bizarre I've ever heard, and I've heard a few, believe me.

Another reason I thought things might not be quite right is that we were often ordered to strip off on the parade ground. One of the things they were supposed to teach us in the Junior Marines was the importance of personal hygiene and one day while on parade we were asked to drop our trousers and then take off our underpants so they could be inspected. If your undies had any skid marks on them you had to do two laps of the parade ground, so you could say that the powers that be were simply fulfilling their brief. Or briefs, in this particular instance. It was a bit odd though. We were barely sixteen, for fuck's sake. It certainly wouldn't happen today.

When they weren't ordering forty-odd sixteen-year-olds to take off their underpants in broad daylight, the people in charge taught us how to act like adults. Or at least adults who could square bash, run a few miles without wheezing to death, iron a shirt and communicate effectively. It was like a military version of a male finishing school, for want of a better example.

In all, the training lasted just under nine months and after passing out we were ready to become Marine recruits. As part of our passing-out parade we had to do a display in front of the officers and parents. You know the kind of thing, lots of square bashing and jumping over vault boxes. After the parade the parents present would then take their triumphant offspring out for a meal to celebrate and, believe it or not, mine had made the journey. To be fair, it was a hell of a round trip for them – 650 miles or there abouts – and I was rather hoping that they might actually be proud of me.

As part of the display we had to jump off a trampette and do a somersault over a Bedford van and when I did it, instead of landing on my feet like the ones before me had, I landed on my head and unfortunately suffered a compressed neck. Fuck me, that hurt! I was taken straight to hospital and when my parents arrived sometime after me they were less than sympathetic. As far as they were concerned they'd travelled 325 miles just to see their son make a complete twat of himself. My father, who was his usual charming self, branded me, and I quote, 'a useless fucking dickhead'.

A week or so later I was told, unofficially, that unless I got myself to the Commando Training Centre sharpish I'd be in danger of being back-squadded. Back-squadding is when you're put into a different platoon than the one you trained with and it can leave you open to all kinds of shit. Bullying, mainly.

I was already aware that Marines who graduated through the Junior Marines were generally treated like shit by the normal recruits and apparently the bullying that took place was on an industrial scale. Some of the normal recruits were in their late twenties or early thirties so it was hardly surprising.

As somebody who'd already suffered more than his fair share of bullying there was no way I was going to allow myself to be back-squadded, and so, still wearing a neck brace and carrying a duffle bag that was as big as a couch (I'm not joking – this thing had all my kit in it), I made my way from Deal to the Commando Training Centre in Lympstone,

Devon. Even today it would take you at least six or seven hours to get from Deal to Lympstone by train but back then it was even worse. I forget how many trains I had to get but there were buses thrown in too and when I finally jumped on the train from Exeter to Ecton, which was the final leg of the journey, I was a physical wreck. Rhyl to Deal had fuck all on this.

The Marine training lasted thirty-two weeks (although you were assessed after twenty-six) so it was a long old slog. Once again, personal hygiene was a big priority, although the spot checks were slightly less perverse and usually took place in the confines of your barracks. The punishment, should you be found lacking in this department in any shape or form, was to be called a crab. This is a strange one and no mistake but basically crabs had to put on a full kit bag, squat down so their arse was almost touching the ground, hold a gun above their head and then walk up a steep hill in that position shouting, 'I am a crab, the king of all crabs.' If that didn't work the other recruits were (unofficially) encouraged to give the transgressor what's called a Brasso bath.

After being stripped off you were put in a bath containing a mixture of cold water and a few tins of Brasso metal polish, which is about 10 per cent ammonia plus some acids, after which an assortment of evil idiots would appear, all brandishing yard brooms. They'd proceed to use the brooms to rub the mixture into your skin. It's one of the more brutal punishments I witnessed. So much so that I always refused to join in. You could leave Marine training at any time, by the way – there was no having to buy yourself out or anything – and one of my fellow recruits left after suffering this. He was in a hell of a state.

The only time I came close to being thrown out during

my Marine training was when I almost hit a corporal. As strange as it may seem, I used to have a photo of my mother in my locker and one day, as he was passing, a bloke called Brian Chalmers stopped and said something like, 'Fuck me, I'd give her one.' The reason I had my mother's photo is because I was proud of the way she looked so perhaps I should have been flattered. Even so, I ended up flying at the bastard and if it hadn't been for a couple of mates who were nearby I'd have killed him, and my career. In hindsight, I should have finished the bastard as from then on I became a target for him and his cronies. Every time I went down on the assault course, for instance, they'd steam in and give me a good hiding. It became a campaign, to the point where they'd hang around waiting for an opportunity. What this did, though, was give me the impetus to get up and keep moving, so they didn't get many. Get up and move or stay down and get a kicking? You'd have to be pretty fucking knackered to choose the latter.

My God, it was tough though. We failed a locker inspection one day – all of us – and as punishment we were ordered to pack up our lockers, which were then strapped to our backs. After being pushed out of the barracks with a kick up the arse each we then had to carry them to a landmark called Three Firs, which was about 3 miles away. It was absolute agony.

The only person who showed me any compassion while I was there was a very hard but very fair man called Sergeant Blackmore. He was easily the most human among the men in charge and he absolutely hated the likes of Bob Chalmers. We were doing a 9-miler one day (without the lockers, thank God) and about halfway through I had a bloody panic attack. While this was happening Sergeant Blackmore walked up behind me and without warning he hit me on the back with a pickaxe handle. This stopped the attack immediately and I was able to carry on. After the run, Sergeant Blackmore took me to one side and, after making sure I was OK, he asked me a question.

'Have you ever had asthma, Edwards?' he asked.

'No sir. Never.'

'Don't lie to me, Edwards. I'll ask you again. Have you ever had asthma?'

In those days asthmatics weren't accepted into the Marines and if truth be known, as it was about to be, I'd been suffering from the condition ever since I was a baby. The way they used to treat asthma in babies was by putting them under an ultraviolet lamp and because my case was quite serious I'd spent literally weeks under one. The reason it hadn't been an issue when I joined is because I hadn't suffered with it much for years and when it came to me having a medical they had no record of it. Incidentally, one thing my doctor did discover when I had my medical for the Junior Marines was that I had a perforated eardrum, and, when it came to it suitability, it had the same effect as asthma. I remember his words vividly.

He said, 'I'm sorry, but I can't sign you fit. A lot of what the Marines do is water based. You wouldn't last five minutes.'

The sensation I felt when he said that was absolutely horrible. It genuinely felt like my stomach had migrated to my feet and I had to stop myself from falling forwards. In a fit of desperation I told the doctor about what had been happening at home and virtually begged him to help me.

'All right then,' he said finally. 'Listen to me.'

Once again the emotions I felt when he uttered those words were intense, except this time my stomach went north instead of south.

'Whatever you do,' said the doctor, 'don't wash that ear, OK? If you let the wax build up, at least for the first few months, they'll never realise. Also, if you think your hearing's going, which you will, just tilt your head in the direction of whoever's speaking.'

The doctor had obviously done dozens of these tests and I had a feeling he'd been here before.

In the end, I had to admit to Sergeant Blackmore that I did have asthma and as I did so I could feel my career as a Marine slipping away from me. I didn't plead this time. There was no point. I was an adult now. A Marine, for fuck's sake. At least for the next few minutes. Having a violent father waiting for me at home wouldn't make a blind bit of difference with this man. 'Hit the fucker back, just harder,' would probably be his reply, and rightly so. I remember looking at Sergeant Blackmore after I'd told him, desperately trying to get a sign of what was to come. He was impassive though. Impossible to read.

'I'll tell you what, Edwards,' he said finally, 'the next time you have a panic attack stick your hand up. I'll brief the team so they'll know what to do. OK?'

I was about to say something like, *But what about the asthma, sergeant?* but just as I opened my mouth he looked at me, as if to say, *Don't be a fucking idiot, Edwards*. It was never mentioned again. I love that man.

The thing I became most famous for at Lympstone, apart from being a human punchbag with a good-looking mum, was polishing boots. Without wanting to sound like a big head I was absolutely brilliant at it and had been since I was at school. In fact, so impressed were my colleagues at Lympstone that they started offering me money to polish their boots. 'Here, Taff. Do you mind doing my boots? I'll give you ten bob.'

'Yeah, all right. Chuck them over.'

Night after night I'd sit there on my own at the end of my bed, polishing people's boots until lights out. There'd be a bloody great big line of them. In the end, I started getting bored and despite the extra income I was thinking of jacking it in. Then, while we were out training one day, somebody suggested I tried using high-gloss spray paint instead.

'Will it work?' I asked them.

'Of course it'll work. It's high gloss!'

'Oh, right. Yeah, high gloss.'

Despite being academically able I was obviously lacking in the common sense department and without even considering the potential pitfalls of spraying paint onto boots I went out and bought myself a few cans and then set to work. If the people paying had been using their boots just the once, or perhaps even twice, then I'd have been home and dry. Unfortunately, this wasn't the case and within a couple of days the paint was starting to crack. Not only was my name now shit but I had to refund every single penny I'd made and I also had to remove the paint. That took absolutely ages, and once I'd removed the paint I then had to polish the boots free of charge.

We were reviewed weekly at Lympstone and if the powers that be thought you weren't cutting the mustard you were out. If you made it to twenty-six weeks, you were then interviewed by a panel. And, if you made it through that, you embarked on a final six weeks training, which, not to put too fine a point on it, made the previous twenty-six seem like a holiday. Well, a holiday for masochists, perhaps.

To commemorate the fact that you'd made it as far as Commando training, which is what the final six weeks were, you were presented with a green woollen Commando hat that you wore during all the training and exercises. I think the worst thing we'd had to endure prior to this, apart from running 3 miles with a locker strapped our backs, was being left on Dartmoor for a few days with nothing but a tent, a sleeping bag and a knife each. It was basic survival training and once you knew what you were doing it was a piece of piss. Like scouting, really. But with more flatulence and lots of bad language.

One of the most amusing things we were asked to do – or, should I say, told to do – during that initial six months was something called hunting submarines. The name is obviously a metaphor and entails you crawling through muddy water that's about 2-foot deep. The first time we did this was in the middle of winter and it was a prelude to us starting two nights' survival training. We were supposed to get some dry kit to take with us for the two days but we got underwear and that was it. The reason they called it submarine hunting is that every so often somebody would jump on your back and push you under. As somebody who dislikes the cold, this was my worst nightmare, I absolutely hated it.

With Commando training everything went up a few notches and was specific to certain situations and scenarios. For instance, instead of being dropped in the middle of Dartmoor and left to survive for three days, which was standard survival training, you were dropped and then given a specific point you had to reach. That could be anything up to 20 miles away and, as you're trying to reach it, a team of about ten Marines would be hunting you down. If you got caught you were interrogated and knocked about a bit so it was supposed to resemble life behind enemy lines.

The only thing I found slightly intimidating about that final six weeks was the endurance course. The Royal Marines endurance course was, and probably still is, the most effective way of separating men from boys – or future Marine

Commandos from Royal Navy servicemen. It's changed slightly now to reflect the difference in fitness (or the fact that everybody back then smoked!) but it was still a killer. First up was a 5-mile run which had to be done in full fighting order weighing about 15 kg. The first 2 miles, which were across rough moorland and through woodland terrain, were interspersed with tunnels, pipes, wading pools and an underwater tunnel that, even to this day, sends a shiver down my spine. As well as being full of water it was as tight as a duck's arse and, once the corporal had pushed you under the water and into it, you had to try and make your way through to the other end. If you were claustrophobic, which I am, it was your worst fucking nightmare and a lot of lads refused to do it. I managed it, just, but as the corporal was pushing me down I could feel my ticker going like the proverbial shithouse door. All I wanted to do was shout, *Fuck that. Pull me up, you twat!* but the alternative, i.e. failure, was enough to get me through. By far the most empowering imaginary synopsis when faced with a difficult situation was the thought of having to live with my parents again, but I kept that one for emergencies.

If you made it through tunnel you then had to run 4 miles back to camp, which was immediately followed by a marksmanship test. Ten rounds from 25 metres if memory serves, and we had to hit at least six. Bearing in mind you were soaking wet, knackered and shaking like a shitting dog with a bad case of constipation, this was a hell of a lot harder than it sounds. Even if you did manage to get the required six or above you still had to finish within the allotted time. These days you have about seventy-three minutes to do the whole thing but back then it was eighty minutes, and when I finished the marksmanship test, having scored eight out of ten, I was a demoralising six minutes over. I was gutted.

The rule was that you could only fail once on the Commando course. Straight after I'd finished, a ginger-haired officer named Captain Ash, who obviously thought I had it in me to prevail, got hold of me and said, 'Right then, Edwards, I'm taking you around again.'

'Can I have a rest first?' I pleaded.

'OK,' barked the captain, 'I'll see you here tomorrow at 0600 hours.'

The next morning, as I was running back to the camp for the marksman test, soaking wet, having earlier emerged from the watery tunnel of doom, Captain Ash said, 'You've got ten minutes, Edwards. Ten minutes.' I was still at least a mile away and with the firing range to get to and shots still to fire it was going to be damn close. A few seconds later, after having deployed my emergency synopsis, I was running at least twice as fast. When I fired the final shot, having scored seven out of ten, I got on my feet and asked the captain how I'd done.

'Seventy five minutes, Edwards. Well done!'

I was elated by my achievement but, after a few seconds, confusion began to set in.

'Excuse me, Captain Ash,' I said cautiously. 'There's no way I could have done that last bit in ten minutes. I was well over a mile away.'

The captain's answer was classic. 'I lied, Edwards,' he said in a very matter-of-fact kind of way. 'You had just over fifteen.'

I thought, *You bastard!*

Looking back, that was one of the most idiotic things I have ever done in my entire life, and there've been a few to choose from. Imagine if he'd made a mistake but hadn't realised. I'd have been the one to tell him! It's like reminding someone you're a twat.

Ultimate Survivor

To prove I was an idiot, shortly after being accepted as a Marine I thought it would be a good idea to get some tattoos done. I decided, because I was good at art, to design my own and drew one featuring the Royal Marine badge, Mickey Mouse and Donald Duck. After designing the tattoo I took it to a tattooist just off Rhyl promenade and had it done. When I first turned up for training it went down like a lead balloon. You had to declare any distinguishing marks for your ID card, and when I showed the sergeant in charge Mickey and Donald he, understandably, thought I was taking the piss out of the Royal Marines. The reason I'd decided to include the two Disney characters was because I could always draw them very well but the sergeant took some convincing. He just thought I was some kind of weird prick.

Before you could take part in the passing-out parade and receive your coveted green beret you first had to complete a 30-mile run over Dartmoor wearing full fighting order. Known as the 30 Miler, it is to this day the final, and some say ultimate, test during the six-week Commando course. Starting in groups of six, you have to complete the run in under eight hours (or seven, if you're an officer) and I collapsed at least twice. In fact, I was probably the weakest of our six, although as a team we were shit hot. Believe it or not, and this was the same for every group, the only time we stopped during the entire 30 miles was when we took a fag break. How mad is that? 'Five-minute burn, boys?' one of us would shout. That's exactly what you need during a 30-mile run, isn't it? A fucking Woodbine.

The worst thing about the run was undoubtedly the heat. It was summer when we did it and it must have been touching 30 degrees. The thing that got me through the run wasn't the prospect of failure or an abusive parent waiting for me at home. It was camaraderie. The realisation that I wasn't alone. Camaraderie really is an extraordinarily powerful weapon. Until then, I don't think I'd realised.

Perhaps it's not surprising, then, but we did the 30 miles in 6 hours and 22 minutes, including fag breaks. That was a new record for the Royal Marines and to this day it has never been broken. In fact, my name is still displayed in the drill hut at Lympstone, as far as I know, together with the five other members of 66 Junior Troop. We celebrated afterwards with some crisps and orange juice in the NAAFI, as we were too young to drink. I remember sitting there and almost falling off my chair. I was that tired. What an achievement though. It was probably the first time I ever experienced any genuine self-worth.

You see. It's not all doom and gloom.

Once again, my parents attended the passing-out parade. This time I managed not to injure myself and I completed the parade with everyone else. I think it was the closest I ever came to making my father proud of me, although all I'd actually done, in his eyes at least, was to succeed in something that was a complete waste of time.

The only time my father ever hugged me is when I left home for the final time about two days after I passed out. It was on a platform at Rhyl station – in public, then – and I couldn't believe it. What made him do it, I wonder? Love or guilt? Perhaps it was a bit of both. Human beings are funny things. I haven't mentioned half of the things he did to me and even today I would class him as being one of the biggest bastards who ever walked the earth. Yet there he was, giving me a big hug.

Something else that's surprising about my father was that he was very much into amateur dramatics. I know, it's ridiculous. Fittingly, though, he played Fagin in *Oliver Twist!* once, and even I was roped into appearing in one or two shows, although never with him. The plays all took place at Rhyl Little Theatre, which isn't far from Gwalia Avenue, and one of the plays I appeared in was *Little Women*. I also played a professor in a play and for that I had to wear some half-moon spectacles, which I borrowed from my grandfather. He said to me, 'Now you look after these. They're solid gold.' I almost shat myself when he told me that.

Despite everything, I don't ever remember feeling hatred towards my father. Can you feel hatred at such a young age? I'd like to think not. It was only later that I started hating him. The thing is, he was always a bit of a contradiction, my old man, or perhaps a paradox. A small, poorly educated control freak from a violent background who enjoyed fishing, photography and amateur dramatics.

In a bizarre footnote to my military training, which encapsulates the abnormality of my life, the guest of honour at the passing-out parade was none other than Jimmy Savile, who, as well as turning out to be Britain's premier paedophile, and, according to some, a necrophile, was an honorary Royal Marine Commando. I've got a photo of him, taken after the parade, with my sister on Exmouth beach. Many years later my daughter, Sian, had her photo taken with him when he visited her school. You couldn't make it up, could you?

FIVE

Straight after passing out I received my first draft. I was going to be in one of three units: 42 Commando, which was based in Plymouth, 40 Commando, which was based in Malta, and 45 Commando, also known as Ski Commando, which was based in Arbroath. The only one I wasn't keen on was 45 Commando as I hate the cold, so when I was handed my draft and realised I'd been assigned to 42 Commando, I breathed a huge sigh of relief.

Rather ironically – and depressingly – within a week of being stationed in Plymouth the entire platoon was on a plane bound for Nova Scotia where temperatures in the winter could reach anything up to – or should I say, down to – minus 40 degrees. Unluckily for me it was January and the reason we were travelling there was to take part in a nuclear and biological warfare exercise with the Canadian and American armed forces before joining the aircraft carrier, HMS *Albion*.

The exercise entailed our company (there were about

two hundred of us in all) digging some hides into the side of a hill, camouflaging them, and then taking part in a long series of ambushes and raids. The Americans and the Canadians represented one side, and us the other. In the hides, which is where we slept, you always had to have at least one person on guard carrying an SMG, a submachine gun; not because of the Yanks or the Canadians, but because of the bears!

We'd come back in from an exercise and the entire place would be turned upside down. Cans of food would look like they'd had 6-inch nails hammered into them: the bears would push their claws into them to get at the contents.

Underneath our uniforms, which was camouflaged ski gear, we had to wear a specially designed suite that was supposed to withstand all kinds of shit such as radiation. These things were like paper and they looked and felt like they wouldn't withstand a fart. The difference between the equipment the armed forces used then and the equipment they have these days is like comparing a twenty-year-old Cortina with a Ferrari. Bearing in mind the state the country was in at the time – this was 1971 – it's a wonder we didn't have to bring our own.

But it wasn't just the equipment that was often below par. Some of the decision making was too. One night, at about two o'clock in the morning, we went out on an exercise that had us walking about 10 kilometres in the pitch black over some hills and through several feet of snow. After we'd done about 8 kilometres the officer in charge led the entire company into a stream that, as well as running like a torrent at the time, was about 5-foot deep. It was situated at the bottom of a very steep bank and by the time he'd ordered us over it there was no turning back. As we all slid helplessly towards the running water I began to realise that there was more to this than just a load of blokes getting wet. To be honest, I think we all did, as when the men started hitting the water the noise they made, which was akin to somebody being electrocuted, created an instant air of panic. We'd obviously been taught about the dangers of hyperthermia and the fact that it had taken us a good two hours to get this far, and it would probably take us longer get back, certainly wasn't lost on me. Worse still, it was now minus 34 degrees, snowing hard, and although we wouldn't have to get back up the bank (it was flat on the other side) the fact remained that an entire company of men were now 8 kilometres away from shelter in sub-zero temperatures and soaked to the skin. Unbelievably, instead of then leading the company back to the hides as fast as he possibly could, the officer in charge made us complete the exercise, which meant walking another kilometre or so before ambushing some Americans.

What an absolute plonker!

Not surprisingly, over three-quarters of us contracted hypothermia and ended up having to be hospitalised. I was one of the lucky ones as I escaped with just some frostbite in the tips of my fingers, but one or two of the lads almost died. The officer was sacked, thank God.

During our time in Nova Scotia I was sexually abused by a corporal who, unfortunately as the bastard's probably still alive, will have to remain nameless. Because it was so cold you had what was called a buddy system where two of you would get down to your pants and share a sleeping bag. I don't want to go into detail, but let's just say this bloke didn't do much sleeping. This wasn't the only time it happened. I've never told anybody about this and I expect the first thing people will think when they know is, *Why didn't he tell him to stop?*

Believe me, I've asked myself that question a

thousand times and the only explanation I have to offer is that the abuse my father dished out left me believing that you just accepted whatever happened to you. In addition to that, you do as you're told in the armed forces (or at least you do when you first start), and because I'd only been there five minutes I didn't have it in me to say anything. That would certainly change but at the time I was, for want of a better phrase, easy meat. The thing is, words like abuse, neither physical nor sexual, didn't exist in my vocabulary. They were just things that happened. This too would change over time and when I'd finally had enough of what was happening – or when it clicked that I had it in my power to bring it to a halt – it all ended quite violently.

When the abuse took place there were other people present and it's my fear that the abuse was systemic, although I can't prove anything.

A few days after the nuclear and biological warfare training had finished I was bitten by some kind of spider and, after watching my arm swell up to the size of an elephant's cock, I had to be hospitalised and put on a drip. This was a bit shit at first as in those days, when you had some leave when you were abroad, a family of locals would take you in for the duration and show you the sights. This was something I'd really been looking forward to so when my arm ballooned I was gutted. Or at least, at first. The family who'd been due to look after me came to visit so I wasn't on my own and the student nurses, who were all French Canadian, seemed to have a thing for men in uniform. I must have had at least four bed baths a day. Talk about coming clean! Even the food was restaurant standard. So, while all the other lads (or at least the ones who'd recovered from hypothermia) were freezing their arses off on open-top buses while being shown the delights of Halifax, Nova Scotia, I was receiving multiple daily bed baths from nubile young nurses while being fed quality grub.

My position once I was aboard the HMS *Albion* was the quartermaster's mate, which in layman's terms is a nautical doorman. Or should I say, gangwayman. If anybody wanted to come aboard while we were docked, they had to get past me first.

While we were still in Halifax, the officers held a shindig one evening for some of the locals dignitaries. I was on duty on the gangway and one of the first people to arrive was a young lady who must have been in her mid-twenties.

'Hello,' she said, coming aboard. 'Who are you?'

'I'm Marine Edwards, ma'am.'

'And what's your first name?'

'Martin, ma'am.'

'Hello, Martin,' she said. 'Before I go to the officer's mess, would you mind showing me around the ship?'

I laughed out loud when she asked me this.

'What's so funny?' she asked.

'You're a guest of the officers,' I replied. 'They'd go mad if they saw me giving you a tour of the ship.'

'But why?' she asked.

'Because we're shit on their shoe . . . ma'am! We're the underlings.'

This time it was her turn to have a laugh and while I stayed in position one of the other Marines showed her to the officer's mess. About ten minutes later the duty officer walked up to me, looking like he wanted to smack me one.

'Edwards,' he barked through gritted teeth. 'You're wanted in the officer's mess.'

'Who? Me, sir?' I asked somewhat predictably.

'Yes you, Edwards! That young lady you were talking to . . .'

'Who?' I said deliberately interrupting him. 'Annie?'

'Miss McLeod to you, Edwards!' snapped the duty officer. 'Her father happens to be a director at the Royal Bank of Canada, and don't you forget it.'

'Well, what about her?' I asked impertinently.

'She's asked you to join her in the officer's mess,' said the duty officer. 'And that's not all. She's asked that you join them for dinner and then afterwards give her a guided tour of the ship.'

The look on his face was a picture. Resentment and jealousy with a nice dollop of hatred.

'That'll be nice,' I said, almost pissing myself.

'There's more,' said the duty officer. 'Tomorrow she's going to show you around Halifax, apparently. Right, off you go, Edwards.'

The look on the officers' faces as I entered the mess was like the duty officer's times a thousand. The thing is, there was fuck all they could do. I was obviously aware of that but I didn't take the piss. After all, once Miss McLaughlin had finished with me I'd be back to being shit on their shoes again and if I'd taken the piss in any way whatsoever there would be consequences – both official and unofficial. God, I was tempted though. I can be a mischievous bastard sometimes and I could have caused havoc, but I acted just as I would have normally (with perhaps some anxiety thrown in) and sat down for dinner. The only thing I remember about this is getting a severe attack of cutlery fear prior to the first course. There seemed to be about four or five of each utensil and I remember looking at them and thinking, *What the fucking hell's going on?* Fortunately, I'd ordered the same as Annie so I just copied her. I could see the officers watching me. They were obviously hoping I'd make a twat of myself so when I didn't I thought, *Fuck you!*

The Making of a Madman

The following morning I was picked up by Annie and off we went. I was only supposed to be gone for a few hours but ended up spending three whole days with her. Three days! Drinking, shagging, taking drugs and visiting Indian reservations were the extent of our itinerary and every time I was due back on the ship she simply called up my superiors and told them I'd be back later. 'Yes, miss, that's not a problem,' they said. They must have been spitting feathers.

A few days after being back onboard Annie came to see me. We'd fallen in love with each other – or at least I think we had – and she wanted me to leave the Marines, stay with her in Halifax, and go and work for her father. Instead of just saying yes like my heart was telling me to do, I told her I'd have to think about it. This all happened about five days before we were due to leave Halifax so I didn't have long.

A couple of days later I still hadn't decided what to do. Until now, the biggest decision I'd ever had to make was choosing what crap to buy after robbing that old bastard blind at the fair and my head was all over the place. I decided the best thing to do was to call Annie and ask her to come over for a chat. This was, in effect, the same as saying yes to her suggestion, but at the end of the day my hand needed forcing as I just wasn't capable of making the decision myself. When I went to find the piece of paper that Annie had written her number on it was nowhere to be seen and for the next two hours I turned my cabin upside down trying to find it. I didn't dare tell anybody on the ship what was going on as I genuinely had no idea what the consequences might be and that scared me to death. I was so bloody naive.

After I was satisfied that the number must have been lost ashore – perhaps on my way back to the ship after our shagathon – I started thinking about what to do next. Fate was a word I'd never heard of then but in hindsight I think I knew what it was, as something inside stopped me from trying to track her number down. And I probably could have, if I really wanted to. That's not to say it didn't hurt. It did. And I was miserable for weeks. As time went on, though, I became more and more certain that the number had been lost for a reason, and that, in language I'd use today, fate had taken a hand.

When we arrived back at Portsmouth we were immediately transferred from the HMS *Albion* to another aircraft carrier, called the HMS *Bulwark*. A couple of weeks later we were on our way to Florida. Sun, at last! Fuck me, was I ready for it.

Two memorable things happened on this trip. First, I got thrown out of Disney World, as you do, and then I put a stop to the sexual abuse I'd been suffering.

Going to Disney World was like a dream come true for me. Until now the Marine Lake Funfair was the closest I'd come to entering an amusement park and entertainment complex, and when we first arrived at the gates I was genuinely speechless. The lads and I were also dressed in full uniform so we were attracting a lot of attention – female attention mainly. After going on a few rides, a mate of mine called Bob Birkett and I caught the eye of two girls who, from the looks of things, seemed to be quite friendly. We ended up going skinny dipping with these girls in the lake around Tom Sawyer Island and, for the first twenty minutes or so, nobody saw us. Then, just as things were getting interesting, we got caught by a member of security and all hell broke loose. I know they can be quite conservative in the States but by the way we were treated you'd think they'd caught us shagging. Another few minutes and they might have. As we were being 'removed' from the premises I saw a sign above the gates that read, 'The Happiest Place on Earth.'

I remember thinking, *Very nearly!*

A few days later a group of us we went out on the town and this time the corporal who'd been abusing me came with us. After a couple of hours he suggested that we go and see some friends of his who had an apartment in the area. Fuck knows why but we all agreed and when we got there we realised immediately that these two blokes were gay. How did we know? Well, apart from eyeing us all up and down they were as camp as tits and, after just a few seconds, we were gesturing to each other that we needed to get out. As we were thinking about how best to do this (well, everyone but the corporal) I spotted an expensive-looking gold ring lying on a table. I again gestured to one of the lads, this time to say that I was going to nick it.

'Go on then,' he mouthed.

'Excuse me,' I said. 'Do you mind if I use your loo?'

'Why certainly not, young man,' said one of the men. 'It's just through that door on the left.'

As I walked past the table I almost took the ring but because I had my back to everyone I decided against it. I came out of the loo as quietly as I could and with nobody looking in my direction I picked up the ring as I walked past the table. Then I said, 'Right lads, let's go and have a beer somewhere,' and led everyone but the corporal and his friends out of the apartment.

The following day we were all lying in a park sunbathing and sometime in the afternoon these two blokes arrived. Fortunately, they didn't mention the ring I'd nicked and a few minutes later I fell asleep. When I woke up, which was about an hour later, I could feel somebody's hand stroking the inside of my left leg just above the knee. Because of the heat, I was quite drowsy at first but when I finally came around I realised that the person doing the stroking was one of the corporal's friends. He was lying next to me on his side and as far as I could make out everyone from the ship had left, bar the corporal. As I was deciding what to do, this bloke's hand suddenly moved up to my bollocks. The moment that happened I got up and started punching him as hard as I could. He bore the brunt of everything that had happened in Nova Scotia, and when I'd finished with him I started laying into his mate. The corporal didn't say or do anything. He just sat there on the grass shitting himself. As sorry as I am for giving those blokes a hiding – and I am sorry – they probably saved me from twenty years in prison as, if I'd snapped with the corporal, I wouldn't have stopped. I'd have made sure he was dead. As it was, the horrible little bastard never touched me or even spoke to me again after that, nor could he make eye contact with me. At last I had realised that what he'd been doing was wrong and, by the time we docked in Portsmouth, I despised the bastard.

The tour to Florida was followed by a four-month tour of duty in Northern Ireland. Lucky us! I'd gone from freezing cold, to sunshine, to constant rain all in the space of a few months. You had to be eighteen to go on a tour of duty so while the majority of the platoon made their way to Belfast, me and a few others had to stay behind. Then, on 26 March 1973, my eighteenth birthday, I was put on a ferry from Liverpool to Belfast. God, I was depressed. I was on my own and it was raining (obviously), blowing a gale, and everybody on board looked like they wanted to top themselves. It was the last time I ever wet the bed.

As I disembarked the ferry, little did I know that in just a few years' time I'd be back in Northern Ireland shadowing one of the IRA's most notorious terrorists. If I had known, I'd have organised a suicide party on the ferry and would have endeavoured to get me and my fellow passengers safely overboard!

The Making of a Madman

My second stint in Northern Ireland was so eventful that I don't remember much about the first one. Apart from the fact that I was bored shitless most of the time and developed a passionate loathing for rain. The entire four months were spent patrolling the streets and the only real highlight was the kindness and generosity shown to me by some of the locals. A lot would give you dog's abuse, obviously, but a lot wouldn't. To be honest, I had very little idea what we were doing there in the first place. I was eighteen years old and was about as politically aware as I was sexually aware prior to going to Canada. I suppose that was a bonus in a way as in some situations ignorance can be bliss. However, when it came to the abuse we received in Belfast I think a little knowledge about the Troubles might have gone a long way. All I knew was that there were Protestants on one side, Catholics on the other, and in addition to them hating each other we were there to keep the peace. In the rain, mainly.

Such was the monotony of that stint in Belfast that after about three-and-a-half months I suffered what can only be described as a temporary lobotomy. Cognitively, I just shut down. Everything was done on autopilot and I became devoid of any kind of emotion. In hindsight, it was probably how most young people would react to a bout of enforced boredom and what brought me out of it was the news that the tour was coming to an end. It took a few minutes to sink in, but when it did it was as if somebody had just injected me with half a gallon of adrenalin. Or, when you consider my behaviour after I left Northern Ireland, as if Dr Frankenstein had just brought his monster to life for the very first time.

Our first port-of-call after leaving Belfast, at which I arrived relieved and with a massive smile on my face, was a holding camp in Poole, Dorset. I was there for about three months in all and during that time I not only became a raging alcoholic – eight pints of scrumpy a day, every day – but started a pattern of behaviour that would culminate in me becoming one of the most notorious men in the British armed forces. That isn't a brag, as when I say notorious, I mean it in it's true sense, i.e. somebody who is well known for doing bad things. Or, in my case, extremely stupid things. Biblically stupid things.

I was actually well behaved in Poole. In fact, I think the worst crime I committed there was turning up on the parade ground half pissed. I wasn't the only one. Due to the fact it was a holding camp there was a certain amount of acceptance of that kind of thing so providing you didn't mouth off at the sergeant major or hit anybody, which I didn't, you'd be sent to sleep it off. It was only when I got to Simon's Town in South Africa and joined the HMS *Bacchante* that my behaviour started to deteriorate and the very first example of this happened approximately six hours after I came onboard.

The officer in charge had a face that was made for slapping and he is one of few people I've ever met who I hated on sight.

'What on earth have we here?' he said when he saw me. 'Bit of fresh blood, eh?'

What a pompous twat. He sounded like something out of Jeeves and Wooster and the only thing that was missing was a monocle and a glass of sherry. Fortunately, some of the lads offered to take me out that evening and we ended up on a train bound for Cape Town. A few hours later, and after a hell of a lot of red wine, we were making the return journey to Simon's Town, but instead of us all sitting in our seats like we had on the way there, one of us was lying on the floor. There's nothing strange in that, of course. We were shitfaced and it had been an excellent evening. The problem is that beneath the person on the floor was a train guard who he'd rugby tackled just moments earlier and, as the non-military passengers looked on in horror and the military ones in amusement, the man in question – me – proceeded to smother the train guard, who was a large black gentleman I found very attractive at the time, in kisses.

As the ten or so South African policemen boarded the train at the next stop and attempted to unclamp me from the train guard and pull me to my feet, I noticed between kisses that several were carrying manacles. *They must be for me*, I thought merrily. And I was right.

My first day on the HMS *Bacchante* and I end up being returned to the ship in manacles having sexually assaulted a train guard while pissed on red wine. As initial misdemeanours go, in the Marines, at least, this was a fucking blinder. The following morning, after being patted on the back a few times and reminded of what had taken place, I was taken to see my friend the commanding officer.

'I'm disappointed in you, Edwards,' he began. 'There was me thinking you were fresh blood, and you end up attacking a train guard and getting arrested. What on earth happened?'

'I was led astray, sir,' I pleaded.

'Well, let's make sure that doesn't happen again, shall we? No shore leave for a month. Now, get out of my sight.'

Not very long after this the HMS *Bacchante* went into dry dock for repairs and so I put in for a transfer to another frigate called the HMS *Danae*. Despite the change of ship and the change of location (the *Danae* was based in Plymouth at the time) things followed in similar vein to Simon's Town. I have an entire folder full of statements from the Military Police regarding my behaviour. The first thing I did was get pissed with some mates and then we gave ourselves a Mohican haircut, each using a bowie knife, before shaving off our eyebrows. We got two weeks' stoppage of leave for that.

In my defence, at least I'm consistent. In fact, you'd be hard pushed to find one piece of paper in that folder that doesn't refer to me being either drunk, drunk and incapable, drunk and disorderly, or all three. All this is nothing, though, compared to the stunt I pulled a few months after arriving on the *Danae*.

Strangely enough, I was stone cold sober when it happened. But I was angry. Christ, was I angry. Angry enough to take an entire warship to siege.

SIX

After being on the *Danae* for not very long I started seeing a local girl called Zoe and after not very much longer she unfortunately became pregnant. Without wishing to make light of the situation we decided we wanted to get rid of it straight away and so an abortion was booked for as soon as possible. After I told my commanding officer what was happening he gave me some time off to accompany Zoe to the abortion clinic and after she'd had it done I decided to go for a couple of pints before returning to the *Danae*.

The first thing I did when I got back was to go for a piss and as I was washing my hands a leading seaman, who I couldn't stand but who was a senior rank to me, came out of one of the cubicles and began washing his hands next to me.

'Been to see that slag have you, Edwards?' he said.

'You what?' I replied.

'That slag of yours. I heard you got her into trouble. Probably not the first time it's happened to her.'

Now there's a rule in the armed forces. It doesn't

matter if they're one rank above you or six ranks, if you hit a senior rank you're court-martialled. There's no arguing. That's it. End of story. Was I aware of this when he said that? Probably. I was aware of a lot of things. That said, it didn't mean I took any notice. With regards to this situation, it wouldn't have made a blind bit of difference as the moment he called her a slag I knew I was going to hit him. The only question was with what and how hard. Because of where we were standing I decided to make use of what was in front of us and so the moment he stopped talking I grabbed hold of the back of his head, pushed it downwards and smashed his face into the taps, at which point his nose exploded.

Leaving the leading seaman to contemplate what he'd just said and how he was feeling after his 'nose job', I walked calmly out of the toilets and then down to the mess deck. In the mess deck, which was oblong shaped, there were twenty-four bunk beds which were lined against the two long walls. At one end of the deck was the entrance, which was absolutely tiny, and at the other end there was a fridge. In the middle there was what's called a mess square, which had some tables and chairs in it.

When I arrived at the mess deck I went straight over to my bunk, got into my sleeping bag and went to sleep. Calm as you like. The next thing I know I was being pulled off my bunk and onto the floor by the duty watch, or the security patrol, as they're also known.

'What the fucking hell's going on?' I asked as I started coming around. Quite quickly, as a matter of fact.

'The duty officer wants you up on the flight deck now, Edwards,' said the one in charge.

As he said that I'd actually forgotten about what had happened, but a millisecond later it all came back to me.

'Fair a-fucking-nough,' I said, getting to my feet.

The duty officer who'd asked to see me was First Lieutenant Blackmore who was one below the captain. It's impossible to forget Lieutenant Blackmore as he was, and probably still is, about six-and-a-half feet tall. When the duty watch frogmarched me onto the flight deck the first thing I did was ask the lieutenant what the hell was going on. I think I must have been resigned to the fact that I was in trouble but as opposed to practising some damage limitation I was obviously in full-on kamikaze mode.

The look Blackmore gave me when I demanded to know what was going on was absolutely fucking hilarious as he'd obviously been expecting some kind of grovelling apology.

'We're actually waiting for the Military Police to arrive so they can arrest you, Edwards,' he said, trying to retrieve the upper hand.

'What the hell for?' I asked belligerently.

'You know full well what for, Edwards,' said Blackmore raising his voice. 'Striking a senior rank. You've done that man some serious damage.'

Now faced with the consequences of my actions – or at least the start of them – I was in what is often referred to as a 'fight or flight' situation in which the person concerned – or in this case the idiot – either stands their ground or buggers off. Not content with just one of these options I decided to take both and after picking up a boson's stool I proceeded to strike Lieutenant Blackmore across the head with it before running for the hatch. As I was nearing the top of the ladder a member of the duty watch got me by the collar but as he did I grabbed him by the shirt, pushed him off and he went straight down and hit his head on a metal hatch cover. That was another one out.

Just as before, once I was away from the melee I

walked calmly back the mess deck where five or six Marines were relaxing on their bunks.

'What's up, Taff?' one of them asked.

'I think I'm fucked,' I replied. 'I've just hit Blackmore with a boson's stool and thrown a member of the duty watch off a ladder.'

None of them seemed especially surprised.

Despite escaping the flight deck I remained in a situation that demanded I either fight or fuck off, as surrender was never going to be an option. Given the fact that we were on a ship and I didn't want to get wet, I decided to fight. The first thing I did was decide to build myself an armoury and the ideal place to do that was around the fridge, which meant I'd be facing the one and only entrance to the mess deck. Even today, whenever I go to a restaurant I always ask for a table that faces the entrance and if I can't get one I'll leave. I have to know who's coming in. It's instinct, I suppose. Instinct and paranoia.

Marines who are stationed onboard a warship are always in what's called a working party and back then the two main pieces of equipment you were issued with before boarding one of Her Majesty's ships were a knife and a marlin spike. If you were on duty these would always be attached to your belt but whenever you were off duty you'd hang them on the end of your bunk. At the time there must have been eight or nine knives and marlin spikes hanging from bunks so the first thing I did was collect them all up and put them behind the fridge. By now the other lads on the mess deck knew exactly what I had in mind and, after pulling themselves into an upright position, they started making suggestions.

'What about the jam, Taff?' one of them said while pointing to a pile of tins by the entrance. 'You could hurt somebody with one of those fuckers.'

The tins that the Marine was referring to were full of strawberry jam and weighed at least two pounds.

'Fuck me, you're right,' I said walking towards the entrance.

'Do you want a hand?' said another spectator.

'No, you lot stay where you are. Whatever happens I'm fucked so best not get involved.'

You should have seen the look on their faces. This was, to all intents and purposes, the build-up to a big fight – the calm before the storm, you might say – and the lads on the mess deck had ringside seats. The thing is, this wasn't going to be a one-on-one contest, which is why I was building the armoury. If anything it was going to be like something out of a WWF wrestling match, but with real violence and a bit more pain.

The first person to emerge through the entrance to the mess deck was a member of the duty watch and before he'd even had the chance to look up, having had to stoop to get in there, I'd thrown two tins of jam at his head. Bang – out cold. By the time they pulled him out of there I had enough adrenaline running through me to send an entire infantry into battle, except that I was also starting to get very angry.

The next person to try and make contact with me was the detachment sergeant major. He didn't try and come in though. He just shouted through the entrance.

'Edwards, don't be a prick,' he shouted. 'You're already in big trouble. It's a case of damage limitation now, so why not do yourself a favour and just give it up?'

'Why don't you fuck off,' I shouted back. 'I can't stand you. You're a twat.'

As I said this I picked up a tin of jam and chucked it at the entrance. 'You idiot, Edwards,' shouted the sergeant major. 'That almost hit me.'

'It was meant to, you dickhead.'

'Right. Fetch the OCRM,' he said to the duty watch.

The OCRM is the officer commanding Royal Marines on board a ship and on this occasion it was a Scouse officer called Steve.

When he eventually arrived at the entrance he did the sensible thing and asked if he could come in. 'All right, Taff,' he said. 'Mind if I have a word?'

The only time this bloke called me Taff was on the rugby field and even then it was only when he wanted the ball.

'No you can't. Now fuck off.' I wasn't going to waste any jam on this twat so I just left it at that.

For the next half an hour or so I was left to my own devices and so I sat cross-legged on top of the fridge and had a couple of fags. The other lads present seemed less enthusiastic now and instead of trying to engage me in conversation they lay down on their bunks facing away from me. Probably for the best.

The next man to request permission to come aboard was the fleet master-at-arms. This was quite a privilege really as the fleet master-at-arms was responsible for the policing and security of every ship in the British fleet! Fuck me, had I reached the big time?

Why they didn't send for this bloke first off I have no idea and the fact that they'd only sent for him now bothered me a little. The fleet master-at-arms didn't ask if he could have a word. He just walked in with a couple of henchmen. He stayed close to the entrance though, which was wise.

'Edwards,' he bellowed, 'what you've done so far will get you two years in prison – minimum – and immediate expulsion from the Royal Marines.'

'And who's going to put me in fucking prison then?' I asked politely.

That foxed him.

'Now look, Edwards,' he said trying a different tack, 'why don't you go upstairs, make us both a coffee, and then we can sit down and discuss this?'

What a 24-carat wanker.

'You are joking, aren't you?' I said, beginning to laugh. 'Either you're stupid – which I'd put money on – or you think I'm stupid, which I'd also put money on. Either way, I'm going to give you ten seconds to get out of here, otherwise all three of you are going down.'

'If that happens, Edwards, you will serve a lot of time in prison, do you understand? At least let me try and talk some sense into you.'

I picked up a tin of jam in one hand and a marlin spike in the other. 'You've got ten seconds,' I said, 'after which I'm going to throw these in your direction as hard as I can. Ten, nine, eight . . .'

'I think this conversation is at an end, Edwards,' he said, ducking down and shuffling out of the mess deck with his minions as fast as he could.

'Yes it is. Now fuck off!'

As the fleet master-at-arms was leaving he shouted to the other Marines.

'Do yourselves a favour,' he said. 'Try and make Edwards see sense, will you?'

'No chance,' came a voice from one of the bunks. 'You upset him, you get him out. We're not going anywhere near him.'

I think me telling the fleet master-at-arms to fuck off and then giving him an ultimatum that would have resulted in me throwing a tin at him rekindled the lads' interest as the boys in the bunks sat up again and started sparking up.

For the next hour or so all was quiet and I nodded off

for a few minutes. My mate Bob Birkett had positioned himself in the bunk nearest the entrance and it was him who woke me up.

'Hold up. Somebody's coming,' he said, sitting up.

It was a member of the duty watch.

'Don't worry,' he said standing away from the entrance. 'I don't want to come in. I've been told to let you know that Legs Diamond is coming to see you.'

Don't be fooled by the cheesy name. Legs Diamond, as well as being over six-and-a-half feet tall, hence the name, ran the dockyard police and was well known as being the hardest man there. He was the scourge of Plymouth dockyard and I hadn't had much to do with him until now. That said, his size and reputation told me that a few tins of jam and a marlin spike weren't going to deter him. Some evasive action was going to be needed and, if possible, a larger missile.

By now the lads in the bunks were behaving like five year-olds at a circus and as I started scouring the mess deck for something substantial to throw at the jolly green giant they started making suggestions again, but from the safety of their bunks.

'How about those boots over there?' one of them said pointing to a pair that were half protruding from underneath one of the bunks.

'Boots?' I exclaimed. 'FUCKING BOOTS! I've got the Navy's answer to the Kraken turning up in a minute and you want me to attack him with footwear?'

'Ah, I see what you mean,' he said.

'Fucking dickhead.'

As I started to resume my search it quickly became apparent that the only thing on the mess deck that might stop the approaching behemoth was the fridge. Just as this began to dawn on me I heard the sound of what I assumed were Legs Diamond's size fifteens striking the steel floor. The corridor outside the mess deck was quite short so if it was him he was literally seconds away. Without even unplugging it I ran over to the fridge and picked it up. Just at that moment the unmistakable head of Legs Diamond came into view at the entrance. Or, I should say, the top of his head. Because of his height he'd had to bend almost double to enter the mess deck so instead of seeing what was in front of him – i.e. a Welsh maniac holding a fridge – he was staring at the floor.

Mistake.

When he was halfway through I ran forward a couple of steps and threw the fridge as hard as I could. After bouncing once it struck the oncoming colossus straight on the head, knocking him out instantly. The next thing I saw was his head disappearing around the corner as they pulled him away. At that moment the audience, who, let's face it, probably weren't expecting this when they took to their bunks earlier in the day, let out a huge cheer.

'You absolute nutcase,' one of them said while clapping his hands. 'They could have sold tickets to this. The other lads will be going spare.'

A few moments later, while having a fag and a can of beer, I heard the unmistakable and thoroughly unwelcome tones of the detachment sergeant major.

'Right, Edwards,' he shouted through the entrance. 'Six o'clock. Gas and dogs. They're coming to take you out.'

I really couldn't stand this twat's voice. It grated on me.

'Fuck off you,' I shouted. 'You're still a twat.'

It was about ten to six when this happened and I knew that the game was up. We were supposed to have been going on an exercise earlier and so on top of taking the ship to siege and injuring half a football team's worth of senior ranks I'd scuppered that too.

After savouring my last swig of beer (I had a feeling I wouldn't be having any more for a while) I got my clean combats on, gave my boots a quick polish, packed an overnight bag and put on my beret.

'Right boys,' I said, walking towards the entrance. 'I'll see you lot later.'

In terms of generating laughter this line was worthy of Ken Dodd, although it was completely unintentional.

'I don't think you will,' said one of the lads, pissing himself laughing.

'Maybe in a few years,' said another.

As I ducked down to negotiate the exit they jumped off their bunks and followed me into the corridor.

'What do you reckon you'll get, Taff?' asked my lookout, Bob Birkett.

'If Blackmore or the detachment sergeant major have anything to do with it, execution!' I replied.

'Might be less painful,' said Bob. 'I just hope the MPs get to you before Legs does. I bet that's the first time he's ever been knocked out by a fucking fridge. Actually, it wouldn't surprise me if that's the first time he's ever been knocked out full stop.'

Joking aside, Bob had a point. In the last few hours I'd knocked out two men (one of whom was a highly dangerous giant) and, as well as busting another man's nose by pushing his face into a tap, I'd hit the first lieutenant over the head with a bosun's stool. I'd never been the most popular lad in the room but at this very moment in time there were at least four men who, unless they'd taken a vow of forgiveness – or were still unconscious – would be after my blood.

'I have a feeling there'll be one or two MPs waiting for me on deck,' I said to Bob. 'At least I hope there will!'

As I walked up the gangway towards the deck I felt like the proverbial condemned man. Legs or no Legs, I was fucked. That said, it had been a right laugh and whatever I ended up doing from now on (or whatever prison I ended up in, which I think accurately describes where most people who knew me thought I'd be spending most of my time), at least I'd have a decent story to tell. How many people have taken a 3,000-ton warship to siege? There can't be many.

When I opened the hatch at the top of the gangway I got the shock of my life. I'm not sure what I'd been expecting – the duty watch, a couple of MPs and everybody I'd injured, I suppose. All throwing tins of jam at me!

What actually greeted me was like the finale to an armed forces recruitment video and featured officers, shore watch, duty watch, MPs, dogs, dog handlers and even a fucking helicopter. What made it really impressive was that the dogs were going apeshit, the handlers were all wearing gasmasks and the blades of the helicopter were still spinning. My God, it was impressive. I felt like Rambo!

The first person I recognised when I started scanning the welcome party was First Lieutenant Blackmore who had obviously come around, more's the pity.

'I hope you're going to come quietly, Edwards,' he shouted.

With the dogs barking and the helicopter still going there was a hell of a racket.

'On one condition,' I shouted.

'What's that?'

'That I'm taken in by Marine police and Marine police only. I don't want any of these fucking matelots touching me.'

A matelot, by the way, is a sailor.

'All right,' said Blackmore. 'Stay where you are.'

Within a few seconds two Marines were marching towards me and in a few seconds more they'd cuffed me and were escorting me to the Royal Citadel. The Royal Citadel, which is on the eastern side of Plymouth Hoe and was built on the site of Sir Francis Drake's fort, is the home to 29 Commando and I was there for about two days.

I wouldn't say I was treated badly at the Royal Citadel but I got the feeling that 29 Commando wanted rid of me as soon as possible.

When the call came for me to be sent back to the dockyard, somebody said, 'It's time for you to be weighed off, Edwards' – weighed off means charged – and before I could say, *Thanks for your hospitality*, I'd been cuffed again and was on my way back there.

When we arrived at the dockyard I was marched straight in to the guard room and who was there to greet me? Legs Diamond. Scourge of Plymouth dockyard and the first person ever to be knocked out by a fridge on a warship. Probably.

Once I've calmed down after an attack of the red mist I can often become quite regretful and this was one of those times. In fact, when I saw Mr Diamond sitting there, and remembered that I was handcuffed, I may even have experienced a few twinges of remorse. Actually, who am I kidding? I was shitting myself. Worse still, he was smiling when I was marched in.

'Have you got a problem with me, Edwards?' he asked, getting out of his chair.

'Not any more,' I said, very quickly.

'All right. Uncuff him please, lads.'

After the guards had uncuffed me he dismissed them and then led me into a small room with no windows. *Oh fucking hell,* I thought. *I'm in for a right drubbing here. He's going to murder me!*

Right in the middle of the room was a small table and two chairs, and on the table were six cans of beer, a packet of fags and an ashtray.

'Sit down,' he said.

I remember thinking to myself, *What the fucking hell are you up to? Surely I'm a dead man.*

Once I was sat down the mountainous Mr Diamond walked to the other side of the table, pulled out his chair, sat down, opened up two cans of beer, pushed one to me, lit a fag, leant forward and with a huge smile on his face said, 'Come on then. Tell me what happened?'

What a relief!

All he wanted was the story of what had gone on.

'But I thought you were going to batter me?' I said, helping myself to a fag.

'Batter you? You're joking, aren't you? We haven't had this much fun in ages. As far as I'm concerned you're a legend. Here, have another beer.'

Over the next hour or so I gave the luckily genial Mr Diamond a blow-by-blow account of what had happened, including me chucking the fridge at him. By this point he was literally in tears and when I told him about his head disappearing around the corner he had to stop for breath.

'You do realise I had a headache for three days,' said Legs once he'd managed to compose himself.

'I'm sorry about that.'

'Fuck me. Don't apologise!'

As agreeable as that meeting was I was still a prisoner and over the next few weeks, while the charges against me were being prepared, I hardly saw the light of day. In the end, I asked Legs if I could do what was called the dinner run, which is when you went to collect the prisoners' meals. There were only about six of us at the time and although it was only about a ten-minute walk, at least you were out in the open.

'Come on,' said Legs, 'I know what you're like. You've gone AWOL before, haven't you?'

'Look,' I said, 'I promise I'll behave. I just need a bit of fresh air.'

'You'll have to be accompanied,' he said, starting to come round.

'Fine by me.'

He ended up chaining me to a cadet who can't have been more than about twelve years old. The poor lad was terrified.

'I heard about what you did,' he said to me on the first trip. 'Can you do me a favour? If you escape, please don't hit me first.'

'Don't you worry,' I said with a growl. 'I'll tell you if I'm going to run. OK?'

'Yes, yes. That's fine.'

After a couple of days somebody informed my fellow Marines on the *Danae* that I was doing the dinner run so and every time me and whoever was lucky enough to be chained to me passed the ship on the way to and from the kitchens they came out for a quick friendly chat.

'They're going to throw the fucking book at you, Taff!' they would shout. 'You'll be lucky to get out before you're sixty!'

'Cheers lads!'

After about five weeks of receiving dog's abuse in the fresh air I was told by Legs Diamond that it was weighing-off time. They'd obviously had to interview everybody I'd injured during the incident and the list of charges they were bringing against me was extensive to say the least. They included several counts of grievous bodily harm plus quite a few lesser misdemeanours. More than enough for one day.

The man in charge of the court was the captain of the HMS *Danae*, Brian Outhwaite, and he'd already got me out of one or two scrapes. In fact, he seemed to specialise in getting Marines out of trouble so if anybody was going to do a job for me, he was. As I was marched into his office prior to the hearing Captain Outhwaite immediately cleared the room.

'Everybody out please,' he said to the guards who'd escorted me in. 'I need a few moments alone with Marine Edwards.'

Once they'd gone he walked right up to me.

'OK then,' he said almost whispering. 'Whatever punishment I give you, you have to accept it, otherwise you'll be facing a lot of time inside. They might even ask for a civilian prosecution, and if that happens, you're finished.'

I was confused now. 'How do you mean, a civil prosecution?' I asked him.

'You mean you don't know?' said Captain Outhwaite.

'No idea.'

'OK, I'll give you an example. If you don't accept the punishment I give you it'll go to court martial and if that happens you'll get two to three years in here, after which you'll be kicked out of the Marines. On the day you're kicked out, you'll be rearrested by the civilian police and charged again with the same offences.'

At this point he picked up the charge sheet and studied it briefly.

'You'd get a minimum of ten years in a civilian court for this lot. Maybe more.'

This brought me down to earth.

Naval law dictates that if you accept the commanding

officer's punishment you don't have to go to court martial, which is why Captain Outhwaite was so desperate for me to play ball. If I didn't agree with the punishment and decided to mouth off – which, given my track record, was eminently possible – he'd have no choice but to send it to court martial. He was trying to save me from myself.

By the time it came to reading out the charges in court the list had shrunk from fuck knows how many charges (perhaps fifteen) to just one.

I soon found out that what had happened was that the ship's master-at-arms, a very good friend of mine called Pete Diablo (obviously not to be confused with my other very good friend, the fleet master-at-arms), had gone to each of the people I'd assaulted and had asked them to drop the charges.

One of the reasons Pete and I had become such good friends was because the moment he found out I could paint and draw he asked me if I'd like to be responsible for producing the plaques the ship gives away to visitors and signatories. Naturally I was over the moon about this and all he did was encourage me. Pete was also head of vent party (which meant he was in charge of the ship's ventilation system) and he used to allow me to commandeer the vent party sub section, which was always nice and warm, to create these plaques. He's a lovely bloke.

By the time it came to court the only one who'd refused to drop the charges was Lieutenant Blackmore, the twat! What a great thing for the rest of them to do though. It was an amazing gesture and I still don't know why they did it. When Captain Outhwaite finally read out the charge he said that I'd assaulted Lieutenant Blackmore, 'under provocation and in fear of my own safety', which was news to me. I was fine with it though.

'The punishment I recommend for this crime is ninety

days,' he said finally. 'Edwards, will you accept my punishment?'

After speaking he looked at me, terrified. Despite what he'd said about a civilian prosecution I think he still thought I was going to protest. Or call him an arsehole.

'Yes, sir,' I said, trying not to laugh. 'I will accept your punishment,'

He didn't say, *Thank fuck for that*, but I could tell that's what he was thinking.

Ninety days though?

It should have been ninety years.

*****

Despite often acting like I don't give a shit, I was quite nervous about spending another three months in prison. Especially as I was the only Marine in there.

It hadn't been a problem while I was on remand as it had all been kept under wraps (from the prisoners, at least) but now I was, 'doing time', after being convicted, everybody would be aware of the crimes I'd committed, charges or no charges. At the end of the day I'd assaulted – grievously, in one or two cases – several matelots, so the chances were they'd be gunning for me. It only took until lunchtime on the first day for things to kick off and the antagonist, if I'm being brutally honest, was me.

Why break the habit of a lifetime?

When I arrived at the galley, which is where we ate, I noticed that the other prisoners had formed a queue but instead of joining them I took a tray, walked past the waiting prisoners, and picked up some cutlery, sauces and condiments, before choosing a table and taking a seat. I wasn't going to wait in a queue with a bunch of matelots. I'd simply wait until they'd been served and then I'd go up and collect my grub.

About five seconds after I'd sat down one of the blokes who'd been serving behind the counter ran up to my table and grabbed me by the scruff of the neck.

'What the fucking hell do you think you're doing, Edwards?' he yelled. His eyes were popping out of his head!

'I'm waiting for the queue to die down. What do you think I'm doing?'

'Don't you dare speak to me like that. Who the hell do you think you are? You don't say or do ANYTHING in this galley without my permission. Do you understand? If you want to sit down you say, "Can I sit down please, SIR?" If you want a knife and fork, you say, "Can I please have a knife and fork please, SIR?"'

That wasn't going to happen. Not in a million years.

'Fuck off,' I said. 'I'm not doing that.'

Just at that moment another man who'd been serving the food leapt over the counter, grabbed hold of this matelot and pushed him against a wall. He was like a fucking gorilla. A talking gorilla!

'He's a Royal. He's mine. Leave him. Do you understand?'

The matelot with the big mouth, who genuinely seemed to be fearing for his life, retreated behind the counter.

'Are you all right?' asked the gorilla.

'Yeah, I'm fine. Cheers for that.'

Not only was this man a colour sergeant in the Royal Marines, but he was also an ex-boxer. Had I landed on my feet? From that moment on I didn't experience a whiff of trouble from anybody.

Bizarrely enough, I enjoyed that three months in Portsmouth Detention Quarters (and not just because I had a minder!). I came out calmer, fitter and happier than I think I ever had been.

Each day started early, which suited me, and as well as getting plenty of fresh air and fitness training we did a lot of drill and were even encouraged to dabble in education. It wasn't too dissimilar to the Marine training, just without the pressure.

If you smoked, which almost all of us did, you were allowed one Blue Liner after each meal and if you didn't smoke you got six boiled sweets. Blue Liners were so tightly packed that you had to light them about sixteen times so I ended up taking the boiled sweets instead. It's the only time I've ever given up smoking and, surprise, surprise, I felt a lot better for it. I started again as soon as I got out, but at least I could say I'd given my lungs a holiday, albeit a short one. Given the amount of time I've been smoking it was akin to a long weekend.

Such was my transformation in Portsmouth Detention Quarters that on my release I was recommended for promotion!

Things had been that good.

This was before I had my final interview though. After that I'd have been lucky to get a kick in the bollocks. Once again it was my gob that got me into trouble. That and the old red mist. I can be a stupid twat sometimes.

When I was marched in for this final interview I stood to attention and the officer behind the desk said, 'Off caps.'

Shortly beforehand I'd been given my berry back (minus the badge as I was still in disgrace) and by law I didn't have to remove it. I certainly could have. You know, in the interests of civility and maintaining good relations with my colleagues in the Navy, etc. But no, not me.

'Are you going to remove your beret, Marine

Edwards?' asked the officer. 'Or am I going to charge you with dissent?'

That was it, I'm afraid. The mist was upon me.

'You can do what you fucking like, matelot,' I said. Sorry, shouted. 'I will not be removing my beret.'

The Marine colour sergeant, who had become my keeper, was asked to come into the office and when the officer told him what was happening he backed me up.

'Marine Edwards is perfectly within his rights not to remove his beret,' he said. 'In fact, the law states that Marine Edwards isn't required to remove his beret for anybody. Not even Her Majesty the Queen.'

Again, in the interests of civility, the colour sergeant could have taken me outside and advised me to relent, but this was obviously a them-and-us situation and it appeared that no quarter was going to be given.

'His badge is off in disgrace,' continued the colour sergeant, 'and I'm afraid that's all you're going to get from him. I suggest you let him go.'

The officer in charge signed the papers and then asked me what draft I'd like. It sounds amazing, but as part of your rehabilitation you're allowed to choose whatever draft you like when you're released from detention quarters and the vast majority of men and women will naturally go for somewhere hot like the West Indies.

'The HMS *Danae*,' I said.

The colour sergeant and the officer looked at each other and then at me. 'I beg your pardon,' said the officer. 'Did you just say the HMS *Danae*?'

'That's right, sir. I'd like to go back to my ship.'

'You mean the ship you took to siege after battering half its crew. Sergeant, have a word with him, would you? He's obviously losing his mind.'

'With respect, Sir, I am not losing my fucking mind, and the law states that I can . . .'

'Yes, yes, yes, I know what the law states, Marine Edwards. I just can't believe what I'm hearing.'

'Would you like me to speak to Captain Outhwaite?' said the colour sergeant.

'Yes, if you would,' said the officer. 'God knows what he's going to say though.'

Although there was often bad feeling between the Navy and the Royal Marines it could also work the other way and Captain Outhwaite was testament to that. I think he liked the idea of having a crack force of soldiers on his ship, which is why he always looked out for us. In his eyes, we were *his* Marines. Apparently, when the colour sergeant told Captain Outhwaite of my intentions, he said, 'Great! Get him back on board. The lad's a nutcase.'

A few days later it was time for me to go back on board and I remember the day clearly as it was absolutely pissing down. I'd been sent up to Cape Wrath in the Highlands for a few days and they'd delivered me back to the *Danae* by helicopter. When I jumped out I ran straight down the gangway and opened the hatch. When I hit the deck I had a quick look around and the first thing I noticed were a load of heads peering nervously around the doors. It was like the Munchkin scene from *The Wizard of* fucking *Oz*.

Come out, come out wherever you are – you bunch of wimps.

'All right lads,' I boomed. 'Have you missed me?'

Just at that moment every single head disappeared and every door closed.

It was good to be back.

SEVEN

My draft on the HMS *Danae* after being released was just six months and at the end I put in for an extension. God knows why but I absolutely loved living on a ship and so even if the extension was refused I'd simply put in for a transfer.

During that six months I'd been a model Marine, all except for one aspect – my drinking. Life on the *Danae* while we weren't on exercise was a bit humdrum and instead of reading an improving book or going for a run I'd go out and get pissed. Very pissed. Subsequently, the extension was refused by Captain Outhwaite and when I then put in for a transfer the matter was taken out of my hands.

In the report that followed it stated that my behaviour may have had something to do with fact that I had far too much time on my hands and this statement was prefixed with the suggestion that, in addition to possessing good leadership skills, I was officer material. This last bit in particular had me scratching my head and jumping for joy at the same time, but what followed had me running for cover. As well as suggesting that I get off ships and become a full-time Marine again it said I should do so with 45 Commando, up in Arbroath on the east coast of Scotland. The reason this had me running for cover is because 45 Commando are also known as Ski Commando and they practise mountain and arctic warfare. In other words, they spend their entire lives freezing their arses off! I'm not sure if it's the same today but back then the battalion generally alternated its time between Arbroath, Norway, Germany and the Isle of Skye, none of which are known for good weather, which was obviously why they were chosen.

My God, I was dreading it. That said, I was more than aware that I needed a big kick up the arse so did as I was told, for a change.

Within my first two weeks of being with 45 Commando I'd had training on the Isle of Skye, where it rained almost constantly while blowing a force ten gale, dug a hole in some snow on the side of hill in Germany before sleeping in it, and had tried my hand at cross country skiing, which, on top of hating every second of it, I couldn't do to save my life.

As somebody who has a strong aversion to all of the above it's safe to say that at the end of that first two weeks I was ever so slightly fed up and would have given anything to get back on the *Danae*. It wasn't going to happen, of course, and I knew deep down that it couldn't. I was also grateful to the powers that be for stepping in and preventing me from becoming an alcoholic.

About six weeks later, although it seemed like six months – genuinely – I saw a sign on the noticeboard in the NAAFI that said something along the lines of, *Would you like to wear long hair, wear civilian clothes and work on your own?* There was a piece of paper underneath where you were supposed to write your name if you were interested, and I most certainly was, as were a few of my mates. There was Mitch, who ended up being my best man at my wedding, a lad called Jessie, who we'd imaginatively christened Jessie James, a short Scottish bloke and a lad from Rhyl who I didn't know and whose names escape me.

That night – it was a Sunday – I decided to go out on the piss to celebrate. I had no idea what we'd signed up for, by the way, and to be honest I didn't give a shit. I just wanted to be somewhere – anywhere – that was further south than Arbroath! The only problem I had in wanting to get shitfaced was that the only place open was the local Quaich Club and I had more chance getting a drink there than I did getting a fucking tan. No matter, in a couple of days' time RM Condor, which was the name of our base, was hosting a dance for the Marines and the locals. I could fill my boots then.

Sure enough, I ended up getting absolutely wankered at this dance, and, according to Mitch, I spent the entire night dancing with a girl called Theresa. I don't remember a thing about this, apart from what Theresa looked like, and Mitch also told me that she and I had arranged to meet each other at 7 p.m. the following evening, which was now tonight.

I may not have remembered much about the dancing but at least I could remember what Theresa looked like. This was obviously going to be essential when it came to picking her out among the crowds at Arbroath station, which is where we'd arranged to meet. So, although I was hungover, I wasn't going to make a twat of myself. Not immediately, at least.

Theresa, on the other hand, who must have been as pissed as I was, had remembered about the date but couldn't for the life of her remember what I looked like and she had to ask a friend of hers – somebody who had been lucky enough to witness our pissed up Fred & Ginger routine – for a description.

'He looks a bit like Omar Sharif,' said Theresa's friend.

'Really?' said Theresa enthusiastically. 'Are you taking the piss?'

As a matter of fact, she wasn't.

I may not have been his double but because I had a black moustache, dark skin and striking good looks, Omar and I did share a passing resemblance to one another, or so I was told.

The reason I was attracted to Theresa – physically, that is, as I couldn't remember if I actually liked her – was because she had Mia Farrow's eyes and I'd always found them quite hypnotic.

By the time I got to the station I was a little bit nervous and when I saw that Theresa was already waiting for me I broke into a trot.

'All right?' I said waving to her. 'Good night last night?'

At the time I obviously had no idea that she'd forgotten what I looked like but in hindsight – and our first date is one of my most vivid memories – it did seem to take her a moment or two to recognise me.

'Yeah, I suppose so,' she replied enthusiastically. 'Shall we go and get a drink?'

We retired to a pub called the Station, where Theresa told me that she'd been working for the knitwear company, Pringle, since the age of fifteen, and, like me, she'd had a fairly hard childhood. No abuse. They just hadn't had much money.

After a few bevvies we decided to call it a day and, because it was late, I was going to have to walk back to the base, which was about 3 miles.

'Why don't you stay at ours?' said Theresa. 'It's snowing like hell out there. You'll have to sleep on the couch but my parents won't mind and it's better than walking three miles.'

I didn't need asking twice.

Because of the previous evening's exertions, not to mention downing a few with Theresa, I started to flag on the journey to her house and after about five minutes I told Theresa that I needed to sit down for a minute. Fifteen minutes later I was sitting against a cemetery fence fast asleep and whatever Theresa did to try and wake me didn't work. This is another talent of mine, falling asleep in random places, and once I'm gone, that's it for anything up to three hours. These days people tend to leave me alone because, if somebody does manage to bring me around, I usually come out fighting. In fact, what people usually do if I fall into a temporary coma is pile all their coats on top of me. That happens a lot these days.

After about twenty minutes Theresa decided to go back to her place and ask her dad if he'd come and try and wake me up, and fortunately he obliged. Her dad was blind, but Theresa still thought he'd stand a much better chance of waking me than she did.

When Theresa and her dad arrived I was covered head to toe in snow but was still fast asleep. God only knows how much I'd had to drink over the last two nights but it was obviously enough to render my nemesis – the cold – completely powerless. Still, he was able to wake me up without me going bananas, and the long and short of it is that, rather than me dying of hyperthermia, I had managed to get myself a girlfriend.

One morning, about six or seven months after I'd applied to grow my hair and plan my own wardrobe, I got a call saying there was somebody at the gatehouse to see me. I'd just got out of the shower and was wearing a towel and flipflops. I had no idea who it was, so I didn't bother getting dressed and just went as I was.

When I got to the gatehouse the only person there who I didn't recognise or who wasn't in uniform was a small bloke in a black suit wearing a bowler hat.

'Excuse me,' I said tapping him on the shoulder. 'Can I help you? I'm Marine Edwards.'

To be fair he didn't bat an eyelid when he saw me standing there in a towel and flipflops and just held out his hand.

'My name is Charles Egerton and I'm from the Ministry of Defence.'

By the look on this chap's face he was obviously under the impression that his name and place of work should have enlightened me as to what he wanted to see me about, but I'm afraid I was at a loss.

'Sorry?' I muttered. 'The Ministry of Defence?'

'Ah,' said the man from the ministry. 'I see you may have forgotten. Is there somewhere we can talk, Marine Edwards? And perhaps you'd like to put some clothes on?'

About fifteen minutes later Mr Egerton and I were sitting opposite each other in an office but I was still none the wiser.

'Several months ago you applied for a role that would allow you to grow your hair and wear your own clothes. Remember?'

Fortunately, I was able to prevent myself from verbalising the first thing that came into my head, which for the record would have been something along the lines of *Fuck me sideways!*

'I can see from the look on your face that you've

caught up, Marine Edwards,' said Mr Egerton. 'Well, I'm here to see if you're suitable for the first step.'

'The first step for what though? I've still only heard rumours.'

'And what rumours might they be?' said Mr Egerton, now hanging on my every utterance.

'Well, there's a sergeant based here who did the same course last year.'

'Is there now? And what did he say?'

'Well, according to him it's a replacement for the MRF.'

Mr Egerton looked disappointed.

'And what else did the sergeant say?'

'Only that last year was the first intake. He wouldn't tell us anything else.'

'I think we'll leave it at that then, for the time being. You don't need to know anything else just at the moment.' He then proceeded with the interview.

The MRF, which stands for Military Response Force, was a covert intelligence-gathering and counter-insurgency unit that was active in Northern Ireland from 1971 until 1973. Charged with tracking down and arresting members of the IRA, they were quickly accused of being nothing more than a legalised death squad as in addition to drawing the Provisional IRA into a shooting match with loyalists, thus distracting the IRA from their objective of attacking the British Army, they also killed a number of civilians. In truth, the unit was overt (or at least it became overt), which became its downfall. This was mainly down to the fact that the unit all wore donkey jackets and drove around in Hunter saloon cars. It worked for a while, but at the end of the day it was just a different kind of uniform and after the Provisional IRA managed to uncover one of the front companies, the unit was dissolved.

The official name of the unit that would be replacing the MRF, which is what I'd inadvertently applied for, was the Special Reconnaissance Unit – the SRU – and would also become known as 14 Field Security and Intelligence Company, and, internally at least, 'the Det' (short for the Detachment).

About ten minutes into the interview, the man from the ministry brought up something that I feared would scupper my chances.

'I hear there was a little kerfuffle on the HMS *Danae* a while ago.'

'You could say that.'

'I also hear you received a great deal of support from your colleagues. Some of whom were even willing to drop charges against you. Is that correct?'

'It is, sir.'

'I've also been informed that you have leadership qualities and aren't easily fazed. You really are a paradox, Marine Edwards.'

I had absolutely no idea what a paradox was at the time but in the interests of my future and being able to grow my hair, I agreed with him. That said, his next question threw me a bit.

'You're a very angry young man, are you not Marine Edwards?' he said, studying some A4 paper that I assume was my report.

'Sometimes,' I said honestly.

Fortunately his manner was neither patronising nor pompous, otherwise it could have got nasty. In fact, he was quite friendly really, so I answered his questions honestly and calmly.

'How are you with fear, Marine Edwards?' was his next question.

'I really don't experience it,' I said after making eye contact with him. 'Not any more.'

I could tell by the look on his face that he was dying to ask me what I was getting at but he left it.

A few minutes later I decided to throw caution to the wind and practise what I now know to be called, in the sales world, a presumptive close.

'Am I in then?' I asked cockily.

This was completely in character for me so I figured it was the best thing to do. When Mr Egerton replied he tried to sound all disapproving, but I could tell he liked me.

'We'll notify you in due course, Marine Edwards,' he said, trying not to smile. 'We're seeing over fifteen hundred people in all so the competition is bound to be stiff.'

Stiff my arse. I knew there and then that I was in but instead of saying so, which wouldn't have been wise, I shook Mr Egerton by the hand, bid him good day, and went to ponder what had just happened. And, more importantly, what I thought was going to happen.

Sure enough, about three weeks later I received a letter from the ministry informing me that I'd been accepted onto the SRU training course, providing I made it through the vetting process. This was almost forensic and went back no fewer than three generations at a cost of about £60,000 per person. That was in 1976, mind you, and today it would be getting on for three-quarters of a million quid. It took me four full days to fill out all the forms I was given. Every single living member of my family was contacted, on both sides, and of course the first thing they did was ask me what it was about. I couldn't tell them, though, which in itself must have given them an idea.

I found out that I'd made it through the vetting process and onto the course proper about halfway through a three-week exercise on the Isle of Skye. The reason I remember this is because I'd just been issued with brand a new pair of boots, which, after I'd climbed up to the top of Cuillin Ridge before scrambling down again the bloody things had fallen to pieces. The amount of money they spent on vetting people was a joke compared to the amount of money they spent on equipment because the majority of it was crap. Later that day the post arrived and the only one for me was a letter from the ministry informing me that I was in.

The next day I went to meet Theresa with the intention of finishing our relationship. It wasn't because we weren't getting on. I just couldn't see the point of continuing as, in addition to having no idea where I was going (although I assumed it would be south of Arbroath), I wouldn't be able to tell her a damn thing.

The reaction I received was a bit of a surprise. The first thing she said when I told her that I was finishing up our relationship was, and I quote, 'No you're fucking not.'

At first I didn't know what to say.

'You what?' I said eventually.

'You heard. Who the hell do you think you are? Nobody finishes with me.'

Just to put mine and Theresa's relationship then in perspective, a few weeks earlier we'd been out on the piss together on a Sunday and had been invited back to a party at a flat belonging to a friend of hers. Like a tit, I'd had nothing to eat all day and by the time we arrived at the party I was starving, and I was very, very pissed.

When this woman opened the door, as opposed to me saying something like, 'Thank you so much for inviting us to your home. Here's a bottle of Black Tower,' I stumbled over the threshold, handed her a carryout of beer I'd got from the pub and belched the words, 'Got anything to eat?' Even then

Ultimate Survivor

Theresa was the only person on earth who could control me to any degree, and she followed me over the threshold and gave me a quick dig in the ribs.

'Marrrrrr-tin! Bloody well behave yourself.'

I didn't argue.

About ten minutes later our hostess walked into the living room while I was leaning against the wall trying to light a fag.

'Are you sure you haven't got anything to eat?' I said belligerently.

'No, I bloody haven't. Now why don't you fuck off, you wanker?'

That was a bit strong.

In those days the only person who could speak to me like that, and live, was Theresa, so with her nowhere to be seen I decided to get involved. To be honest, I'd been itching for some aggro all day so this was exactly what the doctor ordered.

After spotting a big goldfish bowl on the sideboard, I put my hand in, grabbed hold of some goldfish, put them in my mouth, chewed a bit, swallowed, and then licked my lips.

'Don't worry,' I said to my potty-mouthed host, 'I found something. It's a pity you didn't have any tartar sauce though.'

At first I thought she was going to charge at me with her fists flying, but I was wrong. Instead, she walked calmly over to where I was leaning, took her cigarette out of her mouth and pushed it into my forearm. I was too bloody pissed to feel any pain but I was surprised, I'll give her that. And impressed, to be honest. They were hard as nails up there so for all I know she could have been making a pass at me. Regardless of which, it was game on now so as this cow was walking out of the room I took out my cigarette lighter, snuck up behind her and set fire to the bottom of her skirt. Because it was the mid-1970s, her skirt was probably made of something like crinoline and it went up like a tinderbox. I got slightly more emotion out of her this time than I did when I ate her goldfish, but unfortunately I got a similar reaction from Theresa who went apo-fucking-plectic. Once she'd helped put her friend out, that is. Who was unharmed, by the way, save for a couple of burns on her legs.

'What the fucking hell did you think you'd achieve by setting fire to her skirt?' she screamed while bundling me back over the threshold and smacking me across the back of the head.

'I know you're supposed to be a bit of a lunatic Martin, but do you have to be an arsehole too? Do you?'

'But she was getting on my nerves,' I pleaded unconvincingly.

'What? So you thought you'd eat some of her pets alive and then set fire to her? Fuck me, Martin, if that's what you do when people get on your nerves what the hell do you do when they piss you off?'

'I haven't really given it much thought.'

'Don't you get clever with me, Martin,' said Theresa, giving me a proper dig in the ribs. 'I'd ask you to go back in there and apologise but she'd probably call the police. I certainly would. You're an idiot, Martin, do you know that? A fucking idiot.'

And this was the woman who didn't want to finish with me?

She was as mad as I was.

Well, almost.

EIGHT

The last thing I did before starting my training was to spend a few days in Birmingham with my mate Jessie from 45 Commando. He'd also applied to join the Det and had invited me to stay with his family. Basically, we just got shitfaced every day and on the Sunday, which is when we were supposed to report for our first day's training, we went out for lunch with Jessie's sister and his parents. The camp was in a place called Swynnerton, which is just off the M6 and a few miles north of Jessie's home. So, after polishing off some roast beef and Yorkshire puds, not to mention about six or seven pints of Double Diamond, we made our way up there. I can't remember how.

The instruction we'd been given was to turn up after noon and we landed at about 4. p.m. The majority of people may be thinking, *He hasn't even set foot in the place yet and already he's behaving like an idiot.* Nope. Not this time. We took the instruction literally, as in, do not arrive *before* noon, and in the end it saved us getting sent back to our unit.

Of the eighty that started that day (there were 1,500 in all) twenty were sent back for turning up early. They obviously thought they were being clever but they got it so wrong. I saw the staff sergeant saying to one young lad, 'If you can't follow a simple instruction you're no use to us. Now fuck off.' He was gutted.

The first thing we did when we arrived inside the camp was to sign away our human rights. We didn't give a shit because we were pissed but there were one or two people who did have an issue with this and the moment they started asking questions that was it – out.

The colonel who'd asked us to sign these pieces of paper was a Marine colonel and I'll never forget what he said to us when we handed them to him signed. He said, 'You shouldn't have done that boys, because you're going to suffer.' It didn't sober me up exactly but it made me more aware of my surroundings.

After that we were issued with our kit. There was no uniform. We got a gym kit, jeans, underwear, sweatshirts, T-shirts and a jacket, and none of it had our names on. We were then informed that all telephone calls and letters, both incoming and outgoing, would be strictly vetted and so to all intents and purposes – for as long as we were there, at least – we would be owned, lock stock and barrel, by the Ministry of Defence.

About nine hours later we had our first taste of what the colonel had been getting at. The start of what we later found out was called 'make-or-break week' was also the first sifting (if you don't count turning up before noon and questioning having to sign away your human rights). At exactly 1 a.m., just as I was having a lovely dream about doing something disgusting on a beach somewhere, about six or seven soldiers stormed the hut and started screaming and shouting and letting off thunder flashes. I knew what was coming. Basically, we were going to hell.

The first thing they did before taking us there was to give each man his number. Mine was 777 which, when it was shouted out, sounded like an elongated bingo call. All the sevens, seven hundred and seventy-seven. That was the least of my worries.

Over the next week they kicked the shit out of us, both physically and mentally. Our deterioration was hastened by the use of sleep deprivation. We were being observed twenty-four hours a day so if you nodded off, even for a second, you'd have somebody screaming in your ear and pulling you to your feet. It was relentless. Occasionally they'd give you an hour or so, just so you didn't go mad, and the relief you felt when it happened was indescribable. It was what you lived for. It didn't matter where you were, if you got permission to have a quick kip you just dropped and went to sleep.

One of the most brutal things we did during make-or-break week was calling milling. Three minutes of head-to-head bare-knuckle fighting. Anything goes. We were each paired up randomly, but with somebody who was a similar size. The first person I fought was an intelligence lad who ended up failing the course and being RTU'd – returned to unit.

As we lined up I must have had a less than aggressive look on my face as one of the sergeants said, 'Come on 777. You're supposed to want to kill this man. Snarl at him!' Just as his words were beginning to register the intelligence lad smacked me right in the mouth. He chipped one of my teeth, the bastard.

As I wiped some of the blood away I said, 'Right then, you cunt,' and went for him. Three minutes later were on our knees in front of each other attempting to throw punches. We were both as fit as fuck but this had finished us. And in three minutes.

The following day, after we'd had no more than an hour's sleep, they lined us up in the same place as before. With the assumption being that milling was on the agenda, thirteen people refused to get involved. The lad I was up against was a black belt in absolutely everything, which was just my luck, but, even though I was fearing the worst, I wasn't going anywhere. Apart from the floor, maybe.

As soon as the thirteen started to bugger off the sergeant said, 'All right, lads. Murderball.'

We weren't doing milling at all!

Immediately the thirteen deserters all started to walk back to the group but the sergeant wasn't having any of it.

'No chance,' he said. 'You can all fuck off. Consider yourselves RTU'd.'

Murderball involves two teams and an old Land Rover tyre, and one of the teams has to get it past the other. It's rough at times, but not nearly as brutal as milling. Saying that, a mate of mine broke his ankle during that game of Murderball and was RTU'd, so it was still dangerous.

Everything they did was for a reason, so it all makes sense now. Everything was a test. Some things were obvious, such as milling or break week, which were straightforward tests of character and strength, and others, such as asking us to arrive after noon, were less obvious.

One morning in late November, so about a month and a half in, we were all called outside to the training ground.

'Don't bring a thing with you,' said the corporal. 'Not a thing.'

Once we were on the training ground they lined us all up and started hosing us down with cold water. By then, nothing they did surprised me and as I stood there getting pneumonia I did start to wonder what the fucking hell I was doing there.

After that they put us in pairs (I was with the intelligence lad again) and gave us all a pad of paper and a pencil each.

'Right then, lads,' started the corporal, 'in a moment, each pair will be taken to a location where they must stay for the next twenty-four hours. From there, you will record everything that goes on in front of you and you will not move from that position until you are told, is that clear?'

There was no cover. Oh yes, and it was pissing down. On top of that we weren't given any supplies. No food. No water. No fags. Nothing. It was horrible.

When it got to the evening, after which time we'd recorded absolutely fuck all, one of the staff sergeants sidled up to me and pulled out a pack of fags.

'You smoke don't you, 777?' he said.

I hated this bloke. He was a SAS boy called Brown and despite being a fellow Taff, I didn't like him one little bit.

'Yes, staff,' I replied hopefully.

'Well, here you go then boy,' he said handing me a fag. 'You're doing well, you are. Good lad.'

By now I knew what was coming but I had to go through with it, just in case.

'Could I have a light please, staff?'

'A light? I've just given you a fucking fag. What else do you want me to do, smoke it for you?'

I was right. The twat.

About half an hour later he arrived again.

'You hungry boys?'

'Yes, staff. Fucking starving.'

'Here you go then,' he said chucking us a couple of tins. 'There's some rations for you.'

I knew it would either be tins or dried food but at least with dried food we'd have been able to eat it. Dry!

'Silly fucking question, staff,' I began, 'but I don't suppose you've got a tin opener on you, have you?'

'Do you know, Edwards, I don't think I have. I'll tell you what I have got though. I've got an orange.'

With that the evil Welsh bastard pulled out an orange the size of a beach ball (at least that's how I remember it), walked to within about a metre of us, and started to peel the bloody thing.

I don't know if you've ever smelt an orange when you're experiencing hunger but let's just say it accentuates things somewhat.

'Do you what know, lads?' he said, putting a couple of segments in his fat horrible gob. 'The orange is a very underrated fruit in my opinion. It's very tasty. Almost rejuvenating.'

We just walked away in the end. It was either that or kill the bastard. Before eating him.

Shortly after that, we got the chance to record something, as when Staff Sergeant Brown went waddling off into the distance, two of our number started walking back towards the hut. Two down.

About half an hour later, after four more unfortunate bastards had given up the ghost, we heard a whistle.

'That must be it,' said the lad partnering me.

'It'll be a trap,' I snapped. 'You mark my fucking words.'

By this time I didn't trust anything anybody did. I wasn't paranoid, exactly. I was just wary of the fact that you could fail at absolutely any time and without even realising it.

The next thing we heard was Staff Sergeant Brown.

'Are you coming down then, lads?' he shouted to us.

'Fuck off,' I yelled. 'It's obviously a trap. Sorry. I meant to say "Fuck off, staff."'

'Never mind "Fuck off, staff." It's endex, you bloody idiot.'

Endex means end of an exercise but even after he'd said it I was still a bit wary.

'Promise you're not taking the piss?'

'No, Edwards, I am not taking the piss you cheeky piece of shit. Now get down her on the double, otherwise I'll make you stay there for another day.'

We started walking gingerly towards the training ground and once we were satisfied that all was well we broke into a trot. About two mouthfuls into breakfast the door to the NAAFI was kicked in by, who else, but Staff Sergeant Brown.

'Out you go again, lads. I want a security survey of the camp, if you please. Here's some more paper for you.'

Under his breath I heard the intelligence lad say, 'You twenty-four-carat cunt,' and I couldn't have agreed more. We'd been soaking wet and freezing cold for the best part of twenty-four hours and hadn't had a thing to eat or drink, apart from the slurp of tea and half a rasher of bacon.

'Get that fork out of your mouth, Edwards,' cried staff as I tried to sneak another mouthful in before we left. 'You will have breakfast when you've finished the survey and not before. Keep your chins up though, lads. It shouldn't take you more than three or four hours.'

This 24-carat cunt had suddenly gone platinum.

Not only did we have to compile a survey of the camp including entrances, exits and potential weaknesses, but afterwards we had to present the bloody thing to an officer. Four-and-a-half fucking hours it took us and I don't remember a thing about the presentation. By the time we'd finished I was too tired to eat so I went straight to bed. I think everybody did.

Camp One lasted five weeks in total and during that time they sifted out over half the candidates. To be honest, and this isn't just blether, I enjoyed most of it. Does that make me a masochist? Probably. Back then I enjoyed being tested but I was also a tenacious little bastard who disliked authority so completing Camp One was my way of giving the twats at the top the finger. *You'll have to try harder than that, you fuckers!* That would have been my parting shot, had they asked for one. Instead they simply moved us on to Camp Two which was in a place called Pontrilas, outside Abergavenny.

The other reason why I pretty much sailed through Camp One was because Camp Two was supposed to be all about guns and car chases, or so I'd heard. Had I thought beyond the prospect of jumping across car bonnets and doing impressions of Starsky and Hutch, I might have realised that I couldn't actually drive. In a moment of lucidity, perhaps while I wasn't being deprived of sleep, I might have mentioned it to one of my superiors. Instead, I just carried on regardless and didn't realise until I'd arrived at the sodding camp, which was embarrassing.

'Right then, lads,' said my good friend Staff Sergeant Brown almost jokingly on the first morning. 'I take it you've all passed your driving tests?'

It was only then that it dawned on me.

Pointing a finger upwards ever so gingerly I said, 'Erm no, I haven't, staff.'

The look he gave me translated into three words: *You – useless – cunt.*

'Why the bloody hell didn't you tell anybody, Edwards?' began staff. 'You've been with us for five weeks, have you not?'

'I have, staff.'

'And in that time did you not think that, somewhere along the way, you might be required to drive a vehicle of some kind?'

'Yes, I did Staff.'

'Then why the fucking hell didn't you tell anybody?'

'I forgot.'

'You twat, Edwards! What are you?'

'A twat, staff.'

Just then my mate Jay, who I'd met at Camp One, stuck his finger up.

'I'm afraid I'm also a twat, staff.'

'You what? Oh, for fuck's sake. Right, come on then,' said staff addressing everyone else. 'Last orders at the twat bar.'

Fortunately for him that was it. No more twats.

One morning, about a month in, I got called into the colonel's office. It was the same bloke who'd checked us into Camp One and because I was a Marine and a bit daft I think he liked me.

'You've received a letter from your brother Tony, Edwards,' said the colonel. 'He's in rather a lot of trouble.'

'What kind of trouble?'

'Well, let's just say that he's done something that has resulted in him being threatened with a gun.'

'Can I go and see him, colonel?' I asked.

'Yes, you can, Edwards,' he said, 'but if you're away for even a second over twenty-four hours you will be RTU'd, is that clear?'

'Yes, colonel.'

After he handed me the letter I went to pack a bag and, after doing so, I sat on my bed and read the contents. It turned out that my brother had been shagging the wife of a very dangerous nightclub owner and this bloke had had a pistol to Tony's head and had vowed to kill him. My brother had no idea where I was, by the way. Nobody did. He'd had to write to me via a Post Office box. He'd obviously moved back to Rhyl at some point although he wasn't living with my parents.

Later that day I arrived at the address that Tony had given me and luckily he was in.

After saying our hellos and then sitting down, I asked him what the hell was going on.

'As you know, I'm in a bit of trouble,' he said.

'Yes, so I read. Do you think he's being serious?'

'Definitely. The bloke's a nutcase. He's just waiting for the right time.'

'But what do you want me to do about it, Tony?' I asked him. 'I'm in the forces, not the police.'

'I don't know. I'm desperate and there was nobody else I could turn to really.'

'Look,' I said, 'I've only got twenty-four hours so I can't do anything now. Let me go back and have a think about it. I'll also speak to a few of the lads.'

The look on Tony's face when I said I'd try and help him spoke volumes. I'd obviously given him some hope. As time was of the essence, instead of using my full twenty-four hours I went straight back to camp and made some enquiries. The powers that be already knew the situation, having vetted the letter, and shortly after returning I was asked by an officer, who will have to remain nameless, how I'd got on.

I said, 'He's fucked unless I do something. It's just a matter of time.'

'OK,' said the officer, 'there are two things we can do. We can either send some SAS boys down there with a photograph, start a fight, and then rip this bloke apart, or, if you don't think that will work, we can just take him out.'

Ultimate Survivor

To be honest, I'm not really sure what kind of reaction I'd been expecting, but it definitely wasn't that. By the time I managed to track my brother down again he'd done the sensible thing and had fled Rhyl and when I told him what the options were he was as surprised as I was.

'I think I'll take my chances,' he said. 'Thanks though.' It had obviously unnerved him as much as it had me.

The start of Camp Two, which lasted about three months, was all about interrogation and as well as being incredibly intense it really fucked around with our heads. As with Camp One, we'd get dropped off in the middle of nowhere (one by one this time) having been ordered to reach a location and complete a task. After a few hours you'd invariably get caught and those who'd done the catching would then interrogate you. They always wanted to know the same thing: who you were with, where you were going and what you'd been asked to do, and let's just say that despite it only being a training exercise they took their roles very, very seriously indeed. They had to, I suppose.

It always happened at night. On the very first exercise I was captured after about four hours and, after hooding me, they gave me a bit of a kicking and then pushed me into the back of what I assumed was a Land Rover. About five minutes later we came to a halt and after being unceremoniously bundled out they led me into a building and unhooded me. The room, which had a door but no windows, looked like a utility room from an unfinished house and had a concrete floor, breezeblock walls and a plasterboard ceiling with one dim lightbulb hanging from it. It also had four speakers, which were positioned on the floor with one against each wall. Incidentally, nobody had said a word to me by this point, which was making me nervous. I was used to being bawled at all the time.

A few moments later a soldier wearing a balaclava turned me around so I was facing the wall. Straight after that the light went off and a few seconds later the door was slammed shut. There was no light coming from anywhere now. It was pitch black. Nothing happened for about fifteen minutes and then suddenly, out of the blue, white noise started coming out of the speakers. This is designed to drive you bonkers and after standing it for about half an hour I was then taken into another room and interrogated. I managed not to say anything (they should have tried bribery!) but fuck me was I shaken up. The next time I was captured they waterboarded me, which was pleasant, and the longer it went on the more certain I became that these people were the enemy. They were that convincing. After an interrogation I used to think to myself, *Am I still training?* It was a massive head fuck.

The most terrifying method they used on us involved a hood and a helicopter. What they'd do is bring down a helicopter, put you in, walk you from one side to the other and ask you to count the steps. After that they'd push you out, put a hood on you, push you back in again, and then order you to walk from one side to the other and back again. 'Tell us what we want to know otherwise we're going up to three thousand feet,' somebody said when it was my turn. Yet again it was absolutely pitch black, even without the hood, and as I carried on walking from one side of the helicopter to the other while counting to seven each time I suddenly heard the engines start and the blades begin to rotate. We were going up. A few minutes later I'd reached the end of my tether and asked them to stop on what I hoped was my seventh step. At that moment, I felt a hand in the middle of my back and as it started pushing me forwards my entire body became engulfed by pure panic. I'd been in some situations before but I'd never experienced what I thought was imminent death and, had I had time, I would definitely have shat my pants. That's guaranteed. Instead, I started grabbing as I fell but there was nothing around me except fresh air; vital in keeping humans alive normally, but less so when you're being pushed out of a helicopter. The last thing I remember before leaving the helicopter altogether is screaming. That, with the sound of the blades and the engines made for a pretty horrendous soundscape. In hindsight I should have shouted something insulting to the twat who'd pushed me.

'I'm off to fuck your motherrrrrrrrrrrrrrrrrrrrrrr . . .' Splat.

In the end I didn't even have time to finish my scream as, when I was about halfway through, I landed on what was either a very hard cloud or the ground. The first thing I did was rip off my hood and there above me at a height of approximately 3 feet was the helicopter. My interrogators, who had obviously done this before, were almost pissing themselves laughing whereas I didn't know whether to laugh, cry or jump back in there and kill the fuckers. The choice was taken out of my hands as, after telling me to get out of the way and then landing the helicopter, they told me to shut my fucking mouth and return to camp.

To be completely honest, we didn't see the point of all this until we got to Northern Ireland. Then it all became apparent as to reach an observation point you often had to yomp 3 or 4 miles after getting dropped off by car and during that time there was a chance you'd get caught, hence you being interrogated.

The last time I was interrogated I'd had enough and so I talked immediately. Why? Because they tried bribery, that's why. It didn't take much. After being captured they hooded me and took me to a building somewhere. After taking off the hood there in front of me was my interrogator, a cup of tea, a bacon roll, and a fag.

'Right then, 777,' said my captor. 'How about we keep this short? You tell me what I want to know, and I let you have my breakfast.'

This was obviously his opening gambit – a bit of fun more than anything – and he was expecting me to tell him to fuck off – which was usually my opening gambit.

'OK then,' I said. 'There are six of us and we were on our way to observation point four.'

With that I leant over the table, picked up the fag, lit it with this bloke's lighter, took a draw and then picked up the tea and the roll and put them down in front of me.

My interrogator watched me open mouthed and, as I put down the tea and roll, he spoke. 'You weren't supposed to do that,' he said, almost as if I'd punched him in the playground.

'Look, it's just a game,' I replied. 'In real life I wouldn't tell them a fucking thing. You know that. At this moment in time the only thing I care about is this roll, this cup of tea and this fag.'

While he was composing himself and thinking what to say I finished his fag and then tucked into his breakfast.

'You do realise that nobody has ever done this before,' he said eventually. 'Ever!'

'I dare say. I just think it's a bit unnecessary, that's all. You know I'm good.'

My captor didn't confirm or deny this. He just took out his cigarettes, lit one and sat back in his chair.

'What's more, I'm starving fucking hungry,' I continued. 'Or at least I was,' I said holding up the last piece of his roll before shoving it in my gob.

After watching the last bit of his breakfast disappear he sat up and leant forward. 'What I should do in this situation is have you RTU'd, you do realise that, don't you?'

Now it was my turn to neither confirm nor deny. I just gave him a Gallic shrug.

'You are right, though,' he said. 'You haven't even come close to talking. Apart from in the helicopter.'

'Everybody squealed in the fucking helicopter,' I argued.

'Yeah, good point.'

As funny as this was, nobody I've ever spoken to about it – especially those who served in the Det or in the forces – can believe that I wasn't RTU'd, but that's what got me through, I think, humour and honesty. Regardless of the situation I'd always try and make light of it and if the lads were ever feeling down I'd always try to cheer them up. Sometimes it got me into trouble, such as the time I accidentally pushed a staff sergeant into a pond halfway through a route march, and sometimes it worked for me, such as now. Whatever happened, though, I was never going to change who I was and so if I had been RTU'd I'd have been fine with it. Well, not fine, but I'd have just got on with life. Looking back I could have been RTU'd about a dozen times but the powers that be always decided to keep me in.

The last thing I remember doing before we moved on to doing Starsky and Hutch impressions was a lake exercise where we had to, among other things, build a boat and then pull the thing from one end of the lake to the other. When we eventually got to the other side I was shivering like hell and Staff Sergeant Brown took pity on me.

'Are you cold 777?' he asked.

'Y-y-y-y-y-yes, staff,' I replied. 'I'm f-f-f-f-fucking f-f-f-f-freezing.'

'I'll tell you what then,' he said. 'Get out of the lake, take that rope off and give me a hundred press-ups. That'll warm you up a bit.'

When I was about halfway through the press-ups I started slowing down a bit.

'Are you fucking tired, 777?' he asked.

'Yes, a bit, staff.'

'I'll tell you what then. Take one arm away and give it a rest.'

Fifty one-armed press-ups after pulling a boat across a lake while I was soaking wet and freezing to fucking death. He really was a complete twat.

NINE

By the time we moved onto the specialised training involving cars and guns there must have been about twenty of us left. Having got through all the physical stuff was a massive relief and so despite me claiming that I wouldn't have minded being RTU'd I'm glad I wasn't.

We were all issued with a pistol before starting the specialised training and because the vast majority of it took place on the streets we were issued with a code just in case we had a run in with the police. The code was Green Dancer and it was only to be used if they found out you were armed.

We started off by doing some foot follows and then moved onto to staking out pubs. Beforehand we'd be given a photograph of the person we were looking for and we had to wait for them to appear, although sometimes they didn't. That was quite frustrating. Not just the fact that they didn't always turn up, which was obviously true to life, but the fact was that we'd far sooner have been inside the pub looking out. One manoeuvre I did enjoy was sitting on top of the

Severn Bridge looking for a car. We'd been given the make and registration number beforehand and if we spotted it we had to follow the car and then report on the driver's activities. We did eventually spot the car and ended up following it to Cardiff where the driver just fucked about a bit and then collected some dry cleaning. Not exactly *Who Dares Wins*.

There was a hell of lot of waiting around with this stuff and if you had problems coping with boredom or maintaining concentration you were fucked. Luckily for me I had become quite good at both so I enjoyed it.

One of the daftest RTUs we had during that last spell involved two lads getting arrested by the police and then locked up. I forget the exact details of the case but for some reason the police hadn't searched these lads before putting them in the cells, and one of them thought it would be a good idea to hand over his pistol. It's obvious, when you think about it. If you got caught by the IRA would you say, 'Here you go, here's my pistol'? Of course you fucking wouldn't. I know this was the police and not the IRA but the principle was exactly the same. Keep your weapon concealed in case you need it.

Another thing they really went to town on during the specialised training was memory and recall. I walked into a classroom one day and there were about forty items laid out on a table. We had just one minute to memorise them before telling the trainer what we'd seen. It was like the *Generation Game*. Cuddly toy, fondue set, dildo. Actually, there wasn't a dildo, or a cuddly toy, or a fondue set. It was all military hardware and you kept on doing it until you got it right. After that they started showing us some short films of moving cars, but not the entire car. It'd be twenty seconds featuring the bottom right-hand corner of a Datsun Cherry or the front left wing of a Cortina. It was all about instant recognition. On another day we had to watch two of our trainers acting out the scene of a play. Under normal circumstances I'd probably have taken the piss but in this instance we had to memorise what one of the trainers had said, word for word, so this time it was all about concentration.

The most physical part of the specialised training was called CQC – close quarter combat. We obviously weren't SAS attackers but we did have to be able to extract ourselves from tight situations and it was an essential part of the training. The main requirement here was pure aggression and so, if you were ever accosted by somebody, you were taught to punch them three times very quickly, take a step back and then double tap, which is the term we used for firing your pistol twice in rapid succession. So it was shock, step back, draw and fire. Although we used to practise this on each other I also used to do it in the mirror at night. I was a proper fucking John Wayne, I was. We used to have to keep our weapons concealed and most of the lads would have them in a holster just above their arse. I used to keep mine on my left side about halfway around, but I never used a holster. I used to wear one of those old elasticated snake belts all the time so it went in there. The only time I almost came unstuck with that was when I had to play football with the IRA, but we'll come onto that later.

Up next was some evasive driving training and about two weeks before that started Jay and I were reminded of the fact that we were already missing one vital ingredient.

'Right then, you licence-less arseholes,' said Staff Sergeant Brown, 'we've got an Army driving instructor turning up tomorrow and with any luck he'll have you up to scratch within a week or so.'

'But we're all about to go on leave,' I argued.

'You two aren't,' he countered.

'Bollocks!'

The driving instructor was a little Geordie bloke and, after taking us both out for an initial assessment, he delivered his verdict over a cup of tea.

'Yooz lads are two of the worst fuck'n drivers ah have ever seen. Yer shite man.'

'We might be at the moment,' pleaded Jay. 'You'll soon knock us into shape.'

'In a fuck'n week? Yer jokin aren't yer? I'll need a fuck'n yer with yooz two cunts.'

He was right, we were shit. Also, if he didn't feel like he could pass us we'd both be RTU'd, and just before the fun was due to start. The last thing we needed in this scenario was a week on the piss but our instructor had other ideas.

'If I'm down here for a week am off oot,' he said. 'Yer fancy it like?'

'We're not allowed,' I said.

'Aaaah, fuck that man. It's only a few pints. I'll tell you what, I'm staying about two miles away. I'll pick yerz up over there by that fence at about nine o'clock, OK?'

He was only about 5 foot 2 this instructor but he must have been at least fifteen stone. He was full of fucking beer!

Sure enough, we all ended up getting shitfaced every night he was there and by the end of the week we were just as fucking useless. The thing is, because it had all been his idea he had to pass us, and he did. I'll never forget what he said to us before he left.

'Yer still fuck'n shite but am going to pass yerz anyway. I just hope yerz get plenty of fuck'n practice!'

He wasn't the only one. He'd just passed two drivers who experienced little or no fear, had no regard for or knowledge of the Highway Code, and a healthy disregard for the majority of mankind. The fact that we were both about to be trained in evasive driving is terrifying in hindsight but Jay and I couldn't wait.

The situations they were preparing us for by training us on evasive driving were potentially quite alarming but, fuck me, it was fun. One of these scenarios was an illegal VCP (vehicle checkpoint) where some IRA operatives, or boyos, as we called them, would be standing in a road masked and armed, and they'd search people. If you ever saw one of these in the distance you had to either do a reverse flick, which is when you spin a car 180 degrees while reversing, or a handbrake turn. Either way you had to get the fuck away from them as fast as you bloody could. My personal favourite, and one that I had endless fun trying to perfect by using some old cars in the camp car park, was if you got blocked in. In that situation you were taught to ram the car in front of you, which I did. A lot.

Another manoeuvre I enjoyed – sorry, loved – was disembarking and then firing your pistol through a windscreen. What a buzz. It was pure Hollywood. Two of our lads ended up having to perform that particular manoeuvre when we were over there, so as well as being a good laugh it was all relevant.

The only exercise that scared me (and my trainer) was when I had to perform a memory retention exercise while driving on a motorway. I was doing about seventy at the time, which was a miracle given the shit cars we were given to drive, and all of a sudden the trainer leant over and put his hands over my eyes.

'Memory retention exercise,' he said calmly. 'Ten seconds. If you've been paying attention to what's in front of you it shouldn't be a problem.'

Except it was a fucking problem. Because I wasn't expecting it, and because it panicked me a bit, I ended up veering over to the right and colliding with another vehicle. This must have happened within the first three seconds of him covering my eyes but, because he then started to panic, as opposed to taking his hands away he kept them over my eyes! The daft bastard.

Specialised training was to be followed by the final part, which was with the Intelligence Corps in Ashford. Before we left for Kent, the chap who was in charge of it all, Richard Bethell (brother of James Bethell, the racehorse trainer), got us all shitfaced one night. At 5 a.m., just after we'd called it a day, he decided to wake us up and take us all up in a helicopter. After we'd been up for about five minutes he suddenly said, 'Did you know that you can jump start a helicopter?' As soon as he said that the engines stopped and the helicopter began to drop, although not nearly as quickly as you'd have thought. That has something to do with the autorotation of the main blades and as opposed to it dropping like a sack of shit the pilot should be able to keep control, should the engines stop, and may even have a chance of landing it safely. On this particular occasion, the pilot had done it on purpose and about ten or fifteen seconds after cutting the engines he started them again. The jolt that followed was unbelievable and that, coupled with the fact that we'd all downed at least fifteen pints and were more than ready for bed, made us feel slightly bilious. Everybody, apart from Bethell and the pilots, vomited at least once and I'd hate to have been the poor sod who had to clean it up. The lesson he'd taught us was simple: don't go on the piss until five in the morning if you're on duty the next day. What a way to learn though.

The only part of the training that was really at odds with the whole *Starsky and Hutch* comparison was the intelligence gathering in Ashford. Once again, I was really looking forward to it. The way some people had described this part of the proceedings (we'd been told it was all about gadgets and covert cameras, etc.) had made it sound a little bit like James Bond, but after less than a day we realised they'd been taking the piss. If Q had been responsible for making James Bond's gadgets, ours had been made by C, as in crap.

The first thing we covered was covert photography, which included learning how to hide a camera behind the grill in the front of a car before wiring it up to the dashboard. The cameras we used were motorised Pentaxs and they made a hell of a racket. Consequently, if you were driving along and wanted to photograph somebody, the chances are they'd hear you doing it. The things we used to do to try and deaden the sound. We tried packing them with polystyrene and all sorts of things. It was so Micky Mouse. The technology we used to take photographs of what was behind us was frightening. Bleeding edge, I think they call it. We'd cut holes in a pillowcase and put the camera inside that on the back shelf. Incredible! The only things that impressed me slightly were the photograph vans, but only because they weren't what they seemed. They had been converted and had hidden compartments in the back where you could sit – sometimes for days on end – and photograph people. That was about it.

As well as teaching us how to take photographs covertly, among other things we were also taught how to develop the film and catalogue the photographs. Perhaps surprisingly, this was the only part of our specialised training that unnerved me slightly. The reason being that almost every single scenario they prepared you for had you right behind enemy lines. Some of it was from a distance, but a lot of it wasn't, and this was probably the first time that I began to appreciate what might be coming.

One of the exercises we did involved walking through a crowded area with a camera inside your shoulder bag. These days you can conceal a camera pretty much anywhere because they're so tiny but in 1976 they were a bit like televisions – big and heavy. Also, having a camera about my person always made me feel more self-conscious than having a gun – I'm not sure why. Perhaps it was because a gun can protect you, whereas a camera can only put you in danger.

When we arrived back from Ashford, the training staff were unusually friendly and for those last two weeks or so they were forever taking us out for drinks. Because of what had happened previously – and because of what we'd learned – this made us all very, very jumpy and the friendlier they became they more we mistrusted them. Every night when I went to bed I half-expected something to happen. Although it was never confirmed I think most of us realised that this too was part of the training. It was the final lesson. Always keep your wits about you and, for as long as you're doing this, don't trust anybody.

On the final day, the twenty remaining candidates were split up and taken into two rooms. One lot was being binned off and the other had got through. Fortunately, I was in the latter (there were just six of us) and after congratulating each other we all went to the pub and got absolutely hammered. Nobody knew each other's surname, by the way. All we ever knew about each other was our Christian names (if we chose to use them – a lot didn't) and our numbers. That was it.

The following day we all went on a weekend's leave and after arriving back on the Monday we were taken to RAF Brize Norton. There we learned where we were being posted and were flown to the location. All I knew was that it would either be Derry, which was called 8 Det, Belfast, which was

39 Det, or the countryside, which was 3 Det. Those who'd excelled at bush craft were generally sent to the countryside and those more comfortable in a city were posted to Belfast. I, who was neither a city boy nor a carrot cruncher, was posted to Derry, but that was only part of the reasoning.

According to Captain Bethell, who told us of our fate, one of the reasons why I'd passed was because of my looks. Since starting the course I'd taken full advantage of the suggestion on the noticeboard that you could wear your hair long and, because my skin was quite dark, I looked a bit like a gypsy. I don't know if it's the same today but back then Derry had a lot of people with dark hair and dark skin, and Captain Bethell's exact words to me were, 'You look just like a pikey Paddy, Edwards. You'll fit in like a fucking glove.'

The other thing we were given at Brize Norton was a cover and mine was an Ordnance Survey man. Don't ask me why. I thought cartography was the study of cars, for fuck's sake, and I didn't know a contour line from a hole in the ground. These days if you're given a cover in the armed forces you're required to become an expert in whatever it is. Back then it was just a pseudo job title and although I never had to use it, I came very close.

At 8 p.m. we all boarded a Hercules and were flown to Aldergrove Airport, which is now Belfast International. There, we were met by operators, which is what we'd been training to become, and were each driven to our respective compounds. Mine was inside Limavady Camp, on the outskirts of Derry, and comprised of a series of Nissen huts that had been separated from the rest of the military camp by a wall of corrugated iron. The cars were all parked undercover and as well as the huts acting as sleeping quarters we also had a bar, an admin office and a canteen.

The atmosphere in the compound was friendly

enough, but there was also an air of detachment and suspicion running through the place, which in hindsight was both essential and predictable. There was also quite a lot of anger and volatility in the air, which was also no surprise, but the way the operators spoke to each other was quite different to anything I'd ever witnessed. Nothing was really *said*. It was either grunted or shouted and every sentence would contain at least one fuck or cunt. I'd always been a big swearer but as opposed to the swearing being almost gratuitous, like mine usually was, this lot meant every word, all the time. Subsequently, I found the atmosphere a little bit intimidating to start with and so decided to keep my head down. I was also only twenty-one years of age and the rest of them were at least thirty. I had a good idea of how they'd deal with an overconfident youngster and I didn't want to test the theory.

As I said though, everyone I met on that first night seemed to be quite friendly and after throwing me a can of lager in the hut that doubled as a bar, one of the operators started filling me in on what they'd been up to. Fuck me sideways! I may have felt slightly intimidated on entering the compound but by the time I went to bed I was a gibbering wreck. This was real life, not a load of exercises and training courses like I'd been used to. Just a couple of months previously, one of the operators had been shot dead, but not by the IRA. His colleagues had been trying to get him out of an op after it was compromised and he'd been shot by another operator by mistake. I was only in the bar for about an hour but by the time I left I was asking myself what the hell I'd done. My brain was scrambled.

The man I was sharing a room with in the compound was called Graham Dyer. He'd already been there about fifteen months so was over halfway through the maximum two-year stretch. Graham would have been at least thirty then and after mumbling a quick hello he pointed to the end of my bunk.

'We're off out on an op. Look after her, would you? She's about to drop.'

The 'her' that Graham was referring to was a heavily pregnant Jack Russell which, to be honest, wasn't what I'd been expecting to find in a compound full of sweary undercover operatives. I found out the next day that operatives were encouraged to keep dogs as they gave them something to concentrate on other than death and misery. On my very first leave I got myself a cocker spaniel that I named Blueboy. In the meantime, though, I had to forget about spying on possible terrorists and instead try and concentrate on avoiding having my feet covered in puppies and canine afterbirth, which is exactly what happened. There was absolutely no way I was going to try and move this poor dog so I just left her there and at about three o'clock in the morning it started to happen. Graham and the others were still out on the op so I had to deliver them on my own. Not that I actually did much. I just sat there watching them all appear and wondered what state my mattress would be in the next morning.

My first three months in Derry were all about finding my feet and I spent quite a lot of my time at a firing range near Magilligan Prison. The three weapons we were issued in the Det were a 9 mm pistol, an M10, which is a blowback-operated machine pistol that looks a bit like an Uzi, and a Beretta. The M10s, which we kept inside a long coat, were used on what were called 'serious ops', which included things like protecting sources. These people had to be escorted undercover to the source handlers and then back again and as I'm sure you can imagine that was a dangerous exercise. They were obviously risking life and limb and for a variety of different reasons, although mainly money. There was never any patriotism involved and more often than not they hated us just as much as the terrorists did. Poverty was rife, however, and some people thought it was worth the risk. Plenty were killed, of course, as were the handlers, but that was the chance they took.

As well as the training and the hardware, we were also handed a lot of paperwork on arriving in Derry, including a dossier on the people we were likely to be shadowing. Each had their own codename: Gerry Adams was Trout 1, Martin McGuinness was Alpha 11, Gerry McCartney was Lima 4 and Hugh Brady was Delta 7. I don't mind admitting that it was a little bit disconcerting reading the dossier as we were swatting up on people who we'd be following.

Every photograph I've seen of Derry, or Londonderry to even things up, taken during the Troubles is in black and white and that's pretty much how I remember it. I suppose that might sound a little bizarre or farfetched but it's the God's honest truth. If it wasn't raining in Derry, which it usually was, a thick fog would descend and make everything invisible. In some ways that was probably the lesser of two evils but it was depressing nonetheless. We must have experienced the odd sunny day while I was stationed there but I don't remember any of them. The entire place was just fifty shades of fucking grey, and not in an interesting way.

The buildings in the town seemed to consist of either rows and rows of Victorian terraced housing or hastily built office blocks. The latter, which looked like giant cardboard boxes with windows drawn on them, were a result of the 1960s economic boom but they failed to symbolise the prosperity of the era and had been discoloured by smoke from the factory chimneys. The terraced houses didn't need discolouring. They were already dark grey, as were the poorly tarmacked streets. Some of the potholes on the streets of Derry, which seemed to appear every 10 feet or so, were at least a foot deep and you could have trapped bears in them. It was impossible to drive in a straight line.

One of the main focuses of our attentions was the infamous Bogside estate. Situated just outside Derry's city walls, it backs onto a loyalist enclave called the Fountain and was full of either IRA or IRA sympathisers. Eight years before my engagement began, in August 1969, a three-day riot had taken place in the Bogside that is credited for starting the Troubles. Known as the Battle of the Bogside, it erupted shortly after an Apprentice Boys parade, and as well as resulting in over 1,500 serious injuries it sparked similar disturbances all over Northern Ireland. To be fair, things had been deteriorating in Derry for a while, but this was the touch paper. Since then it had been chaos and the vast majority of Derry's major sectarian incidents had taken place in the Bogside, including the infamous Bloody Sunday shootings. This had shifted the prevailing mood in the city from being angry and unpredictable to permanently fucking heated and all the predominantly Catholic neighbourhoods such the Bogside and the Creggan, which is on the outskirts of Derry and is still one of the largest council estates in Europe, had become no-go areas for the Royal Ulster Constabulary and the armed forces. Had the inhabitants of these districts known who we were the same would obviously have applied, and that particular fact did nothing to settle my nerves. Until I arrived there I hadn't appreciated how detested the British forces were by the Catholic population – not to mention many of the Protestants – so walking the streets of Derry as an operator was unnerving to say the least and explained the mood in the compound.

It won't come as much of a surprise that the rest of the inhabitants in Limavady Camp were always curious as to who we were and what we got up to both inside and outside the compound. That said, it wasn't completely cut off as they used to bring us our food and so we were really a colony as opposed to another country. Given our behaviour, if we ever came into contact with anybody while passing through the military camp you'd have thought they would have avoided us like the plague but one day a sergeant major, who was a bit of a pain in the arse and a right nosey fucker, decided to try and make friends with us. To be fair to him, I think one of the reasons he thought he could do this was because there was no obvious hierarchy within the compound and because the Det hadn't been going very long (I was part of only the second intake) we probably lacked structure. If we weren't on an op we'd either chill out, do some fitness, or piss around on a nearby airfield with a go-kart we'd made. We did what we liked, basically.

If we had to do a raid on a suspect's house we'd always wear masks. Not a ski mask, as if you ever wore one of those the chances are you'd get shot by a soldier as they were the preferred attire of the IRA. I used to wear a kind of gimp mask. I guarantee that if our lot had turned up at your house brandishing M10s and shouting the odds you'd have shat your fucking pants.

Speaking of which.

One day this sergeant major came into the compound and asked if he could come over one evening for a drink.

'What the fuck for?' I asked.

'Just being friendly,' he replied.

Just then I had an idea.

'Yeah, OK then,' I said, pretending to be nice. 'Why don't you come over at about 8 p.m.? You know where the bar hut is, don't you? Well, come in there. But make sure you're alone.'

With that he fucked off, looking ever so slightly nervous, and well he might. At about five to eight, twelve operators, including me, went to the bar carrying our masks and a crossbow, took off all our clothes and waited for our friend to arrive. A few moments later the door to the compound opened and in stepped the sergeant major. Before he looked our way I turned off the main light in the bar and told the lads to get in position. On entering, the first thing the sergeant major did was feel for a light switch and on finding one he flicked it. The sight that greeted him wouldn't have looked out of place in *The Wicker Man* and he let out a scream. All twelve of us were standing in a line about 10 feet from the door and, as well as being completely stark-bollock naked below the neck, we were each wearing a gimp mask and held our crossbows across our chests. Without saying a word we all took two steps forward before raising our crossbows and aiming them at his head. I could tell that he wanted to run for it but he couldn't. He was frozen to the floor, petrified.

'This is him,' I said when we took aim. 'Says he wants to be our friend.'

'No I didn't!' he said, suddenly finding his voice. 'I just wanted to come for a drink.'

'You either want to be our friend or you don't,' I said, trying to sound menacing. 'What's it to be? If you do want to be our friend you will have to take off your clothes and pass the initiation ceremony. And if you don't . . . well, let's just say that we'll all be a little bit disappointed.'

That was enough. The moment I stopped speaking the sergeant major turned on his heels and made his retreat. God only knows what he thought we were going to do to him but from that day on the only time we saw anybody from the camp in our compound was when they had to deliver something. Which they always did very quickly.

TEN

My first big scare in Derry, and the closest I ever came to having to claim to be an Ordnance Survey man, happened about five months in, when, much to my surprise, I realised I had a doppelganger. Captain Bethell's prediction that I'd fit in like a glove in Derry had obviously been half-hearted but apparently there was a member of the population who looked just like me. Lucky bastard.

It all came to light during a supervised operation in the city centre. A young lad approached me and, after slapping me on the arm, he said, 'How's your ma doing, Paddy? I've heard she's not too good.' Fortunately, my training was still fresh and so I knew exactly what to do: shrug your shoulders, walk away, and don't speak unless you really have to. I think the only thing I did wrong was blush, but that couldn't be helped. The lad must have been completely nonplussed but fortunately he didn't follow me or call after me.

About an hour later the same thing happened again,

this time with a middle-aged woman. She too was enquiring about the health of my old lady so when I got back to the compound I had a shave, asked somebody to cut my hair and prayed to God that young Paddy hadn't done the same.

I once read an interview with Charlie Watts, the drummer out of the Rolling Stones. He said that in the forty years he'd been in the group (that must have been a while ago then) at least half of it was spent waiting for something to happen either in a recording studio or at a venue. The reason I remember reading that interview is because it made me think, *You lucky bastard, Watts!* As operators we must have spent at least 90 per cent of our time waiting for something to happen. Perhaps more. It was simply the nature of the beast.

The person I spent the majority of my time waiting to turn up, and in all manner of situations and positions, was a gentle soul named Martin McGuinness, or the Butcher of Derry as he was affectionately known.

To be honest, I didn't have a clue who McGuinness was when I first arrived. I was only twenty-one and had all the political awareness of a dead cat. After I'd read the dossier, the first time I heard his name was in my first briefing. I forget in what context he was mentioned but the boys, such as Graham, who'd already been there a while suddenly started paying attention a bit more.

At the time McGuinness's most high-profile crime had been getting caught with a car containing 250 pounds of explosives and nearly 5,000 rounds of ammunition. It certainly wasn't his worst offence but very few of McGuinness's crimes could be either proven or reported, and unfortunately that merely enhanced his reputation. I think he'd served about six months for the car job, but as well as claiming not to recognise the Irish court in which he was tried and convicted, he was also extremely open about his beliefs, his actions and intentions. Back then, that's the only thing I admired about McGuinness, albeit begrudgingly. Regardless of what I thought, he was totally committed to his cause and showed no fear whatsoever. That's where the admiration stopped though.

Some people assume that because he was skinny and looked a bit like a weasel, Martin McGuinness must have been a short arse. Wrong. He was at least 6-foot tall. As well as wearing glasses and looking a bit shifty, he had a short mop of scraggy ginger hair. If you saw him walking down Oxford Street you'd have been forgiven for mistaking him for a Geography teacher or something, but of course he was anything but. His specialised subject involved a lot less theory and at the time was confined mainly to Derry.

Martin McGuinness is still the only terrorist I've ever heard of who was arrogant enough to effectively wear a uniform. Whereas everyone else would be wearing things like donkey jackets and blue parkas in 1970s Derry, Martin McGuinness would always wear a long beige duffle coat come rain, sun, sleet or snow. Mark my words, that man did not give a fucking shit and to be fair to him he never hid from anybody. The phrase 'never judge a book by its cover' could almost have been invented for that twat. OK, so he was quite conspicuous to look at – unique, even – but apart from looking shifty and a bit furtive you'd have thought the closest he'd ever come to committing a crime would have been taking his library books back a bit late or smoking a spliff. How wrong can you be? At the time Martin McGuinness was probably the most dangerous man in Britain and some of the stories I'd heard about him would make your teeth itch. One of the worst of these involved him and a few other boyos kidnapping a para before torturing and then executing him.

Ultimate Survivor

Once the news got out, he then went to a checkpoint where some of this para's colleagues were and started taunting them. He knew full well that they couldn't do anything and he exploited that to its full potential. If it had been me I'd have just killed him and done my time. No question.

Anybody who ever tries to tell me that Martin McGuinness became a reformed character post the Northern Ireland peace process gets told in no uncertain terms that, in my opinion, they are talking out of their arse. He did it to save his skin, end of story, and the fact that so many high-profile people were taken in by it makes my fucking skin crawl. He was an evil cunt.

The first time I ever clapped eyes on McGuinness was when we were setting up a remote-controlled infrared camera behind a wall on some shrubland that was about a hundred yards in front of his home. It was to record his comings and goings, obviously, and had been given the name – as a project, at least – of Petunia. Don't ask me why. I mean, if you were going to construct a spying device and then train it on one of the evilest men in Europe, would you name it after a flower? I thought not. I can't remember if there was any irony at play, but I have an awful feeling there wasn't.

Much of our equipment, including Petunia, was constructed – or, should I say thrown together? – by us (with the occasional help of MI6), so there was usually more guesswork at play than expertise. The camera itself, which was massive and would follow movement while taking photographs, was mounted on a tower made out of large baked bean cans and powered by eight Harrier Jump Jet batteries that had to be buried next to it. The noise this thing made when it started to move and take pictures was incredible, so a man called Peter Lock from MI6 suggested we try and soundproof it.

'But how?' we asked him.

'Actually,' he said, scratching his head, 'I've absolutely no idea!'

What Peter did suggest was that we tried to hide Petunia by using fertiliser on the surrounding shrubs and so we did just that; the irony being that we must have bought enough fertiliser to make about fifty bombs. It did make Petunia slightly harder to spot – eventually – but every time it started moving it sounded like a tipper truck dumping a load. We may as well have shouted, 'Excuse me, Mr McGuinness, but would you mind looking this way? That's it, marvellous. Say cheese!'

The main problem we had with Petunia when we first tried to install it was that we couldn't get a signal from the city walls, which is where the remote control was supposed to be operated from. Instead, we tried operating it from a secret compartment behind the driver's seat in a converted Volkswagen van but it was too bloody hot. In a fit of absolute desperation, we moved the van further up the hill where it was less conspicuous and I ended up jumping up and down on the fucking roof still trying to get a signal! Absolutely fucking useless, I'm afraid.

When me and a colleague of mine called Blue were first setting up Petunia, he grabbed my arm suddenly and pulled me down behind the wall.

'Get up slowly and look towards the graveyard,' he whispered. 'He's just left the house and is walking that way.'

As instructed, I stood up slowly and peered over the wall towards the graveyard. Sure enough, there was McGuinness standing by the gates, talking to a short bloke with no hair. Even from a quarter of a mile away there was no mistaking him and because of his reputation I don't mind admitting that I did feel a bit of a shiver go down my spine.

That feeling wasn't new to me, by the way. In fact, I spent the first four months or so shitting my fucking pants in Derry, and every time I arrived back at the compound having been out in the Bogside I'd be shaking like a leaf. It wasn't quite as bad in the city centre, for the simple reason you had a broad mixture of people there. In the Bogside, however, the only people ever present, apart from us, were about ten thousand or so IRA sympathisers and a few hundred active volunteers, so the consequences of you being rumbled were always heightened. The trick was to be seen enough to be recognised but not enough to be talked to. That was what we all tried to achieve.

The most suicidal thing you could do while either walking or driving through the Bogside estate was to hold your hand up to somebody. That denotes the Red Hand of Ulster and if you were daft enough to do that in the Bogside in the mid-1970s it would have been like signing your own death warrant. Conversely, if you ever raised a finger off your steering wheel to somebody in a Loyalist area you'd receive exactly the same treatment. In an attempt to blend in more, I had my ear pierced in Derry as I was told by somebody that Catholics often wore a crucifix in their left ear.

The point of Petunia wasn't just to take photos of McGuinness. It was to make us aware that McGuinness was on the move, which would trigger us to follow him. This would be done on foot initially and then by car, but in some circumstances we'd throw a helicopter into the mix and that's when it used to get interesting. Whenever I followed McGuinness on foot he'd more often than not end up at the Sinn Fein shop, which had a meeting room in the back. If ever you went in there, which I did only once after following McGuinness from his house, you were always expected to buy something and on this occasion I ended up buying a record called 'Soldier'. It's a Republican song – obviously – and celebrates the death of a British soldier who once leapt on a bomb in order to save a crowd of Irish locals. As you can imagine, the song itself is pretty revolting and legend has it that after the bomb had exploded the locals started cheering and throwing the soldier's body parts around. Nice.

It didn't happen too often but when a helicopter was required I'd race next door to the airfield and try and find Chris, who was our pilot. Chris is the only helicopter pilot I've ever known who can fly one upside down. He could only do it for a second or so, and it was done as part of a roll, but my God was it impressive.

One day, after being triggered by Petunia, I had to drive to an Army base on the other side of Derry as that was where Chris's helicopter was at the time. It was about four o'clock in the morning and because I was undercover, I went by name of 2nd Lieutenant Marshall – Marshall being my mother's maiden name. After arriving at the camp and explaining to a regimental sergeant major that I was due to go up in a helicopter and take photographs he immediately started doing an impression of Hercule Poirot.

'You're not a second lieutenant,' he said smirking. 'You're one of those teddy bears, aren't you?'

'What the fuck's a teddy bear?' I asked.

'One of those secret fuckers. You know full well.'

Actually, I didn't.

'Look,' I said, starting to get annoyed, 'I don't know what you're talking about, OK. But what I do know is that what I'm doing is none of your fucking business. Now, before I go up I'd like somewhere quiet to sit and I'd like to have some breakfast.'

'You'd better go in the officer's mess then,' said my new friend.

Once I was sat down this twat came up again and started asking even more questions.

'Will you please just fuck off?' I said as aggressively as I could at 4 a.m. 'I just want to have some breakfast and be left alone.'

He wouldn't be deterred, this RSM. He just sat down in front of me.

'Must be scary being undercover,' he said. 'Walking around on your own with no back-up.'

I could tell by his manner that he was taking the piss and I'd had enough. I leant forward, grabbed him by the collar, and pulled him half across the table.

'Now look here, you little cunt,' I said before leaning over and putting my face right up to his. 'If me and you went for a walk around Derry, who's going to get shot?'

'What do you mean?' he said in a slightly less self-assured way.

'You're like a figure eleven target in that uniform and you could go at any minute. They don't know who I am though, do they?'

That got the twat.

After shitting himself – well, facially, at least – he got up and literally did a runner.

As I said, when McGuinness was triggered, he'd be followed on foot initially and if he got into a car whoever was tailing him would call-in the make, colour, registration and direction of the car. If it was going in the direction of Belfast, which is along the A6, it would be picked up first by a car and secondly a helicopter. I had a beautiful pair of balanced binoculars that I used to use in the air and as soon as I'd got the car in my sights I'd say over the radio, 'Hotel, I have,' and give the direction it was going. Once you'd locked onto a car you never lost it. Even in traffic. It became like a beacon.

If the helicopter did get involved you'd have one car hanging back from the target and two other cars running parallel in case it turned off. If that happened the helicopter would then guide the car that was closest to the target and once it was in position you'd confirm this by saying, 'OK, you have.' Once that happened we'd usually pull back a bit but stay close enough to come back in if they lost the target. At some point outside Belfast, we'd hand over to 39 Det and this would happen by them liaising with us en route and then getting into position ready to form a trigger. Once that had happened somebody would say, 'We have,' to which we'd reply, 'OK, you go,' and at that point we'd start to pull back completely. At the end of the operation we'd send 39 Det whatever information we'd managed to glean and vice versa.

The thing is – and this epitomises the unpredictable nature of what we did – McGuinness could have been up to absolutely anything when we followed him; from getting tooled up in order to murder somebody to going to see a relative. Regardless of which, all we were there to do was record what he did, so even if he was collecting arms, we'd simply collate that information or, if it was urgent, pass it on. In the case of collecting arms, for instance, we'd want to find out three things: where they were going, who might be using them, and what they'd be used for, and nine times out of ten whatever information we got would link in to some other piece of intelligence. It's probably a bit of a cliché but it was like a game of chess. Put simply, in addition to trying to build a picture of how our opponent operated based on their behaviour, we were forever trying to guess their next move and, ultimately, get one over on them.

There was an operator called Jungle at the compound who had this knack of being able to take in the intelligence – all the photographs, source information and reports – and then suggest not only what he thought was going to happen, but also what he thought we ought to do. Nine times out of ten he was right and so we always did as he said. He just had a brain for it, I suppose, and funnily enough he was also very good at chess. The only thing that would ever dilute Jungle's hypotheses and throw a spanner in the works was the information we received from sources. Ninety per cent of the time it would be absolute bollocks, and we'd often spend hours watching a house that was supposedly a hive of terrorist activity only to find that it was inhabited by a couple of eighty-year-olds with Zimmer frames or sometimes nobody at all. Some sources did it to take the piss and others did it for the money, but because of the 10 per cent of information that was reliable we had no choice but to follow it up. If we thought they were taking the piss we'd usually give them a slap or if they really took the piss they'd get a kicking. Either way, there was no love lost between us and the sources, and in each other's eyes we were just a necessary evil.

One of the most exposed observation points we had was on top of the infamous Rossville Flats, which were opposite Butcher's Gate in Derry. Built in the early 1960s they were comprised of three huge blocks housing, in total, around two hundred families, and because of the height of these blocks (they were each around ten floors) they gave us an unparalleled view of the area, and in particular some of the Bogside's most suspect public houses.

Despite being one of the most exposed observation points we had, this was also one of the most constrained and because of that we always called it the coffin. Just getting to the coffin was an operation in itself as directly below it you had several hundred Republicans all going about their business. Subsequently, it was always safer arriving there in the dead of night and, after being dropped off, you'd quickly make your way to the lift. If memory serves me correctly there were just two lifts serving the Rossville Flats and more often than not at least one of them would be out of order. If that was the case you had to leg it up the stairs as quickly and quietly as you could.

In the early 1970s two soldiers had been murdered on the roof of the flats and since then the Army had closed off the access point. We could get up and down, of course, but only with the help of a soldier. The coffin itself was about 3-foot high, 7-foot long and about 3-foot wide and you'd stay in there for anything up to three days. You'd eat in there, drink in there, shit in there, piss in there and even masturbate in there if you fancied knocking one out. Subsequently, the coffin always had what you might call a certain bouquet that would have scared off a pig with sinusitis. Thank fuck for the airholes, that's all I can say. Over the three days you'd call through everything you saw (within reason) and the relief you felt when your shift finally ended was incredible. Saying that, it still took you several days to get rid of the smell.

One of the most complicated operations I was ever involved in – and one of the most controversial, as it turned out – took place mainly at a primary school in the Creggan. The op started in May 1977, when the British Army had just begun searching for Robert Nairac. He was a British soldier who was abducted from a pub car park in South Armagh before being interrogated, tortured and then killed somewhere across the border. After his death had been confirmed by the IRA, a search for Nairac's body was conducted but it was never found.

Nairac's abduction had been especially relevant to us because about month before he was taken he'd visited our compound and had seen everything. As a result of this, we'd had to cease operations for a few weeks and during that time our cars had been either changed or resprayed. As opposed to getting a new one, which would have been nice, mine had been taken for a respray and when it came back I was gutted. It was chocolate brown. The 1970s really was a horrible fucking decade.

The op got underway after we received some intelligence from MI6. They reckoned that the primary school in question was being used by the IRA to store arms. Because it was a school, we had to be extremely careful as to how we approached infiltrating any of the buildings. The staff, or at least the majority of them, as far as we knew, wouldn't have been aware that the building was being used by the IRA and with so many children coming and going we had to ensure that, not only were they not affected by the operation, but that, ultimately, the IRA's activities weren't putting them in danger. This meant that before we could do anything we first had to stage a week-long surveillance operation as we needed to know the comings and goings of everybody outside of school hours. Only when we had that information could we decide our next move.

Once the surveillance operation had been completed we were able to undertake a recce of the school that would hopefully tell us how to get in. I was told by one of the more experienced lads that we'd need something called a snap gun to break in. This is a gun-shaped lockpick that's used for opening mechanical pin tumbler locks and for some reason I was fascinated by it.

The person who supplied us with the snap gun was a technically minded intelligence officer from MI6 who was a complete pain in the fucking arse. Techie boys always were, to be honest, and if you ever had to take them out on an op with you they were an absolute liability. The reason for this was they tended to take things – themselves included – a little bit too seriously and had no common sense whatsoever. This twat used to put masking tape over his shoes every time he went out just in case somebody recognised the tread. In hindsight, I suppose that was quite sensible. But he was still a twat.

Whenever we went out on an operation, the Army would be told beforehand to keep well away, for the simple reason that we all looked like members of the IRA so a case of mistaken identity would almost be inevitable. Still, it didn't always go to plan.

In order to get to this school covertly we had to make our way along the edge of a ploughed field that was lined by a hedge and, because the hedge was only around 5-foot high we had to crouch down a bit.

When we were about halfway across this field we suddenly heard a man's voice from the other side of the hedge shout, 'Halt. Halt or I shoot.'

As this was said in a very broad Yorkshire accent I knew it was a soldier, as did Blue and Graham who were with me. Our friend from MI6, however, had obviously got broad Yorkshire confused with broad Ulster and he immediately went for his pistol. Luckily for us the stupid twat had left it at the compound, but as he moved to draw his invisible pistol we saw the soldier start to raise his machine gun. I don't know how many tenths of a second it took us to shout, 'Army!' but we managed to do it before he could fire. That, and only that, stopped at least one of us from being killed.

While Blue and Graham went to talk to the soldier, who turned out to be a lieutenant who had about five lads with him, I had a quiet word with the 'intelligence' officer. I made it clear, on behalf of all of us, not only what would have taken place had he remembered his pistol – i.e. a fucking blood bath – but what I was going to do with him when all this was over, which involved some rusty coat hangers, his arsehole, and no lubrication.

Once I'd finished imparting this verbal demonstration to Mr MI6 I went to join the others. It turned out that the reason the lieutenant had been there in the first place was because he'd been told by his superiors that, and I quote, 'the boys would be in the vicinity', and they should all keep their distance. Unfortunately, the lieutenant had misheard this as 'the boyos would be in the vicinity', as in the IRA. He was also quite new, bless him, so together with the masking-taped boffin he'd made a very good stab at getting us all killed. What had saved us, apart from the prat forgetting his pistol, was the lieutenant's Yorkshire accent. Had there been even a hint of Northern Irish in there we'd have opened fire immediately.

Needless to say the operation was aborted and we went back to the compound. I later heard that the Yorkshire lieutenant was sent straight back to the mainland so the significance of what might have happened had obviously been taken very seriously.

A couple of nights later we reconvened at the compound. This time around we managed to make it as far as the school and, although he was still a twat, our intelligence friend went some way to redeeming himself by having us standing in the staff room looking at a ladder that led into the loft within about half a minute of us arriving.

Incidentally, the reason we were there wasn't to do a full recce or remove any arms. It was to gather the information we'd need in order to stage such a mission without anybody knowing we'd been there. This, I have to admit, is where the twat came into his own and after having a very quick look at what was in the loft – it was full of old

Spanish rifles and paperwork – he then started taking photographs of everything, from the paperwork and the stock of one of the rifles to the bottom step of the ladder. After that, we got out of there as quickly as we could and made our way back to the compound.

Because we'd found weapons it was imperative that we went back in there as soon as possible in case they were moved. First, though, the twat's photographs were sent to London and within just a couple of days they sent back exact replicas of the step and the stock. The step had been fitted with a sensor and a transmitter so we'd know when somebody was going up there and the stock had been fitted with a tilt switch which would alert us if the weapons were being moved. The detail of these copies was astonishing and completely belied the inadequacy of our standard issue equipment. On the bright side, at least the fuckers could get something right!

Despite us finding arms in there, the thing that generated the most amount of interest was the paperwork, so when we went back in to switch the step and the stock we also took away the paperwork to be photographed before taking it back again. The initial photographs that the MI6 officer had taken had contained information on all manner of nefarious activities, including executions. Not surprisingly, the name Martin McGuinness's popped up more than once on those photographs and when we started photographing the rest of the paperwork back at the compound, exactly the same applied.

In hindsight, it's a wonder how the hell we got away with going back and forth to that school. We'd already been stopped by a fucking army patrol unit and with it being situated slap bang in the middle of one of Europe's biggest council estates there was every chance we'd been seen. It's a wonder it hadn't been booby trapped.

Ultimate Survivor

The night after we'd finished photographing the paperwork, which had been kept in a large suitcase, we took it back to the school and after packaging up the evidence we sent it straight to Whitehall. Because of the gravity of what we'd discovered, both in terms of quantity and content, we were expecting immediate repercussions, but in addition to nothing happening the Ministry of Defence eventually began denying the existence of the photographs. We obviously couldn't kick up too much of a fuss as we'd have been out on our arses but over time our polite enquiries started falling on deaf ears. This made no sense to me whatsoever until I read a book by a former MI6 operative about a year after I left Derry; he'd been based in Northern Ireland a while before I had. According to him, MI6 had been negotiating with McGuinness since the mid-1970s, which immediately posed two questions: what the hell had we been doing following McGuinness in the first place, and did he actually know we were there? Then it occurred to me that shortly before the end of my tenure in Derry, at least one of these questions may well have been answered.

That's for later.

ELEVEN

One of the biggest near misses I ever had in Northern Ireland – even bigger than avoiding a gun battle with the British Army in a ploughed field – happened soon after we'd given up asking about the paperwork. One of my sources, who was quite reliable, had given me some information as to the whereabouts of a small incendiary device that was due to be planted in a big clothes shop in the city. There'd been a couple of those recently and they'd been slipped into the pocket of either a coat or a jacket. If memory serves me correctly both devices had been detonated via a timer, but they could easily have used either remote control or a tilt switch.

The source had told me that an incendiary device had been hidden in a hole underneath the flyover and was due to be picked up and planted in the city. Providing we got there before a certain time the chances are we could recover it so I asked Blue if he'd like to give me a hand. Every time you volunteered for an operation you could choose who you worked with – providing they agreed – and nine times out of ten I'd ask either Jay or Blue. As Paras, they were both considered to be Teeth Arms, which is a term used for soldiers who are deemed to be the most important when it comes to winning battles. In other words, they were fighters. Rightly or wrongly, that always gave me a certain peace of mind in Northern Ireland. As amenable and reliable as some of the other lads were, such as non-combatants who'd come out of the Intelligence Corps, they just didn't inspire confidence in me. Not when you were faced with a couple of boyos.

When we arrived underneath the flyover on foot, having left the car in a car park about half a mile away, we immediately started looking for holes in the structure. This was 1970s Derry and regardless of how old it was you could almost guarantee that, just like the roads, it would be in a state of disrepair. Subsequently, I had to stick my hand into more holes than James Herriot at a calving convention, except I was looking for a cassette-shaped bomb that could potentially take your fucking arm off. Not that I was worrying about that at the time. In fact, it hadn't even occurred to me.

After about the fifteenth time of trying I eventually found this bloody thing and after slipping it into my pocket, quite nonchalantly, we walked back to the car, drove somewhere quiet, took a few photographs of it, and then put it back. The reason we did that was because we were now using it as a trigger, so if somebody came to collect it, we'd follow them.

When I got back in the car after putting back the cassette I suddenly started shaking.

'What the hell's up with you,' asked Blue. 'You look terrified.'

The truth is, I was terrified.

Hair-raising: The Mohican that cost me 14 days stoppage of leave on HMS *Danae* – surrounded by Bill, Lester and Mick the Butcher

Here we go: Me with the Junior Marines, aged 16, in Deal, Kent

Set fair: Looking like Barry Gibb while having fun at Rhyl theme park, *left*, with my then girlfriend Theresa and my sister, Joanna

Old pals act: Mick and me on HMS *Danae* in the '70s

More antics on the high seas: Youthful high jinks, *left*, aboard HMS *Bulwark* – or was it HMS *Albion*? I forget!

Londonderry undercover – The Det team in 1977 – no names, no pack drill.

Initiation – A sergeant major is about to get a surprise in Derry, 1977. It's not a scene from *The Wicker Man*...

Right: A crossbow lies in wait. No idea who's in the suit

The sheep plot takes a turn – Me, Acky and SF get to work on a close shave in 1978

Above and right: Pissed again, naturally, at my own leaving do in 1978 and making the most of the 'poached pig'

Belfast welcome: Who's that in the gimp mask? This was my cover of choice on raids

Man's best friend – Our undercover dog, Blue. Really just a poodle!

Let my son's killer die!

WIDOW Georgina Jones lashed out last night at IRA sympathisers trying to make a martyr of the man who murdered her son.

The killer is 25-year-old gunman Frank Hughes, now close to death on the 53rd day of his hunger strike at the Maze prison.

Heart - b r o k e n Georgina, 57, said: " Why don't they just let him get on with dying?

" I do not have an ounce of sympathy in my heart for him.

" He has made other people suffer and now I believe it is time for him to suffer too."

Uniform

Her son, 23-year-old paratrooper David Jones was with the S.A.S. when Hughes shot him in an IRA ambush in Londonderry three years ago — just ten days before his wedding.

Yesterday Mrs Jones who has five other sons, took six red roses to David's graveside, in Bromsgrove, Worcs, 500 yards from her home.

She said: " I could never forgive Hughes

Frank Hughes . . . is close to death

" I would not lift a finger to help him. All I want is for them to let him die."

Last night a Northern Ireland Office spokesman said: " The condition of Hughes and the two other hunger strikers continues to deteriorate."

Francis Hughes, *intel photo inset*, makes the headlines after the ambush that left one of our friends dead. Hughes died on hunger strike a few years later

Workforce: I'm about to put the prisoners through their paces in Uganda, 1985

Relaxation: A day's fishing on Lake Victoria with Bob

Party time: Showing off my feminine side on holiday

Stay down: Re-enacting the Iranian Embassy siege, *right*, during a terrorist training session in Abu Dhabi

Teamwork: Me with the Abu Dhabi students, *below*, and Uganda crew, *bottom right*

Dangerous occupation: We trained the police in the hot desert temperatures of Abu Dhabi

...while also making one or two friends

Royal life saver: I leapt to the defence of Her Majesty, *left*, and also met Princess Anne in my time as head of security for P&O

Honorary Royal Marine: That notorious nonce Jimmy Saville

Children in Need – a rare bright spot during our stint at the Post Office in Devon

Police ID: Saudi royalty arranged it so I was able to carry a concealed weapon in Washington DC

ss Theresa McDonald, 13 Fraser Place, Arbroath, and Mr Martin Edwards, from North Wales—St Thomas Church, Arbroath.

Family matters: Our wedding is announced in March 1978 – and we are still together to this day! No-one understands me like Theresa

Kids stuff: With my niece, *right*. Now grandkids keep me young

Ultimate security: Our board in 2010 – They said formal attire ... for the top half!

Big reunion: North Det and 2 Troop get together again at Ballykelly in April 2007

Pride and joy: The kids of Corbets Tey are amazing

BEST SCHOOL OUTING EVE▶

seeing the watercolour by Brian Stonehouse in the ding-room, which shows Diana Rowden and three of walking across the Natzweiler courtyard, the chan heal about the Club and to explore it, which they did huge enthusiasm. We learned afterwards that they us imously judged the trip the best school outing ever one young lady declared that, one day, she would join Club. For us, the highlight was receiving their versi the Northern Ireland haircut photograph by the front e complete with dog, which is printed here with the on for comparison. With initiative like this the member committee may well be meeting them again in a coup decades!

Caroline Ge

Last November nine 11-year-olds (plus teachers) from St Marks Primary School, Hadlow Down, East Sussex, visited the Club having obtained a Lottery grant to conduct research into the life of Diana Rowden, who is commemorated in their village church, she was murdered in Natzweiler in July 1944. Their researches led them, predictably, to the IWM but less so to the Club, where John Andrews, Lois Watson and Caroline Griffith welcomed them. Highlights (apart from the doughnuts provided!) included

SPECIAL FORCES CLUB NEWS, Spring 201

'I've just handled that thing like you'd handle a packet of fags,' I replied. 'What if it had gone off? It could have been on a timer, a tilt switch or anything.'

Blue didn't reply, as I think it had just occurred to him that, had it gone off in the car, he'd have copped it too.

The reason we used to take so many photographs of these incendiary devices was because there were very few bombmakers back then and because each had a different way of working there'd be certain aspects to either the design or the construction that would lead us in the direction of the manufacturer.

There was an operation that was linked to the flyover cassette-bomb and it was absolutely textbook, both in terms of the way it was conducted and the outcome.

Whenever we picked up a new suspect the first thing we did was house them, which meant following somebody until we knew where they lived. A lot of these people were quite transient so even if we'd followed a suspect to the same address once or twice there was still a good chance they were just dossing down there for a few days. Only when we were absolutely sure could a house become a trigger point and once that had happened we could start looking for a suitable observation point.

If a suspect was especially transient with regards to their living arrangements we'd find out what pubs they used and then see if there were any patterns as to when they visited. For instance, if a suspect went to the Bogside Inn at 8 p.m. every Thursday we'd make damn sure we were watching him. By far the most reliable meeting point for virtually every IRA suspect was the dole office, as every Thursday morning they'd be queueing outside for about an hour. It was guaranteed. I used to drive past there in my chocolate-coloured Vauxhall Chevette with the camera behind the grill taking photos of them all. That's after I'd managed to soundproof the fucking thing! I later found out that Vauxhall didn't make chocolate-coloured Chevettes so had any of the boyos been aware of this I'd have been fucked.

Not long after the cassette incident we received some information about a suspect who had recently moved over from Belfast. After following him for days we discovered that he was living in a terraced house in the Bogside (one of seemingly millions) and as luck would have it there was a derelict property just across the road. The houses either side of the empty property were occupied but because of its position we decided to give it a go. We ended up using this place for about six weeks solid and another operator and I spent over a week in there by ourselves. Our diet consisted of cold sausages, cheese and crackers, and because there was no working toilet we had to piss in a bottle and shit in a bag.

If we took any useful photographs while at an observation point or had information that needed passing on quickly, we'd do what's called a live letter drop, which is when somebody would meet you to retrieve it. If it wasn't so urgent we'd do what's called a dead letter drop, which is when you simply leave it somewhere for somebody to pick up. I once had to do a live letter drop in the countryside and after spending about an hour and a half in a fucking ditch by the side of a road in the middle of nowhere a car came along with its lights out and out jumped an operative from MI6. He was wearing night-vision goggles and after spotting me he joined me in the ditch. I had some photographs that were going to trigger another operation so they needed to be passed on quickly. We used to develop our own photographs, by the way, even at an observation point, so we could achieve quite a lot.

In addition to the derelict house we also had

operators waiting at each end of the road for much of the time, which meant if the suspect was going foxtrot – on foot – I could call it through immediately so they'd be ready to pick him up and follow. By the end of the six weeks we'd discovered that the only place our suspect visited regularly was a construction site about half a mile away. What raised our suspicions further was the fact that on the way to this construction site he'd often meet with a known bombmaker who was one of the people who manufactured the type of cassette device we had found under the flyover. Sure enough, when the police raided the construction site that's exactly what they found him doing: manufacturing incendiary devices. In order to formally identify a suspect during a raid the police would take an operator with them and they'd always be hooded so as to protect their identity. The bombmaker got just twelve years for his crime, which in my opinion was outrageous. Then again, what do I know? It was textbook though. A perfect operation.

Conversely, we once led a similar operation in Derry that ended up being a complete and utter disaster. In fact, we had to abort it after a week.

We were watching Hugh Brady at the time, who was basically McGuinness's number two. Brady had been done for possession of firearms in the past but that was just the tip of the iceberg with regards to what we suspected. Like McGuinness, the majority had not been either proven or reported, and because of his reputation he was somebody we took an interest in.

Although he too was quite nomadic we eventually managed to house Brady and soon after that we set up an op nearby. This time we were based in the loft of an empty house as opposed to a derelict one, but just like the last place it had inhabitants either side of it. Suffice to say we had to be careful about things such as noise and even smells so once again it was a case of having cold sausages and cheese and remembering not to move about much. This time around I was swapping shifts with a lad called Spick. He'd arrived just a few months before and was a lovely lad. Unfortunately though, he just wasn't cut out for this kind of work and when I turned up to relieve him after his first shift I got the shock of my bloody life. Bearing in mind this was about 3 a.m. the last thing I expected as I approached the rear of the house was the smell of frying sausages. By the time I opened the back door I was almost salivating. The houses either side of this place were in blackout so the only place it could be coming from was the loft. Sure enough, as I made my way very slowly and quietly up the stairs the smell became stronger, but so did the noise. What alarmed me most about this was that I could hear a lot more than just frying sausages. It was as if there were a couple of five-year-olds up there.

When I finally reached the loft the first thing I saw was the frying pan in the corner on a camping stove and sure enough, there were the sausages sizzling away. The reason I could see it so clearly was because the camping stove was giving off quite a strong yellow and blue flame, which, as well as helping to cook Spick's sausages, was lighting up half the loft.

'Spick, where the fucking hell are you?' I hissed quietly.

'I'm here,' he replied, as if I were about half a fucking mile away.

'SHHHHHHHHHH!' I said, gesturing to him to be quiet. 'What the hell do you think you're doing cooking sausages?'

'Smell nice, don't they?'

'Never mind the fucking smell,' I said pointing to the

stove. 'Look at the amount of light it's giving off. And what was all that noise just then?'

'I went to check on them but I tripped over. They'll be done in a couple of minutes.'

'You fucking what?!'

Given what had happened I had to report that we'd been compromised and we cleared out immediately. Unfortunately, Spick was RTU'd the next day but it was probably for the best. That's not to say he wasn't a good soldier, because he was. In fact, Spick was awarded the Queen's Gallantry Medal sometime after that so he obviously had something about him. He just wasn't very good at keeping quiet!

*****

Something that was far less of a disaster while I was over in Derry was my relationship with Theresa. It wasn't textbook – how the hell could it be given my location and what I did for a living? – but without wanting to sound like a soft arse it was ultimately what kept me going.

At some point during the first year I'd asked Theresa to marry me and she'd been daft enough to say yes. Funnily enough, Jay had also proposed to his fiancée during that first year and just by coincidence we were due to tie the knot on the same day, which was 25 March 1978 – about two months before I was due to leave the Det. We were getting married in different churches, of course, but because we were in it together, so to speak, Jay and I had decided to buy our suits at the same time and have a joint stag do.

The suits, which were £59 each and had a grey pinstripe, were from C&A, which some people will remember, and one Saturday morning about three weeks before the weddings Jay and I drove over to Belfast to collect them. Our mate Blue and I were due at an observation point later that evening just outside a place called Lisnamuck, near Maghera, and on the way back it started to piss it down. The observation point was just temporary so all we had to do was park up, change over, and then sit there in a bush until shortly before dawn. Even so, as somebody who is officially allergic to being wet and cold I was not up for this one little bit and as soon as I started saying as much Jay came to the rescue.

'I'll do it,' he said.

'Are you sure, mate? It's fucking horrible out there.'

'Yeah, I don't mind. I don't fancy staying in.'

'OK then,' I said. 'I'll do control.'

That's how we normally worked as a threesome; two in the field and one on control.

As the Army were always told to stay well away from where we were operating, as far as I was concerned if anybody came at me wearing combats they were going to get shot, end of. If it did happen to be the Army then they'd either disobeyed an order or, as with our friend from Yorkshire, misheard one. Either way, it was my life at stake and right at the beginning of my time there I'd made a conscious decision to eliminate anybody who I considered to be a threat. I know it's a cliché but it was a case of kill or be killed, and I didn't fancy the latter.

Unfortunately, not everybody had thought about this as much as I had and when Jay and Blue were at the observation point they were approached by two men wearing combats and carrying rifles. I later found out that one of them had long blond hair, which should have raised major alarm bells, but instead of blowing the fuckers away Blue said, 'Halt', three times, and on the third occasion the two men opened fire and shot Blue and Jay in the stomach. Blue survived, but had to wear a colostomy bag for a long time afterwards. Jay, though, died in hospital a week after, with me at his bedside. As well as being quite unfit, and so less able recover, one of the bullets had hit his pistol, which had damaged both his liver and his kidneys.

As they went down, either Jay or Blue had opened fire with an M10 and managed to put thirteen rounds in one of the attackers. His name was Francis Hughes, an IRA hitman who at the time was probably the most wanted man in Northern Ireland. Although he managed to flee the scene, we found Hughes a few hours later and, after he was brought to the same hospital that Blue and Jay were in after the incident, the bastard was locked up. He looked nothing like the description we'd received from intelligence, which was par for the course. Hughes ended up dying in the Maze Prison in 1981, while on hunger strike. The other one, a man called Diamond, was never brought to book.

The following week Jay and I had been due to have our joint stag night but it turned into a wake. What we should have done was just cancel the whole thing as the last thing we needed in our mental state was a skinful of alcohol. A few respectful lagers maybe, but not a skinful. Subsequently, but not surprisingly, it ended up being a total disaster and if it hadn't been for an operator called Dave Brewin, it would have been a bloodbath.

I should try and explain that being undercover does different things to different people, but the majority of the time you're able to handle it. I've already mentioned the air of detachment and suspicion that hung in the air at our base, not to mention the anger and volatility. After losing an operator, everything went up five or six notches, which is why replacing the joint stag do with a wake was such a bad idea.

Ultimate Survivor

Instead of just getting either shitfaced and angry, or shitfaced and upset, one of the lads, who will have to remain nameless, went completely fucking bonkers with a fully loaded automatic rifle in his hands.

By this time we'd moved from the compound into a hangar, which was also inside the camp, and instead of Nissen huts we had caravans. Because of the sensitivity of what had happened, not to mention the emotional state of all of us, we'd decided to stay on site for the wake and just drank ourselves stupid in the bar. At about 10 p.m. this lad got up suddenly and left. He was actually mid-conversation at the time. His departure was so odd that we all got up and watched him out of the window. By the time we caught sight of him he was running and, by the looks of things, heading towards his car.

'Where the fuck's he going?' somebody shouted. 'He can't drive like that. He's shitfaced.'

'He's not going to drive,' I replied. 'He's opening his boot.'

As soon as I saw him going to the boot of his car I became alarmed as that's where we often kept our rifles. Sure enough, about a second after delving into the boot he re-emerged carrying his rifle.

'What the fucking hell's he doing?' shouted Blue. 'Look at his eyes. He's going to kill somebody.'

I don't know if you've ever witnessed somebody having an emotional breakdown. It's an invariably heart-rending experience and is often the result of either extreme or prolonged sadness or desperation. I later found out that in this particular case it was temporary madness brought on by what had happened to Jay and life in general, as in life as an undercover operative. God knows how long it had been building up but Jay's death had obviously been the trigger and all hell was being let loose. Instead of immediately firing his rifle, which is what we'd been expecting, he started waving it above his head.

'We're fucking invincible we are,' he screamed. 'Nobody can hurt us. Nobody. WE ARE INVINCIBLE!'

Instinctively (and stupidly, as it turned out) I ran out into the hangar to try and calm him down and the first thing I did when I reached him was grab hold of the barrel of his rifle. I didn't talk to him, like any normal human being would have. You know the kind of thing: *Come on now. Just put the gun down. Everything's going to be all right.*

Oh no, not me. I tried to appease the crazed, rifle-wielding madman by pulling away his fucking weapon. As you'd expect, this had a less than calming effect on the man whose rifle I was clutching and before I could even think about following it up by offering a few words or wisdom or comfort, such as, *Put that fucking thing down, you tit, and come and have another pint*, he pulled it out of my grasp and aimed it straight at my head. Fortunately, I wasn't the only one who'd run from the bar to make a hash of things, and just as he took aim Dave Brewin pulled the barrel and, as he did, the fucker fired it. It must have missed me by literally millimetres, which means Dave saved me by milliseconds. Instead of going through me, the bullet went through the cookhouse and then ricocheted off the water tank. I'd just used up yet another one of my lives.

The next thing I knew about seven or eight operators were on top of this lad, and after disarming him they stripped him. Then, after making sure there was nothing in there he could harm himself with, they locked him in his caravan. He was RTU'd the following morning. We later found out that when he was supposed to have been backing us up during an operation in the Bogside, this lad had actually been across the river in a car park. He just didn't have the bottle and this had probably contributed to his breakdown.

People may expect me to be damning of cowards. In fact, I'm anything but. As somebody who has suffered mental health issues for most of his life, I can appreciate that your brain can often put you through shit, and if somebody doesn't have the bottle you should simply send them home and help guide them into a profession that won't harm them – either physically or mentally. There's no shame in not being able to kill somebody, just as there's no shame in not being able to walk around the Bogside surrounded by boyos. It's horses for courses and the fact that they used to execute deserters in the armed forces fills me with anger and sadness in equal measure. Not everybody's a fucking psychopath. Like me.

When I found out that this lad had been bricking it for so long my heart genuinely went out to him, which is why I haven't named him. I'm just glad that he was able to get out of Derry. It would have been nice if he hadn't almost killed me, but there we go. There was no harm done.

The only other time I ever saw somebody lose the plot while I was there, although this was purely down to anger, was when I went duck shooting with a pal of mine called Terry. Terry must have been at least 6 feet 6 and, like the majority of us, he'd got himself a dog at some point. His was a golden retriever and we used to take it with us on every shoot.

The ducks in question were in a pond about a quarter of a mile from the camp and one day while we were shooting there a farmer, who lived nearby, approached us carrying a gun. Before we could even speak to the farmer he aimed his gun at Terry's dog and shot it dead.

'It's been worrying my fucking sheep,' were the farmer's only words, *after* he'd killed the dog.

This farmer, who was knee-high to a grasshopper, may have had a gun in his hands, but so did the man who's dog he'd just killed and as well as being at least a foot taller than this agricultural scrote, he'd been trained to kill people and was rather angry. Fortunately for him, Terry decided not to take out his revenge directly on the farmer.

First of all, he unleashed a verbal tirade against him that would have woken up an entire graveyard. He used words that even I had never heard of before. The look on Terry's face as he released his outburst was chilling to say the least, and the farmer, who was now walking slowly backwards, had undoubtedly realised that he might just have made a mistake.

When Terry had finished his address he walked past the farmer and on to what was obviously his land. He then shot two of his sheep before putting seven or eight rather large holes in some of his outbuildings. The farmer, who was now about 500 yards away, didn't say a word. Come to think of it, neither did I.

On a slightly less tragic and less heated note, Terry, who had a beard, once had to pretend to be woman while he and I were staking out a bakery. We were there covering MI6 while they were picking a lock and, because women weren't allowed in the Det (they were accepted just before I left), we often had to dress up. Looking back, it's a wonder we were never rumbled because as well as the majority of us being quite tall and very hairy, our disguises were shit. What do you expect from a load of blokes – Vivienne fucking Westwood? If you were in a car you'd wear a wig if you were trying to look young and a head scarf if you were trying to look old, but if memory serves me correctly nobody ever wore a head scarf in Derry, so what on earth were we thinking?

Ultimate Survivor

What saved us, I think, is that the general public were just as naive as we were. Although I was often convinced that people knew who I was or were about to rumble me, the truth was that the vast majority neither knew nor cared.

As tragic as Jay's death had undoubtedly been, my wedding to Theresa went ahead as planned. His funeral had been held in Birmingham the day before and this obviously made it extremely hard to bear. Then again, if it was hard for me, what must it have been like for his fiancée?

At the time of our wedding Theresa still didn't know exactly where I was stationed or what I was doing, and as far as just about everyone else was concerned I was still a Royal Marine with 45 Commando. Unfortunately, the only time Theresa had been given an inkling of what I was up to was when she met a couple of people from the camp in Arbroath who'd been RTU'd from the training course. Naturally, they didn't give her the full details, but what they did tell her was that there was a very good chance I wouldn't come back alive.

To be able to get to Jay's funeral and back to the wedding, Theresa's brother and I had hired a little green Skoda. God only knows how we found the money for it (I was earning just £23 a week in the Det which included an extra ten shillings a week for being undercover) but these were the days when Skodas were really shit so it probably cost us pennies. I used my fake driving licence to hire the car. It was a red Irish licence and I was supposed to be from somewhere in County Down. The licences were quite easy to make back then. Or at least, the inside part was. First of all, you'd put a shilling piece over the photograph and then bang it with a hammer. After that you'd put some black ink over the indentations, smudge it a bit, and Bob's your uncle. Or in this case, Paddy. My first name on the licence was Dominic, which is my middle name. Theresa came with us to hire the car and when the man behind the counter referred to me as Dominic, Theresa piped up and said, 'Oh no, that's just his middle name. His first name is Martin.' I managed to talk my way out of it, but only just. I spent a couple of years successfully being undercover in the middle of the Troubles in Northern Ireland, but one of the closest times I came to getting rumbled was trying to hire a car in Arbroath!

Because of all the rushing around I fell asleep during the wedding feast. I was knackered. The reception took place at Charlie's Bar in Arbroath and cost £3.75 a head for either beef or chicken. To a man who earned probably just enough to buy a chicken but nowhere near enough to buy a cow, this was good value for money but the size of the subsequent outlay, which to be fair was part-funded by Theresa's father, was reflected in the location of our honeymoon. Not the geographical location (although it wasn't exactly Biarritz) but the location of our accommodation.

We stayed with Theresa's sister in Exmouth for a few days where the romantic highlights included a posh meal at a Berni Inn, during which Theresa and I shared a banana split, and a trip to the cinema in Plymouth to see God knows what. Elizabeth Taylor and Richard Burton we most certainly aren't, but unlike them we've managed to stay the course.

Talking of money, which I often did in those days as I never had any, if we ever damaged our cars in Derry we had to pay for the repairs out of our own pocket. Bearing in mind I didn't have a legal driving licence at the time and had never passed a standard driving test (not to mention the fact that when I did drive I usually drove like a lunatic), I used to have to be pretty creative when it came to covering up my mistakes.

Looking back, it's a wonder that any of us ever had any money at all at the end of the week as we used to take better care of our hair than we did our cars. If we finished an op and the helicopter was there, providing it wasn't in daylight, we'd race the helicopter back to Limavady. Chris, the helicopter pilot, was just as unhinged as we were but he had the advantage of, a) being able to travel in a straight line, and b) being a hell of a lot quicker than us. Our nemesis with regards to these races were hedges and we used to bounce off the fucking things like a ball in a pinball machine. We once got back from a race with Chris and, as well as having no bumper, I'd lost my front left headlight. I counted twelve bumps and about half a million scratches. Was I in the shit.

A colleague of mine called Chris England got a brand new red Mazda and about two days later he challenged the other Chris to a race back to the helipad at the airfield after an op. To be fair to Chris England, he equipped himself quite well in the race and by the time they reached the edge of the airfield it was neck and neck. In a bid to reach the helipad first, Chris England decided to go off-road, thus giving him the other Chris's advantage of travelling as the crow flies. What Chris the helicopter pilot didn't have to negotiate, however, were some very large holes – about 5 metres square and about 2 metres deep – which had been dug in the grass (fuck knows why). Subsequently, Chris England ended up driving his two-day old red Mazda right into one of these holes, which spelt the end of our races back to base. What a prat. I don't think I've ever laughed as much in my entire life.

Before that fateful day, sometimes, in an act or sportsmanship, Chris the helicopter pilot would act as navigator for whoever was driving the car, which meant you were ready for anything and could basically go flat out.

'Car coming up in 200 yards,' he'd say. 'Come on, you twat, take him, take him!'

This didn't always work unfortunately, as you can meet more than just cars when you're driving flat out through a corner. I once ended up in a ploughed field after trying to avoid a loose sheep.

Once, when we were coming onto a duel carriageway, Chris called through to say that there was a car coming on the inside lane with a load of traffic behind it, but we might just make it in front if I really put my foot down. Make it or not, that's exactly what I did and there was going to be no backing down. About five seconds later Chris called through again and told us to back off. 'They're too far in front,' he said. 'You don't stand a chance.' *Don't stand a chance, my arse.* Despite driving a shit-coloured Vauxhall Chevette with a crap engine, there was no way in the world I was going to back down but when we finally reached the slip road I could see Chris's point. With a following wind we'd have been lucky to get in just behind the car on the inside lane so I decided to take evasive action. From what I could see the driver of the car was an old man and providing he could hear OK I was pretty sure he'd slow down if he thought he was in danger, and he was! As well as blowing my horn and flashing my lights I wound down my window and started shouting at this bloke just in case he could hear me.

'SLOW DOWN, YOU OLD CUNT! FUCKING SLOW DOWN!'

Fortunately, he either saw or heard the long-haired, bearded arsehole coming alongside and when he looked left and saw me he went from about 60 mph to about 20 mph in three seconds flat. By this time the majority of the traffic behind him had just about caught up so if I hadn't managed to get out in front we'd have been stuck there for ages. In the end, it didn't make a blind it of difference as Chris got back about two minutes before us, but what a fucking thrill. We were like rally drivers without any skill.

The closest I ever came to having to shell out a lot of

money to fix a car happened after we'd been on the piss in Coleraine. This was just after Chris England had written off his Mazda so the team leaders Pat and Tim had been watching us like fucking hawks.

The reason we used to go to Coleraine to get wankered was because it's a university town and, believe it or not, we used to pass ourselves off as students. Students of what, you might ask? The rule was that whenever we went out on the piss one of us had to stay sober and, although we used to practise this at the start of every session, it didn't take long for us to revert to type. Subsequently, when we got in the car to drive back from Coleraine, having been on the piss for about seven hours, we were all paralytic and I took the wheel. I'm not proud of this, by the way. It was simply a cultural thing and although drink driving was frowned upon in those days it wasn't really a lock-up-able offence. Not that we'd have given a shit anyway.

For some reason we'd taken one of the pool cars instead of my Chevette. It was an old Hunter, and on the way back, having already driven the car into fuck knows what, we turned a corner and were suddenly faced with an RUC roadblock.

'Get out of the fucking car now!' one of them shouted while pointing his rifle at the car.

'We're Army!' I shouted. Or slurred.

After making sure I was telling the truth the officer who'd stopped us walked around the car.

'What the fucking hell have you done to this car?' he asked. 'It looks like you've driven it through a forest.'

At the time I couldn't say for sure that we hadn't driven it through a forest, but, unable to engage in a conversation at the time, I kept quiet.

'I'll tell you what,' he said finally, 'between here and

Limavady there's either a hedge or a wall. Try and keep between the two, OK? Now fuck off.'

By the time I got back in the driver's seat I'd sobered up a bit and I drove back to camp like a ninety-two-year-old spinster. It didn't make any difference, though, as the damage had already been done. Instead of parking the car in the hangar, I left it somewhere else in the camp. The following morning, after a couple of hours sleep, I went to inspect the damage and it was even worse than I'd thought. That soldier hadn't been joking when he asked me if we'd driven through a forest and the only thing I can compare it to is something out of a stock car race. Fortunately, me and a couple of the lads who'd been with me had the day off but as opposed to repairing the bumps and scratches, which would have taken days, we just covered the car in more mud. When I drove it back into the hangar later that day, Pat came out straight away.

'Why is that car so dirty?' he asked. 'Get it cleaned, now!'

'Don't be so fucking stupid, Pat,' I replied. 'Somebody might have to use it later on and what's more suspicious than a clean car in Derry?'

I did have a point there and fortunately for me and my bank balance, such as it was, Pat thought so too.

When our cars got either written off or burnt out we used to have to pick the new ones up from Gloucester and, in addition to picking up a shiny new car, we were given two days' leave in which to do it, which was nice. After you'd picked up the car you'd always try and squeeze in a night with the missus, which in my case meant a 420-mile trip to Arbroath. The following afternoon it would be back on the ferry from Stranraer to Larne and that'd be it.

The last time this happened was just after our

honeymoon and, because it was so close to me leaving the Det, I'd been ordered to go to the camp in Lympstone to get my next draft. The welcome I received from the regimental sergeant major was as warm as Arbroath in the winter and I thought, *Here we go again, another cunt with a chip on his shoulder.*

'Who are you?' he said. Sorry, grunted.

'Corporal Edwards.'

'And why are you here?'

'I've been called in about my next draft.'

'Well, you can get your hair cut for a start, *Corporal.*'

He couldn't have said the word corporal in a more condescending manner and, had I not just had a lovely night with my new wife – and, were I not driving a shiny new car – I'd have ripped off his head and shat down his fucking neck.

'Actually, *sergeant*, I can't get my fucking hair cut as I'm going back undercover this afternoon.'

'Oh, I see. You're one of those fucking cowboys are you?'

'You what?'

'You heard me. You lot think you're the dog's fucking bollocks, but you're not. You're just a bunch of chancers.'

Now I'm not really known for my restraint, but in the interests of my new family and my previous record of coming into contact with senior ranks who get on my absolute fucking tits, I decided to do as I was told and go and have my hair cut. There was an ulterior motive, however, as I knew full well that this twat had been motivated purely by malice and deep down he must have known that insisting an undercover operative go and have a fucking haircut isn't going to win you promotion. Subsequently, the sergeant major concerned was reported to Colonel Ian Lapraik, who was then the honorary colonel of the SAS, and he got his arse kicked from Arbroath to fucking breakfast time, the twat. What a ridiculous thing to do though. It was my crowning glory, for fuck's sake!

Fortunately, I managed to persuade the barber not to take too much off but when I got back to Derry I was told immediately that it would be a couple of weeks before I was allowed out on operations again.

Up to that point, the most shit-inducing experience I'd had with regards to coming into contact with a load of boyos – even worse than when I realised I'd a doppelganger – was when Blue and I were forced to play football with about ten of them in the Bogside one day. We were sitting on a wall next to a playing field and had been watching about three of them for a couple of hours. They were playing football with some other lads, who I assume were of a similar ilk, when all of a sudden one of the lads we'd been watching walked straight over to us and asked us if we'd like to have a game. To be honest, I think we must have been chatting and had taken our eye off the ball for a few minutes, pardon the pun, and we only realised what was happening when this bloke was standing in front of us.

'All right there, lads,' he said cheerfully. 'We're a couple of men down. Would you like a game?'

Fuck me sideways. When I realised what was happening and who was standing before us my stomach started going like a ginormous ping-pong ball. I'm almost certain some shit came out of my arse. The first thought that came into my head after I came round was, *Try not to look fucking suspicious!* Bearing in mind we both had an M10 underneath our coats, not to mention a pistol strapped to our ankles, that probably wasn't a bad piece of advice, but short of having a neon sign above our heads saying, 'WE'RE

Ultimate Survivor

ARMED UNDERCOVER OPERATORS AND HAVE BEEN WATCHING YOU AND YOUR MATES FOR SEVERAL DAYS' I'm not sure we could have done anything more to look suspicious.

The only way we could get out of this was by agreeing to play immediately in the hope that he'd not see the beads of sweat running down our foreheads, not to mention smell the shit that was now filling my Y-fronts.

Blue and I were up and at 'em like two teenagers at a gangbang and fortunately this lad didn't seem to suspect a thing. As is the way with any kind of football match, there was a hell of lot of shouting on the field and this made us even more paranoid. Every time somebody shouted for the ball I heard the words, 'They're fucking British. Kill the cunts!' and every time that happened a bit more shit came out. The worst example was when this big blond-haired lad, who I didn't know but recognised, passed me the ball. I'd always been a shit footballer anyway but in this situation I was by far the shittest on earth. Instead of passing it to somebody – anybody! – I hoofed it back to him but I must have got right underneath the ball as it went flying over his head and out of play. The tirade this bloke let out was both biblical and fierce. I dread to think what he'd have said if he'd known who the fucking hell I was. That was enough for me so after quickly feigning an ankle injury I hobbled off as quickly as I could without looking like somebody who was actually just very, very scared. And, who had shat their pants. Playing football with the IRA. Fucking brilliant.

Another unnerving incident I can remember in Derry was when we had to go digging in the graveyard next to McGuinness's house. I can't for the life of me remember what we were looking for – it could have been a cache of weapons – but the very idea of being surrounded by thousands of people who wanted us dead, while at the same time digging up a fucking graveyard full of people who would also have wanted us dead, was sobering to say the least. We didn't find a thing, by the way. That, I do remember.

Shortly after that we received some intelligence that McGuinness was going to be picked up from his house one night at about 7 p.m., but it was nothing special and we weren't expecting much, if anything, to actually happen. Sure enough, when it got to about 9 p.m. we hadn't seen a peep from McGuinness's house so we called through to control and told our team leader, Pat, that we were calling it a day.

'Nope, you can stay there,' replied our glorious leader. He was a fucking nutcase this bloke.

'Fuck that,' I said. 'There are people who've walked past us four or five times now. Do you want to get us both killed? It's just some duff information'.

'I've told you to stay there.'

'And I'm telling you to fuck right off!'

In the end he saw sense and called us off, the stupid stubborn bastard, and sure enough the information came to nothing.

Pat had a habit of either putting us or keeping us in precarious situations, so much so that I once dressed up as a member of the Bee Gees and did a rendition of 'Staying Alive' just for him. I already had the hair and the beard and because it was the 1970s things like flares and open shirts were bang on trend. The only thing I didn't have was the voice (I make Barry White sound like Frankie Valli) which meant I had to mime to a tape. Miming aside, it was a barnstorming performance, if I say so myself, and everybody applauded wildly. Well, almost everybody. Pat may have been a world beater in the putting-other-people-in-danger stakes, but when it came to a sense of humour he was sadly lacking.

Ultimate Survivor

Subsequently, my well-rehearsed rendition went down like a dog in a mosque but it didn't stop us from taking the piss. In fact, because he was such a miserable cunt that made us worse. At the end of the day, though, there was fuck all else to do.

Chris England used to have a tape of a song called 'Suicide is Painless', which was the theme tune to the television show *M*A*S*H*. That had become our unofficial theme tune and every time Pat asked us to do something we weren't happy with or we thought might be dangerous, Chris would play it to him through his car radio. That also used to go down like a lead balloon, which again used to cheer everybody up and was compensation for being put in so much danger. To counter our team leader's morose personality and gung-ho attitude to danger, we also used to play the 'Ride of the Valkyries' whenever he used to come on an op with us. I don't think he had a clue that it was aimed at him.

TWELVE

An event in 1978 helped convince me that Martin McGuinness was aware of far more than the surveillance team ever bargained for. Although I can't prove anything, when I finally made eye contact with McGuinness after trailing him for two years and reporting on his every move, I suspected he had inside information.

The story itself is almost comical, like something out of an old farce. What neutralises the humour, though, is the knowledge of how close I came to being killed by him. To this very day it still wakes me up at night. I'm a shit sleeper as it is and, although it's not the worst nightmare I have – not by any stretch of the imagination – it's one of the most vivid.

The episode took place in the spring, just three weeks before I was due to leave the Det. I'd already decided that I wasn't going to carry on as a Marine and I'd been looking for another job for some time. As a consequence, I was already a little bit demob happy and had my mind on other things.

It was a Saturday morning and I was on a stakeout

that looked like it was going to come to nothing. That was par for the course and, after several hours of doing or saying virtually fuck all, my mind was a bit dead. Then, all of a sudden, I saw McGuinness crossing a road about a hundred yards away. He had his hands in the pockets of his duffle coat and his head down. Spotting him brought me back to life. *Aw, fuck it*, I thought. *I may as well follow him.*

I hadn't been expecting to see McGuinness out so early on a Saturday, which is probably one of the reasons I decided to tail him, rather than stay in my stakeout position. Spotting somebody you intend to follow usually results in a slight surge of nervous energy and, because it was so unexpected – and because I was demob happy and a bit cocky and complacent – I got carried away, for want of a better phrase.

In Ireland, north and south, they have what are called pub-shops and back then the Bogside was full of them. They were often quite nondescript, and were sometimes no more than a front room with a counter and a few shelves. After I had followed him for a few minutes, McGuinness went into one of these places, and, after experiencing the usual surge of nervous energy, I followed him in. At this point, what I should have done, but didn't, was to go foxtrot, which not only meant going on foot, but calling it in. If you ever got out of your car in Derry, even to buy a packet of fags, you were always supposed to ask for back-up first.

As I walked through the front door I entered a narrow hall with a public telephone on the wall. As far as I could see there was only one other door in the hall, which must have led through to the pub-shop. I almost came to my senses at this point but not enough to turn back. I was only supposed to follow McGuinness, not corner the fucker. I had no idea what I was going to find in the next room and walking in there could easily be the last thing I ever did.

The corridor leading through to the pub-shop was only about 3 metres long but it was incredibly dark. Disturbingly so. So was the pub-shop itself, and when I finally made it in there it took my eyes a moment to adjust. The shop part of the establishment took up at least 80 per cent of the space and the pub part was nothing more than a small counter with a table and a couple of stools. More importantly though, there was no McGuinness, just an old man standing behind the shop counter. *Where the fucking hell is he?* I thought. I now felt like I was being drawn into a trap but it was too late to run.

Now back in operator mode, I walked straight up to the counter, picked up a packet of green Wrigley's chewing gum, put ten pence on the counter, nodded to the old man and walked out again. By now I was shitting myself and although I was desperate to leg it, I managed to remain composed – just. But as I stepped into the dark hallway again there, right in front of me, was McGuinness. He had the public telephone to his ear and was looking straight at me. He only said one word but it was enough to make my stomach lurch.

'Gotcha,' he said.

Instinct played a very strange trick on me here because instead of just legging it out of the door and radioing for help I stood there for a few seconds, looked at him, and said, 'Fucking hell!' After that he smiled at me, the twat, which is when I decided to run.

I had no idea what might be waiting outside for me on the street – a gun trained on my head, ready to take me out, or a couple of armed boyos with a hood and a car? Once I was out of the door I started running and reached for my walkie talkie.

'CODE BLACK, CODE BLACK,' I shouted. 'McGUINNESS HAS RUMBLED ME.'

Code black means you've decided to leave a location sharpish. Fortunately, within a minute of giving my whereabouts, I was picked up and escorted back over the bridge.

As I sat there in the back of the car, shaking and sweating my arse off, I remembered what he'd said.

'Gotcha.'

It made me wonder who'd been spying on who.

*****

My final operation as an operative in the Det was completely unofficial and had nothing whatsoever to do with either Martin McGuinness (who I could no longer follow, having been rumbled), the IRA, Republicans or anything to do with the Troubles. It was actually to do with a pig. Had we been collared by either the hierarchy in Whitehall or the owner of the pig, we'd have been in deep shit.

It was all to do with my leaving party, which took place about a week before I buggered off. I've no idea why, but if you lasted the course in the Det and completed your two-year tenure without dying you were given £250 to spend on a party, which in today's money must be about a grand, if not more. That was for food *and* drink, by the way, but even so it was enough for a good bash.

Or was it?

Some bright spark (it wasn't me, honest) suggested that instead of spending any of the money on food we should rustle some and then blow it all on booze. Bearing in mind we had hundreds of farms right on our doorstep and were no strangers to creeping around in the dark in places that we wouldn't normally be welcome, this was bordering on fucking genius. We set about making a list of what we'd like to eat and where we were going to nick it from. Due partly to which farms were most familiar to us, the menu would consist of lamb, goose and pork, and the plan was that over the next three nights we'd rustle them in that order.

We assumed that the first night was going to be a doddle as in our eyes all we had to do was turn up at the field, choose whichever sheep looked the fattest, kill it, and then shove it into the back of my car. Easy.

It just goes to show how wrong you can be.

The first bit went without a hitch. In fact, it was textbook. I knew the farm well and with the field I'd chosen being quite far away from the farmhouse we were odds on not to get caught. That came to pass in the end but the bit in the middle, about choosing a sheep and then killing it – that went slightly awry.

There weren't that many sheep in the field and because they all had full coats it was impossible to tell which was the fattest. We settled on the one closest to us and, after aiming my 9 mm pistol right between its eyes, I fired. I assume most sheep skulls are made of relatively thin bone, but this one must have been born with some titanium in its forehead because the bullet literally bounced off. The impact did knock it backwards a few feet but the blow had obviously been far from life threatening.

Putting the guns away for a second, we decided to give chase and, after executing an impressive sliding tackle from the right, I managed to bring down the sheep and its titanium forehead. After that, we threw it in the back of my car and went on our way. To say that the sheep made its presence felt in the back of my car would be a gross understatement as in addition to kicking the living shit out of my three fellow rustlers it deposited enough piss and shit to fertilise an entire vegetable allotment for a year.

No matter. The main thing was we had the first part of our menu in captivity and all we had to do now was kill it. Fortunately, one of the SAS boys at Limavady had been a butcher in a past life and so he did the deed. After he'd killed and shorn the thing, he said, 'You'll be lucky if there's enough meat on this to feed one of your fucking dogs.' I don't know if it was anorexic, but there was literally nothing on it.

With goose and pork also on the menu, I didn't worry unduly and the following evening the same crack team of rustlers made their way out of the hangar in search of some geese. The place we'd picked was a hut on a green in the middle of a council estate and inside this hut lived about twenty geese. I had no idea who they belonged to but there was at least 500 yards between the hut and the nearest council house, so I figured that even with a bit of noise we'd easily be able to pull off a smash and grab. Absolute doddle.

This hut was no more than about 10-foot square and so, as opposed to all four of us going in, there were just the three of us. Armed with two crowbars and a hammer, we took off some of the planks on the side of the hut first and then crawled in.

A few years ago, somebody told me that for their size geese are considered to be one of the most viscous animals on the planet and should be approached, if at all, with absolute caution.

'Pull the other one,' was my response to this nugget of information.

They beat seven kinds of shit out of us.

It wouldn't have made much difference if we'd been armed with M10s. Seriously, I've never seen anything like it. The idea had been that we'd be able to bend their necks over the crowbars and then clobber them with the hammer. The only creature that came even close to having its neck broken in that hut was Blue. Just moments after I'd retreated and was busy putting the planks back on the side of the hut I suddenly saw Blue running away to the car with what looked like some kind of feathered monster giving chase. Had it caught him, Blue would be famous as being the first undercover operative in the history of the world to have been assassinated by a goose. That's some claim to fame.

With two attempts gone and almost no food in the larder everything was resting on the pig. The option of just buying some food had been and gone as the booze had already been purchased, so it was important that we a) didn't fuck it up, and b) managed to find an animal that wasn't either anorexic or psychotic.

Because of what was at stake, and the fact that the pig farm was in what we called bandit country – a rural area populated by sympathisers and the odd boyo – we decided to execute this like a proper operation so it was headlights off, mask out and night-time goggles on – the works. 'Mask out' means you ensure that as you open the door of the car no light is emitted whatsoever. Otherwise, what's the point of turning up with your headlights off?

Three of us were dropped off at the farm while the driver stayed where he was just in case we had to leave a bit sharpish. We crept around the hedge line and eventually reached the pens containing the pigs. After we very carefully opened the door of one of them, about twenty piglets came rushing out. What a fucking noise they made. It was ear piercing. Blue, who again had been daft enough to offer his services, started trying to hit one of these piglets with his crowbar and in doing so missed and hit his ankle. As soon as that happened he started screaming too, so between him and the piglets we were making enough noise to wake a hundred dead farmers, let alone one live one. Sure enough, in the distance I saw a light go on in the farmhouse so I ran into the pen, found a pig that I was confident I could carry, picked it up and ran for it. The farmer, incidentally, was a right fucking hard-nut Republican bastard who wouldn't have thought twice about shooting us. All this for a few chops and some bacon! It was ridiculous.

As I ran out of the pen with this pig, I told Blue, who was still hopping around clutching his ankle, to call for the pick up but because it was pitch black, save for a tiny house light in the distance, I couldn't see a fucking thing. I decided to dive into a ditch for a few minutes just to get my bearings. All the time, the pig was squealing it's arse off and just as I was trying to pull it into this ditch it farted right in my fucking face. To this day I have never, ever, smelt anything so disgusting. As I continued trying to pull the pig in the ditch with me I started retching. At one point I was hanging on to this pig by one trotter and, as it continued to squeal, I continued to retch. Luckily, the car pulled up right beside me just a few seconds later and although I still couldn't see it properly I managed to bundle me and the pig onto the back seat. Unlike the sheep it seemed to calm down a bit when we started driving, but that didn't stop it from pissing and shitting all over me. I was covered, and so was the car. That was two vehicles we'd wiped out in three days.

Between the pig and the sheep we managed to feed just about everybody but it was kids' portions. That's about all I remember, as we had rather a lot of booze to get through.

*****

In 2005, the Det, or the 14 Field Security and Intelligence Company, to use its correct title, was rebadged with the Special Reconnaissance Regiment and therefore decommissioned. To celebrate both the company's history and existence we had a reunion at Limavady camp. Some of us decided to take a bus into Derry and visit some of our old haunts. A hell of a lot had changed, of course, but a hell of lot hadn't, and in particular the Bogside and the Creggan. Why the hell we decided to go back there in the first place I have no idea. Only three of us were daft enough to do so and despite some of the buildings being different and some of the potholes having being filled in nothing had really changed. Because of the occasion we were all smartly dressed so God only knows what the locals thought. It's a bloody good job they didn't know our history, otherwise there might have been trouble. Fancy us going for a quiet stroll around the Bogside though. It's madness.

On the second day of the reunion we had a group photograph taken on the parade ground at Limavady and in honour of the Det's preference for its trainees to take orders literally, as in 'Arrive after 12pm', I turned up wearing a jacket and tie, as had been requested, and my own choice of attire elsewhere. I think there were about 250 people in all, including brigadiers, generals, and all sorts of bigwigs, and because I was wearing something a bit different I decided to make an entrance. Once everyone else had taken their seats somebody shouted, 'Where the hell's Marty?' which was my cue. With everyone else sitting together and looking my way I marched onto the parade ground wearing a tweed jacket, a pink shirt, a tie, and a lovely pair of shorts and flip-flops. While everyone else was pissing themselves the brigadier stood up and said, 'It could only be fucking you, Edwards! Just for that, you can come and sit here between me and the general,' which is exactly what I did. So, while everyone else in the photograph is looking smart and respectful, I'm looking like somebody who isn't. Well, the top half is.

I was only following orders.

That night I introduced one of my party tricks to the proceedings and ended up getting a fat lip. Not to put too fine a point on it, I put staples in my head and staple my lip to whatever surface I can. That's the top and bottom of it. Why do I do it? Shock value, I suppose. I mean, how many times have you seen a man call for a stapler when he's pissed and then proceed to staple his head and his lip? It's the reactions I like. Some people take it in their stride, some people pretend to take it in their stride – and fail – and some people just lose the plot completely. I think that's probably the jackpot for me, the look on their faces when they see the first staple in my forehead. It's a wonderful experience. Like watching your kids on Christmas morning.

That night in Limavady a young SAS lad challenged me to a staple-off to see who could staple themselves the most. I'd had a proper skinful by this time – we all had – but this SAS lad had probably had too much and, just as I was about to staple my bottom lip to the desk, he came up behind me and hit the stapler with his fist, while it was in my hand. Under normal circumstances I'd make sure that the staple went through my lip and just into the desk, but because of my young helper it went so far in that I couldn't get it out again. It never usually hurts much, but I have to admit that on this occasion it smarted a bit and a medic had to be called. The SAS lad got a kicking for his trouble, although not from me.

As I left the bar, having had the staple removed, two lads were each shimmying up a flagpole. The poles were about 40 feet high and they were obviously having a race to see who could reach the top first. There must have been at least a hundred people watching them and when the first one reached the top it was like a goal going in at a cup final. In hindsight it was more like a dangerous sports convention than a reunion but it was a hell of a lot of fun.

The best part of the evening was when an officer, who had flown himself up from Aldergrove by helicopter, had to fly home. He hadn't touched a drop of alcohol but plenty of other people had and one bright spark had managed to persuade the officer to fly back to Aldergrove naked. To be honest, I don't think he had much choice in the matter and when he hopped into his helicopter stark-bollock naked he was handed what he assumed was his uniform in a bag. Except it wasn't his uniform at all. It was a bag of tea towels. Just the thought of that young officer landing at Aldergrove, opening his bag and realising that he was going to have to make a naked run for it was enough to eradicate any pain from my lip.

THIRTEEN

The first job I applied for before leaving Northern Ireland was with the Manchester Police Force. I sent in the application just after I got married, which is when and why I'd decided to leave the forces for good.

I got time off for the interview and, after meeting Theresa in Liverpool, we hired a car and drove into Manchester. I had to get changed in the back of the hire car – an early Mini Metro – and my interview attire consisted of a grey leather jacket, a pair of black flares that Noddy Holder himself would have been proud of, a pink shirt and a blue kipper tie. I was straight out of *The Sweeney* so it was a good job I was applying to be a copper.

The interview, which took place just before I left Northern Ireland, couldn't have gone any better and they offered me a position there and then. Because of what I'd been doing, the majority of the talk after the usual introductory stuff was about specialising me. I'd still have to go on the beat for a while, but not for very long. They also talked about giving me a house in Runcorn so, as a newly married man who was about to have no job and nowhere to live, it was a dream come true. Theresa was massively relieved as I think she had visions of us living in a bedsit.

About a week later, a few days before I was due to leave, I received a letter from the Manchester Constabulary saying that the Chief Constable, James Anderton, had vetoed the offer and it had been withdrawn. There was no reason, as in those days the police weren't obliged to give you a reason, so I was left scratching my head. I'd been on probation in my teens but despite my rather chequered history I'd never been in any trouble, at least on civvy street.

The first person I told after ringing Theresa was Phil, who was my boss in Limavady. He too was at a loss as to what had gone on and after making a couple of telephone calls he eventually got in touch with a friend of his called Sam Donnelly, who was then the head of the Special Branch in Northern Ireland.

Sam Donnelly was also a liaison officer between the RUC and the SAS and it was reported a few years later that in the mid-1980s he'd blocked a plan by the SAS to assassinate McGuinness by drowning him in the Atlantic. When the SAS men suggested it to Donnelly the first thing he asked was, 'How many people know about the plan?' When the SAS replied, 'Six,' Donnelly, who died in 2008, deemed that to be too many and McGuinness was spared.

Fortunately, Chief Superintendent Donnelly was also puzzled by Anderton's decision and even went over to the mainland to have lunch with Anderton and ask him what his reasoning was. When Donnelly returned he hadn't managed to change Anderton's mind but he had extracted a reason. 'Do you think I'm going to let a man like that loose on my streets after what he's been doing? Not a chance.'

Ultimate Survivor

Over the next few years I tried joining the Fire Service, the Prison Service and several other police forces and despite passing the tests and interviews with flying colours I was eventually refused employment with each. Why? I can't prove this, but it's my belief that there was a Home Office block on me. There's no other reason I can think of why every public organisation would refuse to employ a fit young man with a brain. My time in the detention quarters, had it been an issue, would have been given as a reason in anything but the police force, but it never was. The only refusal that ever really upset me was when I went for a job at a young offenders centre in Chelmsford. I've always been very good with young people because of my history and background, so I thought I'd be able to achieve something and perhaps make a difference. I would eventually get my chance to do that later down the line, but it would be no thanks to any of the public services. To them, I was simply *persona non grata* and probably still am.

When I arrived back on the mainland, having been shafted by James Anderton, or God's copper as he was known, I had £200 in my pocket, no job and nowhere to live. Theresa was staying with her sister and her husband in Exmouth at the time and they very kindly allowed me to stay too. The only money coming in at that time was from Theresa, who was working as a machinist in a clothes factory.

As soon as I got to Exmouth I started looking for a job but, Christ, was I in for a shock. The fact is I'd already become institutionalised and becoming a Marine, and especially an operator, had stripped me of reality. I can understand completely why people leaving the forces often have problems adjusting and I can't even imagine what it must be like after twenty or thirty years. Where the hell do you start? Fortunately for me I wasn't short on endeavour and had just enough common sense to see me through. So, after scouring the streets and job centres for a few days I eventually came across a construction company called Fowlers. I'd seen some signs for a new estate they were building called Green Acres and so I doorstepped them and asked if they needed a labourer. Like virtually every other company I'd visited, I received a polite but ultimately meaningless *We'll let you know,* and went on my way. As I was leaving the building I saw a huge Jaguar pull into the car park and after watching it park up I noticed that it had gone into a space reserved for Henry Fowler. *Lucky twat,* I thought. *He obviously owns the company.*

For many years now I've always gone for an early morning walk and the following day, as I was doing just that, I spotted the Jaguar I'd seen yesterday coming towards me. Luckily there was a bit of traffic around so it was moving quite slowly and when it was about 20 feet away I walked into the road and raised my hands gesturing him to stop. Fortunately for me he did stop and immediately started blowing his horn. To ensure that he didn't go anywhere I then lay on the bonnet with my face almost pressed against the windscreen.

'What the bloody he'll do you want?' he shouted through his wound-down window.

'I came to your offices yesterday about a job as a labourer and got fobbed off,' I shouted. 'I've just come out of the forces and desperately need a job and you're building houses all over the fucking place. What's the problem? All I want to do is work!'

'Tomorrow morning at 8 a.m.,' shouted Mr Fowler. 'Come to the offices first and I'll take you to the site and introduce you to the foreman.'

By this time there was about a mile of traffic behind

him so instead of saying thank you or trying to shake his hand I just got off his bonnet and let him drive away. It was a different approach, I grant you, but it was effective.

The following morning I arrived at the offices bang on 8 a.m. and after making me sign a few forms we got in the Jag and I was driven to my site. I earned £32 a week for Henry Fowler and can say without fear of contradiction (as he must be long dead by now) that I was the best labourer he ever had. I was there for about two years in all, and not long after I started working for him I got another job as a petrol pump attendant at a local Jet garage. My wages at the Jet garage was a pound an hour, which wasn't too bad, but I still managed to supplement this by nicking half an ounce of Old Holborn and some papers every week, which just about covered my fag money. The owner of the Jet garage, who was a bit of a jack the lad, then opened a restaurant and he asked me if I'd like to do all the painting and decorating, again for a pound an hour.

Within just a few weeks of arriving in Exmouth I was working ten hours a day, seven days week, and I loved every fucking minute of it. The money was obviously nice but it was such a contrast to the stop/start life in the Marines and as an operator, and although I was always fine with that it was nice to be busy for a change.

The only problems I had people-wise while settling into civvy street were my fellow labourers on the site. They'd all been used to working at a certain pace and when I came in it upset the equilibrium. Sorry, allow me to rephrase that. It exposed them as being a bunch of lazy bastards. All I wanted to do was work and all they wanted to do was sit on their arses smoking and slagging off the foreman. I was fine doing the last two. It was the first bit I had a problem with and when one of them first approached me about it I gave him short shrift.

'What you fuckers do while you're here is entirely up to you and what I do is entirely up to me. Now fuck off or I'll beat you to death with a fucking trowel.'

This was obviously fed immediately back to the rest of them as within five minutes I had an Italian lad standing next to me brandishing a knife. Before he could even speak I had him up against a wall with the knife touching his throat. I told him that this was an end to the matter and that I should be left alone.

Although I didn't have much contact with the labourers after that I got friendly with some of the tradesmen and became good friends with a lad called Jeffrey who was a JCB driver. My favourite part of the job was doing something called oversights, which involved running with bags of cement up to the mixer, mixing it with aggregate, and then putting it into a dumper truck before laying it. There was slightly more to it than that but as a way of keeping fit it was incredibly effective and, after a few weeks, I was eleven stone, very lean and the fittest I'd been in a long time.

Because of the speed in which I performed these oversights Henry Fowler ended up giving me a bonus. The foreman must have told him about my rather controversial work ethic and, after opening my wage packet in the Portakabin where we all scoffed our lunch, I found the extra money and mentioned it to the fellow labourers that I was just about on speaking terms with.

'Fuck off,' said one of them. 'Henry Fowler's never given a bonus in his life.' Jeffrey the JCB man confirmed this, so just to be a clever cunt I got up to show them all.

'Look at that,' I said, waving the extra fiver around. 'That's what you get if you work hard, you bunch of lazy bastards.' Strangely enough, I think that was the end of us being on speaking terms.

One day, while I was working at the Jet garage, I overheard the owner mention to somebody that he had a 40-foot caravan for sale and, without even thinking, I interrupted the conversation and asked him how much.

'Four hundred quid,' he said.

'I'll take it,' I replied.

When I got home that evening I immediately told Theresa the good news.

'I've found us somewhere to live,' I said enthusiastically.

'Really,' she replied eagerly. 'Where is it?'

'Erm. Anywhere you want it to be, really.'

'What do you mean?'

'It's a caravan.'

'Oh, for God's sake Martin!'

I'd already arranged for the caravan to be towed to a place called Wimpole Caravan Site and once Theresa had come around to the idea, which didn't take very long, we got our stuff together and moved in. Once the caravan had been paid for and I'd forked out for the first month's site fees, I was left with exactly £37.50, but not for long. The caravan still had to be connected and when the site owner, who was a cunt of the first order, had finished it all I had exactly 14p, which had to last me almost a week. Theresa was also skint at the time so despite having a roof over our heads, albeit one made of fibreglass, we had nothing in the cupboard except a few cubes of powdered soup which you used to melt in hot water. We managed to get a small loaf of Hovis with the 14p.

Although we didn't eat very much that week, at least we were on our own for the first time. Being alone with me in a 40-foot caravan would be some people's idea of hell, but to Theresa, who is the only person on earth who can handle me at close quarters and over a long period of time, it was less so (slightly!). The best way of describing us at this point is poor but happy.

That was until we heard a rapist lived on the site.

Wimpole Caravan Site was the British equivalent of an American trailer park, in that it wasn't so much a tourist destination, more a place that was inhabited by people who couldn't afford a house. Like us. Subsequently, you used to get all kinds of banjo-playing arseholes living there and one day word went around that a convicted rapist had moved in. As we were new to the site and didn't know a new banjo-playing bastard from an existing one, I decided to play it safe and tell everybody, one-by-one, and while brandishing an axe, that if they came anywhere near my patch I would chop them up into little pieces. There were all kinds of people on the site, including some hardnosed gypsies, but I couldn't give a shit. Tell one, tell all. That was my motto. Or, threaten one, threaten all. That would be more accurate.

It's hard to overestimate just how hand-to-mouth our life was back then and every penny we earned was accounted for. This isn't a fucking whinge, by the way. There's no need to start humming the music from that Hovis advert. I'm just saying how it was. It was character building if anything, and I learned a lot from our time in Exmouth.

One night, this must have been a Sunday, I went to the restaurant that I was decorating, which was called Noshers, to find the place completely deserted. This was strange as the owner was usually around, but instead there were just a couple of tins of paint on one of the tables. At the time I couldn't manage without my decorating money and after deciding that the paint must have been meant for the ceiling, I started work. I didn't leave that place until about 3 a.m. and the following day after work I popped in for my money. The owner went red as soon as he saw me.

'That paint was going back, you stupid arsehole. It's the wrong fucking colour!'

He made me pay for the right paint, the bastard. And I had to repaint it for free.

The only member of my family who I really kept in touch with after I'd left the Royal Marines and Northern Ireland was Uncle Peter. He was still living in Kensington with his partner Andrew, and Theresa and I would visit him whenever I was on leave. On one occasion a fellow Marine called Acky tagged along and after arriving in Kensington we all went to the pub. It was a gay pub and so you occasionally got the odd gay-hating wanker in there causing trouble. This, unfortunately, was one such occasion and as Acky and I were playing pool three blokes at a table started making homophobic comments. I will not tolerate homophobia in any shape or form, and on hearing one of them say something along the lines of, *Look at them, bunch of faggots*, I decided to have a word.

'Have you three got a fucking problem?' I asked.

'Oh, you're one as well are you,' came the reply.

Whenever I know that I'm about to fight I always take out my false teeth, so I took them out and placed them on the pool table. I was going to ask them if they'd like to step outside but as I was already without my teeth I decided to forgo the invitation and instead I beat the living shit out of them, with some help from Acky, and then threw them out. After that, I put my teeth back in and we carried on playing. That wasn't the first time I'd had to sort out a gay basher or three, and Uncle Peter used to love it. Not the people getting beaten up. He used to love the fact that a straight man was prepared to stick up for gay people. The fact that it was his nephew was the icing on the cake.

I once got £50 from one of Peter's friends for letting

him feel my bollocks. Theresa was there at the time. Again, it was in a pub and this bloke, who was some kind of Russian aristocrat, put his hand on my bum while I was talking to somebody. Peter was standing at the bar with Theresa so I said, 'Hey, Peter, have you told this bloke who I am?' I then looked down to where this Russian's hand was and then back at Peter. Now aware of what I was getting at Peter said, 'He's a Marine Commando, he's straight, and I'm talking to his wife.' You'd think with that information at your disposal you'd at least consider moving your hand but this bloke wasn't bothered. He just stood there with a slightly lewd grin on his face and with his hand still on my left buttock. I decided to call his bluff in the end and said, 'Right then. If you want to go around the front it's going to cost you fifty quid.' Peter looked at me, as if to say, *What the bloody hell are you doing?* but that was about two weeks' pay for me. Without even flinching this Russian pulled out £50, handed it to me and then put his hand on my bollocks. By now the entire pub knew what was going on and they were pissing themselves. Not the Russian though. He was having the time of his life. 'Right, stop there,' I said to him after a few seconds. 'I'm getting a twitch!' Fifty quid though, just to feel my bollocks.

The first person from the armed forces to visit me in Exmouth was a lad called Mick who'd been a chef on the HMS *Danae*. The most interesting thing I can say about Mick's career in the armed forces, apart from the fact he eventually became a major, is that he used to wank into the liver and then serve it to the officers. The dirty bastard!

A few years ago back in Arbroath, Mick's wife had died from a blood clot in the brain shortly after giving birth, and ever since then he'd been struggling a bit. He just turned up one day in a hell of a state and so I took him down the pub. Theresa and I had just sold the caravan as I'd got a job in London doing some bodyguard work. She was going back to live with her sister for a bit while I got myself sorted, and I was going to be living in a loft in Belgravia, which is where my new employer was based. At least some of the time.

I'd managed to get £1,100 for the caravan, which was like winning the lottery for us and so I was in exactly the right frame of mind to try and cheer Mick up a bit. I had a good job waiting for me, at last, and I'd made £700 profit on the caravan. And, I was newly married to a beautiful and understanding wife, of course. The pub, which was the only one in the area, was about 2 miles from anywhere and so everybody drove there, regardless of what they were drinking. Mick and I had been there at least a couple of hours when all of a sudden four policemen ran in.

'I don't care if you've been drinking,' one of them said, 'but if you live at Wimpole Caravan Site please get back there as soon as possible. One of the caravans is on fire.'

When the site came into view on the way back I could tell by the flames that the fire was in the vicinity of our caravan and I had an awful feeling that my £700 profit had just gone up in smoke. I think Mick was OK by this point as I'd managed to cheer him up with a few jokes. It was me who was starting to get desperate.

When we arrived back at the site I saw immediately that it was the caravan next door to ours that was on fire but, with a gap of only 2 metres and a full gas canister inside that I'd bought the day before, ours was far from being out of danger. It sounds a bit mercenary but all I could think about at the time was the £700. Fuck the people next door!

Normally I wouldn't dare go anywhere near a burning caravan, especially one that might have a couple of gas canisters in it. With so much at stake, though, I decided to throw caution to the wind and, after running into ours, I managed to undo the canister and remove it in no time at all. After that I just prayed that there were no canisters sitting next door and, fortunately, there weren't. My precious profit was safe.

*****

The job I'd managed to line up was as a bodyguard to Prince Bandar bin Sultan Al Saud who is a member of the Saudi royal family and who was Saudi Arabia's ambassador to the United States of America between 1983 and 2005. The reason I got the job was because one of my old bosses in Northern Ireland had become a partner with the company who arranged Prince Bandar's security and the first people he turned to when he was on the lookout for new staff were former operators.

Incidentally, when Stella Rimington became director general of MI5 in 1992 one of the first things she did was to recruit more spies. After seeing one of the adverts, I wrote to Miss Rimington informing her that there were hundreds of former operators still of working age who, as well as having experience in the field, had already been vetted. They would obviously have had to be retrained, etc., but surely it was worth exploring?

Never heard a thing back from the old bag.

In the past Prince Bandar had used a couple of former SAS boys but apparently they'd been a little bit impatient and patience is one thing that operators all had in spades. Bodyguarding is all about situation awareness. It's not about fighting or killing people. Spot the people you don't want and where they might be coming from. Then keep the fuckers away. That's the aim of the game. It helps if you can look after yourself, of course, but it's all about prevention. There were about sixteen of us on this job and we all slept in camp beds in the loft of one of Prince Bandar's offices, which was just behind Sloane Square. Some of the lads I knew, and some I didn't, but they were a great bunch, and although we were always professional (there was no fucking about with this bloke) we still managed to have a laugh.

One of the directors of the security company, who was also a Lloyds underwriter, owned a huge five-bedroomed house on Sloane Street, which connects Sloane Square and Chelsea with Knightsbridge, and about a month after I started with the company he asked me if I'd like to look after the place for him while he and his family went on holiday. He also said I could invite Theresa to come down and stay with me. We had to sleep in the servants' quarters, naturally, but as much as I enjoyed sleeping on a camp bed with a load of sweaty bastards in a loft it was slightly more preferable.

Just because we slept in the servants' quarters didn't mean we couldn't make ourselves comfortable in the rest of the house. We bloody did. The only complaint I had when he got back after the two weeks was the tea.

'You could have told me you only drank Earl fucking Grey,' I protested. 'I had to buy my own.'

It was disgusting. All that money and he couldn't even get me some proper fucking tea.

People sometimes ask me how Theresa and I coped with being away from each other for so long at the beginning of our marriage but because that had always been the norm – even before we got married – we were both used to it. In fact, the only potential problem then would have been whether we could cope with each other long term and in the same house! We'd tried it in the caravan for a while but it remained to be seen as to whether that would work as well as being separated for long periods. If you gave Theresa the choice now, I shudder to think what she'd say. *Let's go back to how it was at the beginning*, probably. *Now piss off!*

After the Prince Bandar contract came to an end I was offered another contract with the same company guarding a high-end jewellery shop called Bond that had just opened in Mayfair. It was being partly financed by the Hyderabad royal family and it had been given the name Bond because Sean Connery also had a stake in it. I think he got out soon after it opened because the price of gold went up, but he did come in once while the shop was being fitted out. He was a big bugger.

Shortly after Bond opened, which, incidentally, had an address that also shared a name with its famous investor's character as it was based at 125 Bond Street, I was asked to attend a press junket and photo shoot. I was there to look after the valuables, of course, and at one point during the afternoon I had on my wrist a watch that was worth over £750,000, which these days would be, at a rough estimate, about £3 million. The strap of this watch was just leather but the watch itself had a 23-carat cut diamond on its face. I felt almost as paranoid wearing that as I had been walking around the Bogside with an M10 under my coat. Everybody was under suspicion and if anybody I didn't know came near me while I was wearing the watch I'd stand up quickly, as if to say, *Stay where you fucking well are, you potential watch-pinching bastard*. It was a different world. I'd come from less than nothing and never had two pennies to rub together. Then, all of a sudden, I'm looking after princes and wearing watches that would have cost more than the town I was born in. It was a laugh though. Something to do.

Because I was quite good with people, after a few months the owners of Bond offered me a job selling jewellery and I bit their hand off. This meant that as opposed to being somebody who'd been contracted in I was a member of staff, and that was the first time I ever had an employer, so to speak. Apart from Her Majesty the Queen.

One of the other owners of Bond was a giant of a man called Mehmet Birgen. As well as being a driver for the CIA at some point in his life he'd been at school with Salem bin Laden, Osama bin Laden's elder brother. Despite being a multi-millionaire who drove a Ferrari he always wore combats, and regardless of his wealth and position this gave me licence to take the piss out of the giant playboy. And I did. A lot.

In hindsight, this could very easily have worked against me, i.e. he could have sacked me on the spot. Instead, he used to allow me to abuse him verbally and regardless of what I said to him he'd just laugh at me. Whenever he came into the shop, providing there was nobody there, of course, I'd say something like, 'Fuck off, Bergin, you fat spick twat. Get out of here before I kick your arse right down Bond Street.' He always sounded like a Middle Eastern Santa Claus and after ho-ho-ho-ing for a minute he'd smile and say, 'You shouldn't speak to me like that, Martin.' 'Fuck off, you fat twat.' What can I say? Some people obviously like being verbally abused.

One day Mehmet walked in and after giving him some shit for a few minutes he asked me if I'd like to do a job with him. 'Sure, what will we be doing?' I asked.

'Taking some stones over to Paris.'

It turned out that the stones we were taking were cornflower-blue sapphires worth about £3.8 million – then! When he opened the case I almost fucking fainted.

'First, we must get to Heathrow,' he said.

Now, I wasn't naive enough to believe that we'd be

taking the fucking tube to the airport, but by the same token I also wasn't expecting us to drive through the backstreets of west London at 100 mph. Mehmet never told me what the actual security risks might have been but given the mood he was in and the way he was driving he obviously wasn't taking any chances.

After arriving at Charles de Gaulle airport we took a taxi to the Champs-Élysées and, after delivering the sapphires to some high-end jeweller, he asked me if I'd like some lunch. I remember standing there in my C&A wedding suit, which was still my best one, thinking, *What the fucking hell's going on?* I was twenty-four years old and I'd just helped to deliver almost £4-million worth of precious stones to a high-end jeweller in Paris with a man who could have cleared the national debt with the change in his back pocket, and he's asking me what I want for lunch?

'Fish and chips,' I said.

'What?' he replied.

'Fish and fucking chips. That's what I want for lunch.'

'What do you mean, fish and chips?'

'I mean fish, batter, French fries and peas. Fish – and – fucking – chips!'

Ever the obliging sort, Mehmet took us straight to his favourite Parisian restaurant and, after he had a word with the maître d', I was eventually served a very posh version of fish and chips, minus the peas. Unfortunately for Mehmet and the maître d' I was as obstinate and determined as they had been obliging and, after calling the maître d' over, I took him to task.

'Where are my fucking peas?' I asked.

'Pardon, monsieur?'

'Peas!' I exclaimed. 'You know. Petit pois.'

The look on his face said to me that if Mehmet hadn't

been so wealthy I'd have been out on my fucking ear but with moneybags still sitting opposite I was onto a good 'un. Two minutes later a silver salver was brought to the table carrying a lovely mound of petit pois. I stopped short of asking them to be mushed as that may have been going too far. Taking everything into consideration, I'd have to say that it was one of the best plates of fish and chips I've ever had and definitely the most expensive.

I saw Mehmet again about ten years later in Cyprus and he had three women on each arm. After shaking him by the hand I said, 'You're a lucky cunt you are, Mehmet.'

'No, no,' he said. 'I am a handsome cunt. Ho, ho, ho.'

After I'd been selling jewellery for a few months one of my colleagues moved out of his bedsit and asked me if I'd like to take it on.

'How much?' I asked.

'£35 a week.'

'Go on then. I'll call Theresa and tell her to come down.'

The bedsit was in South Kensington, which is a lovely part of London. Unluckily for me, though, the block in which the bedsit was situated was full of IRA sympathisers. This meant that every time a bomb went off they all had a party. If it hadn't been for Theresa persuading me not to every time it happened, I'd have committed mass murder.

Funnily enough, shortly after moving into the bedsit we made friends with an Irish couple called Jimmy and Breda. Theresa had managed to get a job in a clothes shop called *Just a Second* that specialised in high-end seconds, and had got to know Breda there. Jimmy, who was a builder, had Irish plates on his van and one day he said he'd take us up to one of the pubs he frequented in Kentish Town, in north-west London. The first thing that happened after walking through the door was somebody pushed an IRA collection plate under my nose.

'What the fucking hell's that?' I said, pushing it way. 'Get that fucking thing out of my face.'

The next one of my senses to be infected by something to do with the IRA was my hearing.

'Are they singing rebel songs?' I said to Jimmy.

I was referring to a band who were playing in the corner and I was sure I recognised the song.

'That they are, Martin,' said Jimmy. 'Just ignore it though. They serve a good pint and that's the main thing.'

'Get me out of here now,' I said, grabbing Jimmy by the arm. 'Otherwise, I'm going to start hitting these cunts.'

To be fair to Jimmy, I hadn't told him about Northern Ireland. I'd just told him that I was a Royal Marine. Mind you, that alone should have made him think twice about taking me into a fucking boozer full of boyo supporters.

After finding a boozer with a jukebox, as opposed to a couple of twats with tin whistles, we got stuck into a few pints and, as was still the way back then, drove home when we were done. I was pretty legless so as opposed to sitting up front with Jimmy I decided to have a lie down in the back. On the way, we were stopped by the police and the moment I sat up and saw the lights flashing I thought, *Irish fucking plates!* Of course they were going to stop us.

In the early 1980s there were bombs going off all over the fucking place so if you had a vehicle with some Irish plates on it, especially at night, the chances are you were going to get stopped.

Jimmy wasn't quite as far gone as I was but he was on the merry side all the same. And he was talkative.

'Good evening there, lads. Would you be having a good evening? What can I do for you?'

203

Ultimate Survivor

'I don't care if you've had a drink sir,' said the officer. 'We just want to check the van if that's OK.'

'Of course it is, lads, of course it is. Just open the back there if you would.'

Given Jimmy's profession they were probably hoping to find tools. Well, they certainly found *a* tool, as they only thing in the back of that van was me, pissed as a twat.

FOURTEEN

After about a year living in this bedsit we'd managed to save up enough money to put down a deposit on a house, or at least that's what I thought. The trouble is, not being from London I had no idea where to look given our budget. We may have lived in South Kensington at the time but that was way out of our league. What we needed was somewhere that was cheap and on the up, but commutable into London. An electrician friend of mine suggested we look at Essex and, in particular, Brentwood. The houses were in our budget (although they wouldn't be now!) and it was just thirty minutes into Liverpool Street station.

Perfect.

One of the first places we looked at was 11 St Peter's Road; a two-up two-down that was on the market for £18,500.

'That'll do,' I said to Theresa. 'Let's buy it.'

Unfortunately, I couldn't get a fixed rate mortgage for the full amount so had to borrow the balance on an endowment mortgage. We didn't have any money for furniture either, so apart from a mattress and a sofa that we already had I made everything we needed out of MDF.

Once again, every single penny of our money was accounted for at the time so when I got a call from the building society one morning asking where our payments were, my arse started to speak more than somewhat. Then I realised that it was the start of the bloody month and our payments weren't due until the end of the month.

'Ah, but that's only on the fixed rate mortgage,' came the reply. 'The payments on the endowment mortgage are payable in advance.'

'You what?' I said.

'They're payable in advance. You did read the terms and conditions, didn't you?'

I stopped short of saying, *Of course I fucking didn't!* Which would have been the truth.

After telling the caller that I didn't have the money they called me in to see the manager so it was out with the old C&A suit again and off I went to the building society.

After reiterating to the manager that I wouldn't have the money for another three weeks his exact words were, 'Beg, borrow or steal it, Mr Edwards. Otherwise, we'll have the house back'.

The moment I left the building society, having told the manager exactly what I thought of him and what I was going to do with him once I'd paid off my mortgage, which involved a very sharp knife, some boiling water and his tiny fucking bollocks, I went straight across the road to Lloyds Bank and took out a loan to pay part of my first mortgage payment. At least we had a house. That was the main thing. And a mattress.

In 1984 Bond went bust so I went back into security via a company called Consolidated Safeguards. The reason

I'd got in touch with them was because they were linked to another company, Citadel, which did special projects but because there was nothing going on that side of things I ended up having an interview for a job as a chief inspector, which is like a supervisor, on the guarding side just to earn some money. I ended up being offered a different job, which was chief inspector of mobile security, and this meant working nights and weekends, a bit of a bugger. On my first night in this job I accidentally drove the wrong way around Trafalgar Square in my little yellow van and the cops came at me from absolutely everywhere. I was surrounded by the fuckers.

'What have I done, what have I done?' I squeaked while getting out of the van with my hands up.

'You are aware that Trafalgar Square is one way, aren't you?'

'Obviously fucking not!' I replied. 'Sorry, officers.'

Fortunately for everyone concerned, but especially the local constabulary, a job came up with Citadel in Abu Dhabi but before I could fly out there I had a sexual encounter with the current Prime Minister. Yes, you read that correctly. I had a sexual encounter with Margaret Hilda Thatcher.

One of the other jobs I did while working for Consolidated Safeguards was acting as a bodyguard for the Saatchi brothers, Maurice and Charles. At the time the brother's adverting agency, Saatchi & Saatchi, were responsible for at least some of the Conservative Party's PR and marketing campaigns and occasionally some of their campaigns would require a speech from the blessed Margaret. These speeches were all recorded in a building behind Oxford Street and the room where Margaret delivered them was done up to look like an office in Downing Street. One day Margaret and her team turned up to record one of these speeches. As always, she was accompanied by members of Special Branch and she had with her a bottle of champagne and a box of chocolates. Everything went smoothly until it came to finding her speech. The chap writing it was a man called Brian Walden who some of you may remember as the presenter from a programme called *Weekend World*. Old Brian was nowhere to be seen when he was called for and after about half an hour trying to locate him he rolled in pissed as a fart having obviously enjoyed himself a bit too much at the club or whatever. Anyway, about two or three hours later Maggie and her team emerged from the makeshift office and pissed off back to Downing Street. Out of curiosity, I popped my head around the door to the makeshift office and there on the desk was the bottle of champagne. It appeared to have at least a glassful left inside, which gave me an idea.

Maggie had been sitting on her seat for about three hours during the recording, and as far as I know she'd been doing the same thing at least once a week for ages. What's more, it had been very, very warm that day so all things considered, that seat would be literally swimming in Maggie Thatcher's juices. Without even thinking I took the bottle of champagne, knelt down next to her chair, poured the champagne onto the seat and proceeded to suck it out. Every last drop! I have no idea why I did it, but I bet you any money you like that Denis never did the deed which makes me the only person in history to have tasted the blessed Margaret. Well, possibly. How's that for a story?

I was flown to Abu Dhabi to help train their special police force in counterterrorism, including anti-hijacking and riots. I'd discussed it with Theresa first, of course, and although the money wasn't brilliant it was a long-ish contract and it could well lead onto something else.

The man in charge in Abu Dhabi was called Major

Peter John, who had been a sergeant major in the army. He'd been responsible for writing the majority of the parade ground manual for the British Army and although he'd reached sergeant major in that capacity, as far as Citadel and the Abu Dhabi police force were concerned he held the rank of major.

Despite being just a corporal in the Royal Marines, I'd been elevated to captain for this job and I brought with me three men: Bill and Gavin, who I knew from the Marines, and a lad called Ian Singer, who, as well as being a Sandhurst-trained officer, was a gigantic fucking twat. I ended up driving my car at this arsehole in London one day. I'll come on to that.

So anyway. That was us.

To be honest, the job was a bit boring and there was no fun to be had in any shape or form. Drinking was strictly forbidden and whenever we had any free time we were encouraged to spend it learning Arabic.

Whoopee! Or, in Arabic, ﺹﺎﺧﺑ!

I had a driver out there called Ali and in return for him helping me learn Arabic I helped him learn English. Well, my version of English. Basically, I taught him a load of swearwords. Things like asshole, piss flaps and bastard. I didn't tell him what they meant, of course. In fact, as far as he was concerned, asshole meant, *Yes, sir*, piss flaps meant, *No, sir*, fuck off meant, *I don't know*, and bastard meant, *I'm fine thank you, how are you?* There were a load of other little gems.

Ali had to go into a meeting one day with the directors of Citadel who were visiting Abu Dhabi and he lasted about five minutes.

'Would you like to sit down Ali?'

'Asshole.'

'And how are you, Ali?'

'Bastard.'

I got the blame in the end, not him. There really was sod all else to do though. It was desperate.

I don't know if this was in revenge for my bogus linguistic tuition but one day Ali had to drive me to a firing range that was about 50 miles from the nearest town and the little twat left me there! He fucking drove off. Three-and-a-half hours I was up there and when he finally came back I chased him around the car a few times, pleaded for some fucking water and then asked him where he'd been.

'Fuck off,' he said, as if saying, 'I don't know.'

The cheeky little twat.

When I was in Abu Dhabi the locals still believed in an eye for an eye so if you killed somebody from one village they would come and kill somebody from yours. It might still be same, but I remember waking up one morning in the barracks to find that half the students had disappeared, and that the armoury had been emptied.

'Where the hell are they?' I asked somebody. 'And where are the bloody guns?'

It turned out that somebody had attacked and killed a villager from wherever these students came from and so after tooling themselves up they'd gone looking for revenge.

About five hours later they all came back but because they'd left without permission – and, because they'd killed somebody – I put them all in jail. The police colonel, who was the man in charge of these buggers as well as our contracts, went absolutely fucking mental with me for that but I had no idea it was all legal.

When it came to teaching the students how to deal with sieges I didn't realise that Peter John, one of the other men who was in charge of us, had told the Abu Dhabi police colonel that I had been one of the SAS troopers involved in the Iranian Embassy siege. He was obviously trying to butter the colonel up for the next contract but as opposed to him merely being impressed by Peter's enormous fucking lie, he insisted I stage a re-enactment of the entire siege!

'But what for?' I asked.

'Because he wants to know how to react if it ever happens here,' replied Peter.

'You mean he's seen it on fucking television and fancies seeing it live?'

'Possibly.'

'Why did you have to tell him that I was involved? I wasn't even in the SAS!'

'I know that and you know that, but he doesn't.'

I didn't know what the hell actually went on in the embassy. I specialised in taking British warships to siege and knocking out naval gentlemen using marlin spikes and large tins of jam, not abseiling down buildings, freeing hostages and killing terrorists.

I tried to run Ian Singer down because, just before we were due to fly back to the UK, he told the police colonel that the captains and majors who'd been teaching his special police force about counter-terrorism were nothing more than sergeant majors and corporals. It was in the contract that the people doing the teaching had to be *officers* from the British Army (hence the elevated ranks), so we were shopped. To us, going forward at least, this meant the difference between earning £15,000 and a Range Rover per contract as Captain Edwards, which is what I was due to receive when we taught the rest of the Emirates, and jack shit, which is what I'd receive as a sergeant or a corporal out there. In other words, a lackey. Singer was a typical fucking Rupert, which is what we used to call officers, so we should have expected it.

Ultimate Survivor

To be fair to the colonel, he took the news quite well. We'd done a bloody good job and the students had responded really well to what we'd taught them. Which had all been agreed beforehand, by the way, and sanctioned by the relevant authorities. It wasn't just something we'd made up. The company had merely elevated one or two of us to a higher rank in order to get the best people for the job.

The only other snag – apart from the fact that thanks to this fucking Rupert I'd lost about three years' work on very good money (and a Range Rover) – was that the colonel was now refusing to pay the remainder of the contract unless I agreed to stage a re-enactment the Iranian siege.

'You must be fucking joking,' I said to Peter. 'I'm due home any day.'

'You'll be going without any money if you don't stage this siege.'

The police colonel must have thought I was Lewis Collins or somebody, and on hearing about his ultimatum I didn't know whether to punch him in the face or sign him a fucking autograph. 'Also Peter,' I continued, 'I must say, once again, that in addition to never having been in the SAS, at the time of the Iranian siege I was working in a fucking jewellery shop on Bond Street! In fact, my only link to the siege, apart from working alongside the SAS in Northern Ireland, is that I was living in a bedsit in South Kensington at the time, which is where it took place. Is that tenuous enough for you?'

Ever the professional, Peter then came out with a classic line that was obviously meant to pacify my fears and inspire confidence.

'Don't worry,' he said. 'We'll fudge it.'

'Well, you'd better get the wives out here then because that's the only way I'm going to agree, regardless of how much money I'll lose.'

'Done,' he said. 'I'll go and book the tickets.'

I had a horrible feeling he was going to say that. Never try and bluff a bluffer.

Poor Theresa, who must have been about five stone wet through at the time, had never been abroad before in her life and when she found out she was coming to Abu Dhabi she started to get ever so slightly nervous. And with good reason, as it turned out. First of all, she had to go and have some jabs before flying and the needle they used was the size of a drainpipe. As a result she fainted twice, but that was nothing compared to what almost happened to both of us shortly after she landed.

When Theresa and the rest of our wives stepped off the plane we were all standing there in uniform waiting for them. Whether it was just the fact that she'd missed me or the sight of me in uniform, as soon as Theresa saw me waiting for her she ran up and gave me a kiss. In Abu Dhabi. Where it was illegal to kiss anybody anywhere in public. Even your wife.

The moment it happened about ten armed guards started shouting and aiming their rifles at us and yet again a bloodbath was only just averted. It was my fault, though, as that's the first thing I should have told her.

'Welcome to Abu Dhabi, love,' I said, leading Theresa away as quickly as possible. 'The people are very friendly.'

While the wives were over in Abu Dhabi we were all put up in the Ramada hotel, which was rather nice, and while we were busy training people and trying to recreate sieges that we'd never been involved in they were looked after by a bodyguard and had a driver at their disposal.

We ended up staging the siege on the parade ground in the police barracks and used a building that faced the parade ground as the embassy. By now the powers that be had decided that the siege re-enactment would be included in the training programme when it was rolled out to the other Emirates, and so all the relevant sheikhs were there to watch. They were all sitting there in armchairs. The only thing missing was popcorn and a massive Pepsi!

As part of the re-enactment we had two dummies made up; one that we hung from the flagpole, which was supposed to be a hostage, and another that we covered in tomato sauce. That one, which was supposed to be a terrorist, ended up being thrown at the feet of the sheikhs almost symbolically. *Here you go, lads. Have a dead dummy terrorist!*

Just as we'd hoped, they absolutely lapped this up and despite the minor variances between our effort and all the argy-bargy that had taken place in South Kensington a few years earlier, it went down very well.

We had actually studied the siege quite carefully so, despite the dummies, which was just a bit of pantomime, we did produce something that would have resembled it. Or at least the parts that had been caught on camera, which is what they really wanted.

My final task in Abu Dhabi was to choose a winner for the best student on the course but instead of giving it to my first choice I had to give it to the nephew of Sheikh Zayed, who was the ruler of Abu Dhabi. If I'd had my way, which is what I'd been expecting, it would have gone to a bloke called Sergeant Ali who was a green beret and a royal guard. He'd shat all over the competition but before I could award him the prize I was told by Peter John that for the sake of future relationships, not to mention getting our bloody money, it should go to a lad called Faisal, who had been mid-table at best yet was shitting cash and had an uncle who was the most powerful man in the United Arab Emirates. With my own chancellor of the exchequer standing next to me, i.e. Theresa, I had to relent.

The day before Theresa and I left for England the police colonel organised a get together at the barracks. The rest of the wives had gone home by then but Theresa had stayed on and we were told sometime during the festivities that this was the first time a woman had ever been allowed into a police barracks in the UAE. What a claim to fame, eh? At the end of the party the police colonel presented the instructors with a set of silver coffee pots each that fitted inside each other like Russian dolls, followed by a Longines gold watch each bearing the Abu Dhabi royal crest on the face. As well as the wives leaving early, many of my team had too, so Theresa and I had to smuggle these back into the UK by wearing them up each arm.

*****

When we arrived back from Abu Dhabi I decided to take a few weeks off. As well as wanting to refamiliarise myself with things such as alcohol and fun, I was physically and mentally exhausted and just wanted to unwind for a bit.

After about two weeks, during which time I had a sneaking suspicion that I'd started getting on Theresa's nerves, I received a call one day completely out of the blue – from Blue.

He was acting as a personal bodyguard to Prince Bandar, who was now based over in Washington as the Saudi Arabian ambassador, but was also negotiating the AWAC deal (airborne early warning and control) which at the time was going to be the largest arms deal in history. Israel was against Saudi Arabia having AWAC, so Prince Bandar was considered to be a possible target for Mossad and thus it had been decided that he needed more bodyguards.

'Do you fancy a job?' said Blue.

'Absolutely,' I replied. 'In fact, your timing's perfect. When do you need me there?'

'Tomorrow.'

'Really? Bloody hell.'

I think Theresa was ironing at the time and after putting the receiver down I said casually, 'I've got a job, love,'

'Oh aye,' said Theresa. 'Where is it?'

'Washington.'

'As in America?'

'That's right.'

'And when do you go?'

'Tomorrow morning.'

'Bloody hell, Martin!'

Two days after I flew to Washington somebody was murdered just around the corner from where we lived and, after receiving a visit from the police, Theresa was naturally a bit nervous about being on her own. After voicing her concerns to the members of the constabulary, one of them said, 'They'll get you if they want to madam,' and then they just buggered off!

Bloody marvellous.

You have two types of personal bodyguard: one that stays with the person you're guarding at all times and never lets them out of their sight, and one that prevents the wrong kind of people from approaching them. It's two lines a defence. Prevention, followed by a cure. Or a bullet, in our case.

Prince Bandar wouldn't use any other car than a BMW 7 Series and they'd all been fitted out with magnetic blue lights and a siren that went through the sound system. The latter was totally illegal in Washington but that didn't make a blind bit of difference to us and, fuck me, did we have some fun.

Only the people who were on duty stayed at Prince Bander's residence and if you weren't on duty you stayed at the Highland Hotel, which was just across the road from the Hilton Hotel where John Hinckley Jr had tried to assassinate President Reagan in 1981. You could still see the bullet marks on the wall of the hotel from my bedroom window.

It's a good job the assassination attempt failed as while I was over there President Reagan had the good fortune of speaking with me over the phone, albeit against my employer's wishes.

I should explain that Prince Bandar is very Westernised and in his youth he'd been trained to be a fighter pilot in Alabama. Incidentally, it's illegal to carry concealed weapons in Washington unless you're a police officer and Prince Bandar had managed to get around this by asking the commander of the Alabama police force, who was a friend of his, to make all his personal bodyguards temporary police officers, which he did. I've still got the card and the badge at home.

One day during the AWAC negotiations, Prince Bandar came back to his residence from the White House absolutely raging. Blue had been with him and when he followed Prince Bandar back in he looked at me as if to say, *Don't say a fucking thing!*

Sure enough, before disappearing upstairs the apoplectic prince turned to us and said, 'If anybody from the White House calls you are not to put them through under any circumstances. Is that clear? I don't want to speak to anybody from the American government ever again.' With that he slammed the door and disappeared upstairs.

Even Blue, who'd been the prince's personal bodyguard for a few years, had never seen him like that before.

About an hour later the telephone rang and because I was the only person there I answered it.

'Hello. Prince Bandar's residence.'

'This is the office of the President of the United States,' came a voice. 'Could I speak to Prince Bandar please?'

'I'm sorry,' I said, 'but Prince Bandar has given me strict instructions not to put anybody through from the White House'.

'Did he appear slightly angry when he arrived?' asked the voice.

'Angry? That's an understatement. He was furious.'

'OK', said the voice. 'Let me call you back.'

Two minutes later the phone rang again.

'Hello, Prince Bandar's residence.'

'This is President Reagan,' said a voice sounding just like President Reagan. 'Do you think I could speak to Prince Bandar please?'

What I wanted to say at that moment was, *For you, Ron, anything,* but I didn't dare. Instead I told him what I'd told the secretary.

'I've never seen him so angry,' I explained.

'Oh, I'm sure he'll speak to me', said the president.

'Yes, I'm sure he will, sir,' I agreed, in what was possibly the most sycophantic voice ever heard by a head of state. 'Just one moment please.'

As much as I respected Prince Bandar I had on the phone the most powerful man in the world and saying no to him wasn't going to be easy. Then again, calling up Prince Bandar and telling him a member of the American government was on the phone wasn't going to be a walk in the park, even if it was the top dog. In the end, I decided an earful from Prince Bandar was going to be preferable to saying no to my mate Ron, and so I put Ron on hold and called the prince. 'What is it?' he barked. 'I thought I told you I wasn't to be disturbed.'

'Prince Bandar, there's somebody from the White House on the phone,' I said.

'WHAAT! WHAT DID I TELL YOU? I NEVER WANT TO SPEAK TO ANYBODY FROM THE AMER . . .'

'BUT IT'S PRESIDENT REAGAN,' I shouted, desperately trying to save the situation. And my life.

'OK,' said the Prince. 'Put him through.'

'Just putting you through now, Mr President,' I said. I think I'd assumed an American accent by then.

'Thank you, young man,' said Ron.

'My pleasure.'

About forty minutes later Prince Bandar walked in and Blue and Bill, who was his other personal bodyguard, took him back to the White House.

And they all lived happily ever after.

Apart from having a police badge, carrying a gun, staying in a posh hotel and chatting with the president, the best thing about the job in Washington was the money. The salary itself was more than competitive but it was the tips that made it a proper earner. Prince Bandar's secretary would often give us $500 each, just out of nowhere. Back in the 1980s $500 was a massive amount of money but it didn't stop there. After I'd been there about four months, Theresa became ill and so I asked if I could go back and look after her. Not only did Prince Bandar give me the week off but he gave me $500 and wished me all the best.

Theresa had started having fits. When we went to see a doctor on my first day back and he found out what I was doing, he immediately pinpointed that as the reason.

'So you're saying that if I come home from Washington they'll stop?' I asked.

'I think so,' said the doctor.

By the end of the week Theresa hadn't had a single fit so as far as I was concerned the doctor had got it spot on. As a result, the first thing I did when I got back to Washington was to explain what had happened and I resigned. True to form, Prince Bandar was very understanding and as well as a nice bung he also handed me a first-class plane ticket home. He didn't have to do that and I was very grateful.

While handing it to me he said, 'I know exactly what you're going to do with that, Martin.'

'What do you mean, Sir?' I said innocently.

'You're going to cash it in, buy a standby ticket, and pocket the difference. You think I don't know? That's what they always do.'

The first thing I did when I got back was walk into the building society where I'd taken out the endowment mortgage and pay it off with cash. I threw it over the counter in a bundle as a kind of protest to the twat who'd called me in. 'There you go,' I said. 'And you can tell that fucking manager of yours, thanks for nothing.'

It was a little bit dramatic, I suppose, but it felt good.

FIFTEEN

As soon as I started getting under Theresa's feet again I began looking around for another job and once again it was a mate of mine from Northern Ireland who came up trumps. This one was called Dai and the job he thought I'd be suitable for was as a night operations manager with a security company he was working for called Sterling Guards. This was a very similar job to the one I'd had prior to going to Abu Dhabi and, once again – this time before I could drive a van the wrong way around Trafalgar Square – something more specialised came up almost immediately.

The *Achille Lauro*, a cruise ship, was hijacked by members of the Palestinian Liberation Front in October 1985, which resulted in one of the hostages, a disabled Jewish passenger in a wheelchair, being shot dead by one of the terrorists and thrown overboard. The company who owned Sterling Guards was P&O and in the light of what had happened on the *Achille Lauro* they asked Dai and me if we'd do a survey of their fleet and advise them on what could be improved with regards to the measures they had in place to combat hijacking and terrorism. As a project, this was right up my street.

The first ship I was assigned to was the SS *Canberra*, one of the most famous cruise ships in the world. Due to the extremely sensitive nature of what I was doing there, I had go undercover and when I spoke to the staff I obviously had to do so privately. Can you imagine what would have happened if I'd gone on board carrying a clipboard?

Passenger: 'What are you up to then?'

Me: 'Just doing a survey on how vulnerable you all are to hijackings and terrorism in general. To be honest, it's not looking good!'

There'd have been a mutiny on board, and rightly so.

My first point of contact on the ship was the captain, a man called David Jones, and when we both sat down after I'd completed the first part of my survey it was scary how different our opinions were as to what you should do to prevent a hijacking. That's not to say that everything I said was correct. I was just there to make recommendations. It was up to the captain and P&O if they wanted to take them on board, pardon the pun.

'What would you do if you saw somebody who wasn't a passenger or a member of the crew in distress?' I asked first.

'You mean at sea?' replied the captain.

'That's correct.'

'Well, we'd obviously try and help them.'

'What do you mean, obviously?'

'Exactly that. We'd obviously try and help them.'

'So, what if that person was a hijacker or a terrorist and they were trying to get on board? Do you have a gun on board the ship?'

While I was aboard the SS *Canberra* I must have put the fear of God into the captain and his crew but not unnecessarily. I'm not saying they were blind to the dangers of terrorism but despite what had happened on the *Achille Lauro* there was certainly an air of 'it could never happen here' about them. What they really needed was a little scare, just to bring it home. If it had been the Abu Dhabi police force they'd have asked me to recreate the entire *Achille Lauro* incident singlehandedly, but fortunately that wasn't necessary on this occasion. In fact, all we had to do was dock in Haifa for a few hours. That was enough to scare anybody, including me.

Because the *Achille Lauro* had been hijacked by members of the PLF, trying to weigh anchor in a port in Israel was always going to subject to some pretty stringent security checks. That in itself would, I'm sure, have adequately driven home the importance of security and preventative measures to the captain and his crew. In fact, the only thing that could have trumped this was if Mossad were doing the security checks and, as if by magic, they were the ones who sent out the greeting party. Unfortunately for me, I was the one who had to let them in.

Mossad are to counterterrorism what I am to saying the F word, so if you ever want a lesson on how to search a ship for terrorists or incendiary devices, they're the ones you'd choose. If they actually gave lessons. Which I doubt.

Because my role on the ship was all about counter-terrorism it made sense for me to greet the pilot ship and when I opened the hatch I immediately made a friend by asking one of the Mossad agents if I could look inside his bag.

'No you can't,' he snapped, quite clearly affronted.

'You're not coming on board then,' I replied.

With that he pulled his jacket open so I could see his pistol.

'I've got one too, mate,' I said, tapping the bag I was carrying.

In hindsight, and regardless of how brave I might be, creating a stand-off with Mossad while they were trying to search a ship attempting to dock in an Israeli harbour probably wasn't the best idea I've ever had, but in terms of an adrenalin rush it was incredible. Like something out of *Gunfight at the O.K. Corral*.

Fortunately for me, and for our chances of being able to proceed on our journey, I realised early on that I had several members of Mossad in front of me and not a couple of cowboys. Subsequently, the man with the bag and his friends (they also had dogs with them) were allowed to come aboard and over the next four hours they did a clean sweep of the entire ship. Under the watchful eye of yours truly, of course. After all, I had to earn my keep.

I don't know why but we weren't allowed to leave Haifa until the following morning and all through the night all I could hear was explosions going off in the water. I later found out that the explosions were mines that were being dropped into the sea – they were designed to stop terrorists swimming ashore. What did the damage, though, wasn't the explosions themselves. It was a high frequency noise the mines made that could burst a human's eardrums at a radius of about 500 yards.

As time went on some rumours started going around the passengers as to who I was and what I was doing on the ship. I used to turn up for dinner every night in my black tie but because I was always on my own people had started asking questions. Despite not carrying a clipboard around, I have to admit that I was probably quite conspicuous. Especially as I suspected everybody of being a terrorist and probably looked at them all as if they were about to plant a bomb. Without any help from me or the crew they'd come to the conclusion that I was some kind of nautical James Bond and over the course of the cruise I'd chatted to quite a few of them.

On the last night of the cruise when I turned up for dinner I sat down at my table as normal. I'd been used to people staring at me but tonight seemed to be different: as opposed to one or two pairs of eyes looking my way every so often it seemed like everyone in the room was eyeballing me. It was also a lot quieter than usual so I knew something was up.

About five minutes after I'd sat down the passengers started looking just behind where I was sitting and they were all smiling. I looked over my shoulder and walking towards me was the maître d', who was carrying a large silver tray. As soon as I saw the tray, I knew exactly what was coming.

A few days earlier, while chatting to some of the passengers, one of them had asked me what I thought of the food on board the ship and I said that I could have murdered a chip butty. I wasn't kidding. I really could.

Sure enough, when the maître d' arrived at my table he deposited the poshest chip butty I'd ever seen in my life. Because I always drank pints, this was accompanied by an empty pint glass and a bottle of Moët & Chandon, and when the whole lot was on my table a great big cheer went up from 2,000 passengers!

When we got back to the UK, I continued working for P&O for a while as its head of security and in the short time I was in the position two memorable things happened: I saved Her Majesty Queen Elizabeth's life, and I swore at her daughter.

Let's go with the daughter first. What's she called again? Anne? Everybody likes Princess Anne. She's a good 'un. Well, she came on board one day for an event of some kind and as she was the first British royal I'd ever catered for I decided to go to town a bit on the security. In addition to sanitising the lift, which I did personally, I had an officer posted at every single lift hatch on every floor and even in the lift itself.

When Her Royal Highness came up the gangplank I was nervous but confident. Lord Sterling, who was the executive chairman of P&O, was a friend of Princess Anne and that was another reason why I took so much care. Always keep in with the receptionist and the chairman. That's what I've always been told.

As she stepped on board, Princess Anne was greeted by Lord Sterling and then guided to the lift but literally two steps before she reached the bloody thing she stopped and asked if she could take the stairs!

'You absolute fucking cow,' I said under my breath.

At that moment I felt like the world had caved in on my head and, as soon as I'd finished cursing Lord Sterling's well-connected mate, I called through to the guards and told them to reposition themselves at the top of each flight of stairs.

I could have fucking killed her!

Not too long after that Anne's mum turned up for an event – one of many, as it turned out – to mark the 150th anniversary of P&O. Given the status of our special guest, who had one or two people looking out for her, I had very little to do with the security surrounding her visit. When she was ready to leave the ship a colleague of mine called Mike and I had been asked to stand halfway up the gangway, which was actually two gangways fixed together. As the Queen approached the top of the first gangway I noticed that the sea had become a bit choppy, and that the length of the gangway had been decorated with a string of lights on the inside.

'Those lights are stretching a bit, don't you think Mike?' I said.

'Yeah, I suppose they are a bit,' he replied.

'And what's going to happen if they snap?' I snapped.

'Somebody's going to get a shock,' said Mike.

I didn't need to say anything else. The look on Mike's face when he realised that Her Majesty the Queen might be about to receive a few hundred volts up her skirt and through her tiara after a lovely afternoon on board the SS *Canberra* was hilarious. While Her Majesty and her entourage carefully negotiated their way down the first gangway, Mike and I used every ounce of strength we had to keep that and the other one as close together as possible, and, more importantly, keep some slack in the string of lights. Thank God she didn't look at either of us as she passed. If she had she'd have been forgiven for thinking we were both shitting ourselves. Which we were. Almost.

*****

In early 1985, before my stint on the SS *Canberra*, I was offered a job by another former colleague of mine from 8 Det called Johnson. To be honest, I never liked him much (I always thought he was a bully) but because some of the other lads were involved I decided to hear him out.

The office of the company he was working for was above a shop in north London so it wasn't exactly salubrious. Then again, neither is security work in general so if it had been at a flash address I'd probably have been suspicious. I was just a bit underwhelmed and when I walked through the door the last thing I was expecting was to be offered a job in

Africa. Acton, perhaps, but not Africa. It was Uganda, to be exact, and we'd be installing surveillance equipment for President Milton Obote's secret police force and then teaching them how to use it.

On paper it wasn't too dissimilar to the engagement in Abu Dhabi in that we'd be teaching a secret police force. That, however, was where the similarities ended as regardless of what the job entailed the economic and political situation in Uganda was at the opposite end of the spectrum, and that would become a contributing factor when it came to trivial things such as getting paid and staying alive.

Just to put these differences into perspective; the population in Abu Dhabi at the moment is about 1.5 million, the GDP is $170 billion and it's been run by the same family for generations, whereas Uganda has a population of population 41 million, a GDP of $88 billion and has been in a semi-permanent state of political unrest for decades. Things weren't much different back in 1985. In fact, since 1981 a bush war had been going on in Uganda between the government and a rebel guerrilla army called the NRA, or the National Resistance Army. Intent on overthrowing President Obote, the NRA were based in the bush and would often appear out of nowhere, causing chaos. Obote had already been toppled by a *coup d'état* by Idi Amin back in 1971 and although he'd managed to seize power again in 1980, the bush war, which had started soon after, had made his position precarious to say the least. There was even talk of another coup.

Because we were over there installing surveillance equipment before teaching a group of people how to use it, we were, in effect, creating a Det for the Ugandan government. The enormity of the undertaking meant that we invited some of the government members over to north London to discuss the plans in more detail. It was January

1985 when they arrived and the poor bastards were freezing their fucking arses off. We were going to be running a selection process over there and when one of the delegates asked me for an example of what we might be doing, I decided to have some fun and give them a practical demonstration.

'I'll tell you what, gents,' I said, 'let's start off with some basics, shall we? Have you brought a tracksuit?'

They looked at me blankly.

'Never mind. We'll sort you something out.'

After kitting them all out with some sports gear I marched them to a local park and started warming them up with a few sit-ups and press-ups. Despite only being in their thirties or forties they were all as flabby as fuck and, after helping them firm up their man-tits for a while, I jogged them up to a churchyard about a mile away. Once there, I made them sprint to the edge of a pond in the middle of the churchyard and then told them to get in.

'I beg your pardon?' one of them said when he'd managed to catch a breath.

'Get in the pond,' I repeated.

It obviously wasn't that deep but it had a thin layer of ice over it and was the same colour as oxtail soup. Subsequently, dissent wasn't far away.

'I'm sorry,' said the fattest one, 'but there is no way we're getting in that pond, Mr Martin.'

'You what?' I growled.

'I've told you. There is no way we are getting in that pond. No way!'

'GET IN THAT FUCKING POND NOW,' I screamed. 'RUN, RUN, RUN, RUN, RUN, RUN. AT THE FUCKING DOUBLE!'

That shifted the fuckers.

Sure enough, the water only went up to the middle of their shins but you should have seen the look on their faces. It was as if I'd murdered their mothers or something.

I tried jogging the fat bastards back to the office but they were having none of it. Once they were back in civvies again and had a glass of wine in their hands they set about cancelling the contract.

Needless to say I was not Johnson's favourite person that afternoon. It took the ignorant twat several hours to talk them around. The only outstanding issue at that point was payment and after a lot of to-ing and fro-ing the company settled for a certain amount upfront and the balance via a performance-related bonus scheme. This obviously affected everybody so the deal was that while we were out there the company would cover our mortgages and then cough up the balance once they'd been paid. It certainly wasn't ideal but I had fuck all else to do at the time and so I agreed.

About two weeks after the weighty delegation had returned to Uganda, about ten of us followed with some of the equipment and they put us up in a villa on top of a hill about 5 miles outside Kampala and overlooking Lake Victoria. The villa also overlooked the notorious Makindye Prison where Idi Amin had done a lot of his dirty work back in the 1970s. There was a slide running from the prison into Lake Victoria and after clubbing inmates to death with a hammer they'd then throw them onto this slide and they would slip down into the lake in their own blood. Apparently the crocodile population in Lake Victoria trebled while Amin was in power and it's estimated that he killed tens of thousands of people in that prison and up to half a million more outside it.

While we were there the plan was that once we'd knocked these fuckers into shape we'd then install the communication masts and repeater stations. A guy called Matt was the technical wizard, while I was there to oversee fitness first and foremost and then help out with the other stuff.

Speaking of fitness, which there didn't seem to be a lot of in Uganda in the mid-1980s, I had a heck of a job trying to get these bastards into shape and all they used to do was moan about being tired. I took them out for a run one day but instead of joining them for the whole thing I sat in a Land Rover for some of it and shouted at them. Sorry, encouraged them. If I thought they needed a kick up the arse I'd jump off for half a mile and jump back in when I was done. The cries that went up from these twats when I jumped back in was incredible and anyone listening nearby would have been forgiven for thinking Idi Amin had made a comeback. Bunch of girl's blouses.

As part of the deal the Ugandan High Commission were supposed to pay us a certain amount of money to live on and this would be requested as and when we needed it, which was about every other day. If we'd spent even half as much time training the recruits as we did trying to extract the cash they'd have been as good as Mossad. As it was, we used to spend about three or four hours every day at the High Commission banging on doors, and at one point we had to suspend the operation indefinitely because they simply didn't have any cash. Either that or they'd spent it all on cakes.

The company who'd employed us back in England were stuck between a rock and a hard place and had no choice other than to send us some Ugandan shillings in lieu of us getting paid by the Ugandans. Thinking back, it's a wonder they didn't just cut their losses and bring us home because ever since the bush war had started the country had been in turmoil.

While we were waiting for this cash to materialise we did little other than keep fit and drink alcohol, and the latter tended to take place in Kate's Bar, the closest watering hole. The only beer they served was called Nile Beer, Uganda's version of Fosters. The name obviously has something to do with the fact that the River Nile starts in Uganda and, judging by the taste, it made a pitstop at the brewery. It must have changed now, but back then the bottles they used were returnable and I'm adamant that they never washed them. There were always bits floating around in Nile Beer – it was famous for it – and the chances of you receiving a bottle that wasn't chipped were almost non-existent. You had a good chance of getting the shits though. Somebody always had the shits.

The food menu at Kate's Bar was just as minimalistic as the drinks menu: if you didn't like boiled eggs and rock salt you were fucked. It was exactly the same with the music. In the seven months I visited Kate's Bar I only ever heard one song being played and that was Tina Turner's 'What's Love Got to Do with It?' Whenever I hear that song now I always smile, open a beer and do myself a boiled egg.

I've actually done the menu a disservice as one night when I was particularly pissed I decided I wanted an arachnid with my boiled egg. As I was sitting there, out of the corner of my eye I saw a spider about the size of a 50p piece. It was a sac spider, which are round and yellow, and after spotting it I got up, put it between my thumb and my forefinger, told everybody to watch closely and then bit through the middle of it. As I started chewing the bit that was in my mouth and the insides from the other half started dripping onto my chin, some members of my audience started vomiting. Mission accomplished, I dropped the rest of the spider into my mouth, wiped its insides off my chin, licked my fingers and took a nice swig of Nile Beer to swill it all down.

About two days later I was doing some exercises around the hill where the villa was situated when suddenly some children from a nearby village ran past. The moment they saw me they stopped, dead in their tracks. It sounded like they were shouting 'Mullaloo! Mullaloo!' Later that day I asked one of the recruits what *mullaloo* meant.

'It means crazy man,' he said. 'They must have heard what you did to that spider.'

Behind Kate's Bar, which was full of all kinds of people, there was another bar that was frequented by locals mainly and all they used to sell there was Ugandan hooch, or waragi, as it's known, which means 'war gin'. I've still got a bottle of this stuff at home but I daren't drink it because the last time I did it burned the roof of my mouth. I dread to think what percentage it is but, in 2010, eighty people died from multiple organ failure after drinking waragi, so fuck knows what they put in it. Paint stripper, probably.

One of the reasons we used to drink so much, apart from extreme boredom, was because the villa we were staying at was infested by rats, cockroaches and buzz bombs, and I mean infested. There was obviously no pest control in Uganda at the time and if you ever went to bed sober you were either kept awake by the noise of these bastard things, which was constant, or by them crawling all over you or landing on you. I could just about stand being crawled over by a rat or a cockroach, although depending on how pissed I was I'd usually take a pot shot at the rats. We all did. As a result the walls and doors in the villa were covered in holes, but it was a shithole to start with so nobody really cared.

The ones that really made me drink myself into oblivion were the buzz bombs, or cockchafer beetles, to give them their correct name. About 2 inches in length, these things would fly with their backs against the ceiling and make an awful whirring sound. When the whirring stopped, it meant they were diving to attack, and if you were the only person in the room when that happened and the lights were out, it was fucking horrible. I used to wake up covered in bites and scratches and would even have rat shit on my bed sometimes. It was still preferable to lying awake sober and waiting for the buzz bombs to stop buzzing, which would have resulted in something far worse than rat shit.

The only thing more populous in Uganda than rats, cockroaches or buzz bombs in the mid-1980s were rebels, and with tensions running higher than ever between them and the government we were never far from trouble. We used to fire rounds of bullets down a street (from cover) just to see what the reaction would be, and nine times out of ten we'd get a round back. It was incredibly volatile.

Because of the money situation, or lack of it, somebody from the company would have to fly out occasionally and give us some sterling. We'd then take the sterling to a flip-flop factory to get it changed into Ugandan shillings. Not a bank or a *bureau de change*, but a flip-flop factory. At the back of this factory was a fat bloke who was surrounded by sacks of Ugandan shillings and we used to walk away with rucksacks full of them. We could have gone to a bank to get the sterling exchanged but the rates were half what they were on the black market.

One night, shortly after receiving a delivery of cash, we all went out to a nightclub to get shit-faced. There was a big group of ex-SAS lads in Kampala at the time who were also supposed to be training the High Commission and we'd got to know a few of them. Subsequently, we ended up giving these lads one of our radios so we could keep in touch.

The only people who'd taken against us since our arrival in Uganda were President Obote's bodyguards. Apparently they thought that we were going to take their jobs or something, and every time we'd come into contact with them it had almost kicked off. That night at the club it did finally kick off with these wankers and one of them tried pulling a pistol on me. The reason I say 'tried' is that while he was attempting to remove the gun from its holster I knocked about ten of his teeth out. It was at that point that we decided to leave.

We'd arrived at the club in an old van, and after making our escape to the car park we piled in. Despite us making a run for it, Obote's bodyguards had decided that our quarrel was far from over and as we began to reverse out of our parking space they started taking pot shots at us. I don't know if it was just incompetence or the fact that they were pissed but not one of them hit the van. We only had one pistol on us so while they were firing bullets into thin air we started firing at their feet, just to get the fat fuckers dancing. Instead of running away like I thought they would, they all ran to their cars and gave chase. All except one, that is. Just as we were leaving the car park, the side door of the van opened and in leapt one of the bodyguards. Talk about the element of surprise. We were so surprised to see this lad that by the time we were ready to take action he was already laying into us and it took us at least ten seconds to get him under control. As soon as he was, one of the lads opened the side door again and out he went. We must have been going at least 60 mph at the time and the chances of him making it would have been slim to non-existent.

With that lot being armed to the teeth we decided to go straight to the police station and on the way somebody had the bright idea of calling the ex-SAS lads who'd been in the club earlier that evening. Fortunately, they were only about a mile away from the police station when we called and by the time we pulled up outside they were waiting for us. Obote's bodyguards were only about thirty seconds behind us, but that gave us enough time to get out of the van and take cover while the SAS lads, who were armed with machine guns, prepared the greeting party. After spotting our van parked up, the bodyguards did the same and got out of their cars. Just as they did so the SAS lads took aim and fired a few round into the sides of their cars.

'You've got ten seconds to get in your cars and drive away,' one of them shouted. 'And if you don't, we'll kill you. Ten. Nine. Eight . . .' By the time he got to seven they were all back in their cars and as they began to screech away he let off a few rounds just to say goodbye. Just goes to show that it's not what you know, it's who you know.

After fuck knows how many weeks of getting pissed every day and winding up Obote's bodyguards – and making the fuckers dance – the money started coming through from the High Commission so without any further ado we started installing these masts. Because I'd worked on a building site before and had experience of doing oversights I was considered to be a construction expert and was put in charge. It was like being back in Abu Dhabi, except that instead of me having to recreate *Who Dares Wins* it was *Auf Wiedersehen, Pet*. The first may have been more dangerous with regards to execution but, when it came to sourcing the materials we required, Uganda was on its own. We needed aggregate, concrete and steel rods, which in Uganda were about as rare as rocking-horse shit. We also needed labour and after putting in a request to the High Commission they sent fifty prisoners and a small fat man wearing shorts, wellies and pith helmet. He looked like a black Dr Livingstone.

Once the labour had been sorted we set about trying to find the materials and over the next few days visited every builders yard in the Kampala region armed with a pistol each, the prisoners, who were going to have to carry what we bought, and sack of Ugandan shillings.

When it came to mixing the concrete prior to construction we'd have to do it on the side of a road as the masts, which we were supposed to be installing all over Kampala, had to be positioned at the top of a hill. So, after mixing it on the side of the road the prisoners would then shovel the concrete onto a piece of corrugated iron and carry it to the summit. The main problem we had, apart from these poor bastards having to carry half a ton of concrete uphill with no path for a quarter of a mile, was the heat. It was never less than 40 degrees and so by the time they got it up there it was far from dry. Remedy? We just chucked a load of rocks in with it. At the end of the day I wasn't going to be there in five years' time, so what the hell?

The concrete was for the anchors that went below the masts and the structures of these anchors were built with the steel rods. When it came to building the masts, this had to be done in sections and the final height of these things was about 250 feet. One of the lads got attacked by an eagle while bolting on the final piece of one of the masts and he refused to go up again after that. Fortunately, I was in charge so could delegate it elsewhere.

By the time all the masts had been put up I'd been in Uganda for about six-and-a-half months and despite the fact that I'd spent much of that time on the piss I was due some leave – to sober up and see my family. When I walked through the door at home one of the first things Theresa, after giving me a huge hug, asked me was what I wanted to eat. When we'd spoken on the phone one of my main gripes had been the food and she knew what I was going to say. 'A toasted mushroom and bacon sandwich please love,' I said, already drooling. 'Actually, make that two!' To this day it's one of the best meals I've ever had and it was definitely the most welcome. I can still taste the bacon.

As we were still making up for lost time in Uganda I only took a few days leave. I didn't want to go back, though, as I had a feeling it was about to kick off. Funnily enough, that's actually the reason I did go back as me and the lads were all in this together. Staying at home would have been akin to desertion.

By now we had a daughter, Sian, who was two years old. Before I left she gave me a hug that lasted about two hours. She would not let go for love nor money. It was almost as if she knew what I was going back to. As I made my way to the airport bound for Kampala I was in two minds whether to turn around and go home. The Ugandan bush war had gone into overdrive before I left and there were rumours circulating that another *coup d'état* might happen. Even so, there was absolutely no way I was going to drop out and leave everybody in the shit, so I got on the plane and just hoped for the best.

Bush wars notwithstanding, when I arrived back in Uganda we had to crack on with what we were potentially being paid to do and so an hour after I landed we went out to erect one of these masts. When we were about half way to the location I saw what I thought were some rebels on the road about a mile in the distance. Not willing to take any chances I decided to head back and without even considering what might be in front of us I drove off the road and into the elephant grass in order to turn around. Unfortunately the elephant grass was hiding a twenty foot drop and after taking a bit of a tumble we ended up landing roof-first. Despite being only a few metres from the road, to all intents and purposes we were now in the bush and given the noise we'd just made there'd be people coming to investigate. People who would have no problem whatsoever killing a bunch of white men in a Range Rover.

After dragging ourselves from the vehicle (one man was knocked unconscious but came around after a couple of minutes) we heard a helicopter that appeared to be coming our way. Without any transport and being miles from anywhere we were literally at the mercy of whoever was flying this thing and if they didn't stop or were on the wrong side we'd be fucked. Nobody driving a car would stop on this road, especially to help out a bunch of white men. There was literally a fifty-fifty chance of us being slaughtered.

When we got to the road and saw the helicopter we had no idea at first which side they were on. We figured that if the rebels did have a helicopter it would probably have been nicked from the military, so we just had to stand there and hope for the best. Luckily for us the helicopter belonged to Obote's Forces and had been sent out to disperse the rebels up ahead. After landing on the road and picking us up they took us to their camp and after checking our credentials they offered us lunch. I was absolutely fucking starving by this point so their offer was gratefully received. The person in charge at the camp was a colonel and he was our host.

'A drink, gentlemen?' he said after sitting us all down. We just nodded furiously and smiled at him.

He clapped his hands a second or so later a waiter appeared carrying a tray of half pint glasses that were all filled to the brim with what looked suspiciously like whisky. My taste for whisky had been spoiled somewhat after taking an inch off the spirit bottles at my friends house all those years ago and, after taking a small sip, I almost puked.

'Is there something wrong with the refreshments?' asked the Colonel.

'Not at all Colonel,' I lied. 'It's very refreshing.' I was just going to have to grin and bear it.

About five minutes later the food arrived and at first glance there appeared to be two elements to it, kidney beans and something else.

'What have we got here Colonel?' I asked. 'I recognise the kidney beans.'

'That is correct,' said the Colonel. 'Kidney beans and chicken entrails! It is a Ugandan delicacy.'

Had I not had to down half a pint of whisky I'd have been ok with this, but unfortunately I did. I lost count how many times I puked in my mouth and had to swallow it again. It must have been at least ten. Mercifully, we weren't offered a refill by the Colonel and after asking to be excused before puking for real we were driven back to the villa. Incidentally, the only part of the Range Rover that we managed to salvage was the number plate.

Within about three days of me arriving back in Kampala we were told that a coup was now inevitable. As far as the rebels were concerned this would play right into their hands as, with the government in turmoil, they'd be able to make a move for power.

In expectation of this we kitted out our new Range Rover with a roof-mounted machine gun and just waited. Sure enough, within a week of me landing we received word that the rebels were on their way down the Bombo Road, which leads right through the middle of Kampala, and within a few hours they'd flooded the entire city.

This left us well and truly in the shit. For a start, we were a bunch of armed white blokes, which wouldn't go down well, but if the rebels got word that we were also working for Obote we'd be goners.

The first thing we did was contact the British High Commission but in their eyes we were mercenaries and so basically they told us to fuck off. This was news to me as I'd been informed that everything was above board. Perhaps that was naive of me, but there you go. This was a real game changer, as with no protection we were going to have to get out the back way. Had we been recognised by the High Commission as official military training staff we'd have been flown out immediately, but as it was we were considered to be worse than criminals.

In the end help came from the strangest of places. One of our blokes, who shall remain nameless, was sleeping with a local woman called Liz at the time. She happened to be a niece of – wait for it – Yoweri Museveni, the leader of the bloody rebels! Museveni is now the president of Uganda but back then he was, I suppose, the closest thing they had to an opposition leader.

Because of her connections, Liz was privy to a lot of inside information and fortunately she was able to show us a route where we might make it out alive. The deal was that she'd come with us as, like so many, she was desperate to flee the country. It actually tuned out to be the same route Obote had taken when he fled with some of his bodyguards, which was ironic.

Before we left, one of the men we'd been training, a man called Anthony, turned up and asked if he could come with us. As a member of the secret police force he was obviously going to be high on the rebels' list so the first thing we did was get rid of his secret service ID and tell him to use his cover ID, which was a teacher. None of us knew this at the time but if you were a black man fleeing the coup (they didn't care about women) you were considered to be the enemy and this was made clear to us at the first checkpoint we came to. Our own cover was that we were British Telecom engineers, so we obviously had to remove the machine gun from the roof.

The bloke in charge of this first checkpoint was as pissed as a fart and when we got out of the Range Rover he started screaming at us and waving his gun around.

'Who are you?' he yelled. 'Come on, who are you?'

'We're just telecom engineers,' I said trying to pacify him. 'We've been over here for about six months.'

'Who's he?' he said, pointing at Anthony.

'I don't know. We just gave him a lift.'

'You,' he said pointing at Anthony. 'Lie down on the floor.'

The moment Anthony touched the ground this bloke shot him in the back of the head.

'There,' he said. 'Dead.'

I wasn't expecting that.

'You know him?' said the pissed-up nutcase, waving his gun in our direction.

'No,' we said putting our hands in the air. 'We just gave him a lift.'

The next checkpoint we came to was about 2 miles further on and it was like a big compound. Just to get our bearings we decided to pull up about a hundred yards away. There were cars and wagons everywhere so pulling over wasn't too conspicuous. What was conspicuous, however, was the arrival of a lad that we all knew from the secret police called Chris.

'Captain Marty,' he said walking towards me. 'My Royal Marine friend! It's good to see you.'

Before he could say anything else I ran forward and put my arms around him as though giving him a hug. I then turned him around as if I was playing with him, silenced him and pushed him under a wagon. Had I not done so, we would have been dead.

Whenever I tell people this story the first thing they usually say is, 'It must have been horrible having to do that,' but it wasn't. The Ugandan secret police force were bastards of the highest order and would think nothing of butchering a child for fun. In fact, I once saw three generations of the same family slaughtered for a bag of charcoal. We were training some men on the side of a hill at the time when all of a sudden there was a commotion somewhere down below. When we looked down we saw one of Obote's men get out of a car and grab this bag of charcoal from somebody who I assumed was a civilian. Moments later the car ploughed into this man and his family killing at least four of them.

The behaviour of people such as Idi Amin had obviously permeated throughout the Ugandan establishment and authorities and, even though he was no longer in power, his legacy was alarmingly prevalent. Then again, Obote was no angel (his regime was responsible for 300,000 deaths as opposed to Amin's half a million) so the fact that people like this were still operating was hardly surprising. I wasn't aware of this when I first went to Uganda, but some of the stories I heard later were horrendous and this particular man was one of the worst offenders. As far as I'm concerned, he deserved to die.

Thanks mainly to an inordinate amount of luck and a not inconsiderable amount of charm we finally got to within a stone's throw of the Kenyan border. The person in charge there described himself as a colonel, but he wasn't. He was just a fat fucking chancer who'd come out of the bush because he was told to and was now killing and robbing anybody he fancied. When we turned up in the Range Rover he must have thought all his Christmases had come at once and the first thing he said after ordering us to step out was, 'Money. You give me money.'

Fortunately we had about six million Ugandan shillings in the back of the Range Rover, which was about £3,000, and if we hadn't had that – and the Range Rover, which the bastard also took – there's no way he would have let us cross. He was very similar to the man I bumped off. He was just vermin.

'OK,' he said eventually. 'You go.'

It was about 200 metres to the Kenyan border yet it

seemed like 200 miles. We obviously couldn't walk quickly as that would have drawn suspicion so we had no choice other than to try and walk at a leisurely pace. The most off-putting thing as we attempted this was the Ugandan's radio, which seemed to go off every few seconds. Every time it did I was certain it would be somebody warning him to keep an eye out for five blokes masquerading as telecom engineers. Not that he would have needed an excuse to shoot five men in the back. I was aware of that too.

When we finally stepped over the Kenyan border I looked back at Uganda, hopefully for the last time. It had been a mistake taking the job and an even bigger mistake going back there after my leave, but there was fuck all I could do about that now. I was just grateful I'd got away with it.

The first thing the Kenyan authorities did when we walked across the border was search us. One of the lads had left a magazine of bullets in his bag and what followed was probably one of the greatest pieces of ensemble acting there has ever been. Bearing in mind what we'd just been through, you'd have been forgiven for assuming that we might have shat ourselves when the soldier who was searching us pulled out this magazine, or at least turned a bit crimson. Not a bit of it. Without any consultation whatsoever (there wasn't time) we all looked at the magazine as if it was something from another century before one of said, 'Ah, yes. I found that last week. I have no idea what it is though.' We then proceeded to ask the soldier a series of innocent – bordering on clueless – questions about the magazine which meant we couldn't possibly have been anything other than five telecom engineers from the UK. The *pièce de résistance* of our performance was asking the soldier to keep the magazine as we obviously had no use for it.

Hook . . . line . . . and sinker.

After leaving the border-control building – at a leisurely pace, of course – we walked down some stairs and came across a seven-seater taxi. Money wasn't a problem as I'd managed to smuggle about £3,000 in a money belt so we jumped in and asked the driver to take us to Nairobi. The drive was going to be at least ten hours but after about twenty minutes we suddenly came to a halt.

'What's wrong?' I asked the driver.

'No gas,' he said giving me a Kenyan equivalent of a Gallic shrug.

'Didn't you think about checking this before we set off on a ten-hour fucking drive?'

He just repeated the shrug.

In the end we had to push this seven-seater three bastard kilometres to the nearest petrol station and every time one of us moaned another would say the magic words, 'It's better than being in Uganda.'

When we finally got to Nairobi the first thing we did after checking into a hotel and then calling our loved ones was get absolutely shitfaced, not surprisingly. I think we'd forgotten that not all lager tasted like Nile Beer and the last thing I did before going to sleep that night was pull down my jeans and moon out of my window. Why? Because my room was facing Uganda!

The following day we managed to catch a flight from Nairobi to Heathrow and with the coup in full swing – and with the vast majority of the people fleeing Uganda making their escape via Nairobi – the press were absolutely everywhere. The first person to approach us when we came through customs was the journalist and now Channel 4 television presenter, Jon Snow. The first thing he did was ask us where we'd come from and when we told him we'd been in Uganda for seven months he basically offered us a blank cheque. One of the reasons they were so keen to speak to people who'd been in Uganda was because the African news agencies were reporting it as being a non-violent, bloodless coup and they knew that was bollocks, as did we. There were several reasons why we turned down Mr Snow's offer but the main one was the fact that we were still masquerading as telecom engineers, and if the UK authorities had smelt a rat and found out the truth – which to be fair wouldn't have been too difficult – we'd have been arrested as being mercenaries. Which we weren't, of course!

Yoweri Museveni's niece Liz ended up staying with us in Essex for about three months after we returned and almost became part of the family. She then managed to get political asylum in Sweden. When she finally moved over there she robbed us for everything we had, or at least everything with value. The cow!

Strangely enough, I didn't really begrudge her this as, like it or not, that's how they lived over there. I obviously wasn't pleased, but it made me chuckle. Then, about two years ago, my son, Bryn, who makes an appearance in the next chapter, received a message on Facebook from a black woman in Sweden asking if he was related to Captain Marty Edwards who had been working in Uganda sometime during the mid-1980s. 'Don't fucking answer,' I said to him. 'I can't afford to refurnish!'

SIXTEEN

Taking the job in Uganda was undoubtedly one of the poorest decisions I've ever made. That said, it pales into insignificance compared to a decision I made in Devon one day about three years later. We can laugh about it now – just, and with a drink – but for a while it created a living hell for us all and Theresa still has nightmares about it.

By now we had three children: Sian, who was born in March 1983, Bryn who was born in May 1986, and Rhian, who was born in July 1987. After returning from Uganda I'd gone back to Sterling Guards and they'd had me working for all sorts of people. The boss there, an amazing man called Charles Gorer, wasn't known for taking people back on again once they'd left, but with me he knew he'd be getting reliability and value for money. I know that makes me sound a bit like a Ford Escort, but it's true. Subsequently, I think I'd been back to him about four times by this point so it was becoming a habit. Speaking of Ford Escorts, one of the first things we did after my return to Sterling Guards was go out and choose which car I'd be using. This ceremony had happened on every occasion so far and it always ended the same way.

'Let's take a walk, shall we?' Charles said to me. He'd been a Major in the army and sounded like a cross between Terry Thomas and Kenneth Williams. 'Now then,' he said, when we got outside. 'Let's see if we're on the same song sheet when it comes to which car I think you should have.'

'That one,' I said, pointing to the shittiest car.

'How on earth did you guess?' he said, chuckling.

'Luck, most probably.'

The car in question was a yellow Ford Escort Economy and what a shit heap it was. Go above 50mph and a yellow light used to come on, to signal you were using too much fuel. It also had no shelf at the back and awful plastic seats.

'I'm sure you'll be very happy together,' said Charles, handing me the keys. 'Happy driving!'

Until now, I'd never actually realised that Charles had been doing me a favour by giving me the old bangers, but it turned out he had. Or at least he said he had.

'I've always respected you,' he said, after handing me the keys. 'And you've always worked very hard for me, which is why I always give you the shit cars.'

'How do you mean?' I enquired. I was intrigued.

'Well,' continued Charles. 'Which cars are the first to be replaced Martin? That's right,' he said before I could answer. 'The shit ones. You always get the new cars first, because you always start with the shit ones.'

I had a feeling that hidden somewhere inside that statement was a compliment, though I had trouble finding it!

I spent a good two or three years working for Charles this time around, but after three years or so, which would take us up to 1988, I was knackered. And, I was bored. Very bored. Then one day, and completely out of the blue, Theresa suggested that we should move down to Devon, which is somewhere we'd spent quite a bit of time over the years and a place we all loved.

'When can we go,' was my answer.

The first thing I did after having this conversation was ring up a couple of security companies down there and ask them what the form was. We'd spent plenty of time on holiday in the south west, but when it came to things such as employment and what the average wage was, I was clueless. The reaction from these companies was generally positive and, after seeing my CV, two of them offered me a job. The problem was the money. The most I was being offered was £12,000 a year, half of what I'd been earning in London. With three small children to look after Theresa couldn't work, so this would be our only income.

I worked out that the only way we could make it work financially in Devon was if we bought a business that had accommodation with it. The idea being that we wouldn't have to worry about having somewhere to live, which was obviously our primary concern, and could live on the profits.

After settling on this as a course of action I called up some estate agents and told them what we were looking for: a shop or business with accommodation that was situated no more than 5 miles outside Sidmouth, which was where Theresa's sister and her family were now living.

The first thing that came up was the post office in a village called Otterton, some 3 miles down the coast from Sidmouth. From the photos they sent us it looked the dog's bollocks. It had a thatched roof and oak beams everywhere. It was perfect.

The next day I drove down to Devon to have a look

at it on my own and was so taken by what I saw that I put an offer in, which was £120,000 on an asking price of £130,000. When I arrived home later that evening I told Theresa what I'd done and, despite being slightly taken aback, she was as excited as I was. I think we had about £80,000 in equity on our property at the time so we were going to have to get a mortgage of about £40,000. That didn't matter though. After all, this was our dream home.

Once the offer had been accepted Theresa went down to have a look at it and, with no issues, we decided to sign on the dotted line. Before that happened, I sat Theresa down and told her that the chances of us ever being able to move back to Essex were non-existent so she had to be completely sure. I also had to ask myself the same question and, although there was a part of me that wanted to stay in Essex, the two previous years had been a nightmare and I think I'd probably persuaded myself that we needed a clean break.

A few weeks later, after the contracts had been exchanged, we packed up our belongings and drove down to Otterton. If the first night was anything to go by we were going to be in for a bumpy ride as the first thing Theresa did when she sat down on our bed, having unpacked the essentials, was start to cry.

'I don't want to be here,' she said. 'It just doesn't feel right. I'm telling you, Martin, there's something wrong with this place.'

'For Christ sake, it's a bit late now, love,' I cooed, sympathetically. 'We've just unpacked!'

Theresa's premonition that we might have moved to the wrong gaff gradually began to come true over the next few days. By the end of the first week we were all on the verge of nervous breakdowns, even the kids!

A friend of ours called Steve, who'd been my number

two at Sterling Security and a neighbour in Brentwood, had helped us move in and he was one of the first to realise that we may have bought – for want of a better word – a complete fucking shithole.

It was the day after the move and he and I were in the post office trying to do some cleaning. The glass on the counter was yellow and seemed to be smoked. 'That's strange,' said Steve. 'Why on earth would you have smoked glass on a post office counter?'

On further inspection he realised that the glass was actually clear and the yellow smoke effect was just dirt and nicotine. That was just the tip of the iceberg. The cold fridge, which by the looks of things had been leaking for weeks, had been blocked up with fag butts and all that was left now when you tried to drain it was a trickle of black and yellow sludge. One of the worst things we encountered was the slicing machine, which we took apart to clean. At one end of the machine there was a lump of what we assumed was fat but as we started taking it apart the lump began to move.

'What the fucking hell's that?' Steve asked, taking a step back.

I picked up a pencil and prodded it with one end. 'They're maggots mate,' I said.

Although the apartment wasn't exactly a palace it was liveable once it had been cleaned, so with the shop and post office now free of things such as maggots, fag ends and nicotine-stained glass, I set about getting it ready to open. The amount of time, effort and money that was needed to achieve this was at odds with my original estimation and over the next week or so I received a host of expensive surprises. The worst of these happened when the lino started moving underneath my feet in the shop one day and, after pulling it back from the wall, I discovered that the previous owner had put plasterboard over the floorboards. They obviously must have thought that the original floorboards weren't strong enough, which is why they put down plasterboard, but after several weeks of having a fridge leaking onto it the prognosis had changed.

The first thing I did was call the Post Office authorities to tell them that we wouldn't be able to open.

'That's not possible,' they said. 'You have to open, otherwise you'll be fined.'

After much searching we managed to find a carpenter who could do about two hours a night, and every night he worked we had to empty the entire shop first. The shop wasn't small, by the way – it was about 30 foot x 15 foot – and it was full of fucking shelves. Even so, every night as soon as we closed we had to take everything out and then put the whole lot back again afterwards. It took about two hours in all.

Once the floor had been sorted we started making plans as to what we might sell. The bloke who'd had the place before us had been a chronic alcoholic, hence the state of the place, and all he'd ever sold apart from fags and a few essentials were things such as buckets and spades for holidaymakers. If we were going to make this work we knew we had to concentrate on the locals. The first thing we did once the floor had been sorted was put a pad and pen on the counters of both the shop and the post office, and when people came in we asked them to write down what they'd like us to stock.

The thing I hated most about being a shopkeeper – apart from all the shit we had to deal with at the start – was doing the papers. They'd be left outside the shop at precisely 4 a.m. every day and once I'd brought them in I'd then have to mark them up for the paper boys. When I started it was a nightmare as I didn't have a clue what I was doing, but once I'd got used to the process ... it was still a fucking nightmare.

Of all the suggestions re what we should stock the funniest came from a posh old duffer from the village who I used to enjoy winding up from time to time. He'd asked us to sell – wait for it – lambs tongues in aspic, for fuck's sake. And when I dared to question their popularity among the population of Otterton he went bananas.

'Oh, balls to them,' he said. 'That lot wouldn't know quality if it jumped up and hit them on the arse.'

'But where am I supposed to get them?' I asked.

'Only one place you can get them,' said the duffer. 'Harrods!'

In the end I had to decline his request but the mention of Harrods must have put an idea into his head because a few weeks later a parcel arrived for him at the post office from that very shop. It was supposed to have been collected from us but, after a week or so, he still hadn't been in, which is when it started to smell, and I mean *really* smell. In the end, I dropped the parcel over to him and, when he opened it in front of me, I realised he'd ordered a hamper.

'Look at that,' he said. 'Bloody ruined.'

'Why the hell didn't you tell me that you'd ordered a hamper?' I asked.

'Well, I thought you'd have brought it round the moment it arrived.'

'What did your last slave die of, Rupert? I'm not your fucking batman.'

That riled me, that did.

Within about six months of opening I'd been named locally as the mad postmaster from Otterton, and – à la Basil Fawlty – people used to come from miles around to be abused by me. I think what drove my new character was a mixture of sleep deprivation, mischief and an extreme desire to shock people and make them laugh. One woman from

Ultimate Survivor

Birmingham got a right roasting one day, although I don't think she'd travelled down especially. It was a bank holiday and she'd come in for some milk.

'That'll be 30p please,' I barked.

'I can get it for 20p down at Norman's,' she replied.

Norman's was a local supermarket chain that Norman Wisdom used to do the adverts for, and that's where the majority of people did their shopping.

'Is Norman's open today?' I asked, leaning towards her.

'No.'

'Well that's why it's 30p, you daft cunt.'

With that I grabbed the milk and went to put it back in the fridge.

'Hey,' she said. 'I want that milk.'

'You can fucking whistle for it,' I said, waving her out. 'I'll tell you what. Go and wait outside Norman's. They'll be open in about fifteen hours. Now get out of my fucking shop.'

The biggest mistake anybody ever made in that shop, apart from me when I bought the fucking place, was when a Rupert walked in one day and started complaining about his newspaper delivery. I was in the post office at the time and the first thing he said was, 'Hey, Edwards. I want a word with you.' That was his first mistake. The only people who've ever got away with calling me Edwards are school teachers and officers (and maybe the odd policeman), but that's it.

'What the fucking hell do you want? And it's Mr Edwards to you.'

To any normal person this would have issued a warning signal advising them to alter their tone, but this twat was oblivious.

'You've delivered a copy of *The Times* to my address and I take *The Telegraph*. What the hell is going on?'

'There's been a problem with the *Telegraph* today,' I

said, 'so for the twenty or so wankers who take the *Daily Telegraph*, I swapped it for a *Times*.'

'Are you thick, Edwards?' he said, trying to sneer. 'The fucking *Times* is nothing like the *Daily Telegraph*.'

Without even thinking I picked the till up and threw it at his head. Luckily for him one of our neighbours – a big ginger bloke – was in the queue behind this twat and he diverted the till with his hand just before it hit him. After that the Rupert ran for his life, but he didn't cancel his order. And he never complained again.

Despite me not killing the old fart, the incident triggered an outburst that resulted in me smashing up the shop. It was a culmination of everything, but mainly the long hours and frustration. I have a tipping point that applies to many situations and once I go over that tipping point it's better to make yourself scarce. Once again, I'm not trying to appear like some kind of hard man. Far from it. I've been at odds with myself mentally for most of my adult life and when that becomes too much for me I explode. I'd be a psychiatrist's dream if I ever decided to get on the couch, especially with everything that's happened to me.

I'm afraid I made quite a professional job of smashing up the shop. When Theresa and the kids came home they found me sitting on the floor with the till in my lap. I was crying my eyes out and, after sending the kids upstairs, Theresa helped me to my feet and told me that everything was going to be OK.

*****

Once I'd cornered the market in till-throwing rural postmasters who have a talent for saying the F word, I decided it was time we tried to become an off-licence. Getting up at 4 a.m., seven-days-a-week, wasn't enough for me. I wanted to go to bed at midnight too. Unfortunately, the rewards on offer if we opened an off-licence were too great to ignore (especially as the mortgage interest rates had recently doubled to 15 per cent) and so, after talking it through with Theresa, we went ahead with the application.

The only person who opposed our application to run an off-licence from the shop was the local butcher. Fuck knows how, but he'd been running an off-licence for years from his place and because he'd had a monopoly on it had been ripping off the locals left, right and centre. He really was a horrible little wanker and when he told me one day in the street that he was going to take me to court over the application it took all my legendary calm and restraint not to rip his head off. The twat.

When we got to court I was informed by the Justice of the Peace that there was a rule in place in rural areas that prevented similar businesses from opening within a hundred metres of each other. When it came to the crunch, this was the butcher's only argument, except that we weren't within a hundred metres of the butcher. In fact, we were almost 400 metres from him. You should have seen the fat bastard try and argue it.

'I've counted my steps,' he said. 'And it is my belief that the distance between the butcher's and the post office is just under 100 metres.'

Fortunately, the JP knew the area well and once he'd got it into his head exactly where we were he squashed the argument dead.

'You would have to have the legs and the stride of an ostrich in order for that to be a hundred metres. You can have your licence, sir. Good day.'

The butcher almost exploded. You could almost see

his bank balance disappearing. And his blood pressure rising. I do hope he was OK.

With the mortgage rates staying at 15 per cent we decided to convert the stables at the back of the property into a cottage and then let it out. We managed to get a father-and-son team who were local to do the job but, because of their workload, they could only do it on evenings and weekends. Also, because the shop was situated on the side of a road, instead of having the building deliveries such as sand and bricks dropped at the rear of the shop, where the work was going on, they had to be dropped on the road itself. With me based permanently in the shop, Theresa had to fetch a wheelbarrow and shift these deliveries as soon as possible and she did quite a good job. The day after the cottage had been finished we let it out to some students and from then on it became an earner.

I don't want to overstate our progress at this point as we were making just enough money to be able to eat, pay the mortgage and have a little bit left over. We were just about scraping by, with the main advantage being that because we were a new business and weren't able to get credit, we had no debt apart from the mortgage.

My next battle at Otterton was with the Post Office authorities as opposed to one of the locals. What a bunch of obstinate, arrogant bastards they were. Nevertheless, I still went into it with the same kind of sweary determination as I always do and, without wanting to big myself up, they didn't know what had hit them.

It all started during our first Christmas. The deluge of parcels we received to be posted was incredible and the scales, which had been provided by the Post Office, were at best inadequate. Because of this the queues were becoming ridiculous and tempers were beginning to flair. People with parcels would put their head around the door when Theresa was there and whisper, 'Is he in a good mood?' If Theresa said no they'd whisper, 'OK, I'll take them to the next village.' If they didn't do that and caught me in a bad mood I'd just throw the parcels at them. It was Basil Fawlty to a tee, but with a bit more violence.

By this time most of the locals were aware that whingeing would get them nowhere in our shop and so, instead, some of them started making suggestions, the best one being, 'Why don't you get some digital scales?'

The following day I rang up the Post Office and told them what was happening. 'It's absolute chaos,' I told them. 'We can't go on as we are. Could you send us some digital scales please?'

'Nope. You're not big enough,' came the reply.

'Haven't you been listening? People are walking out and it's all because the scales aren't adequate for the job.'

'I'll repeat it. YOU – ARE – NOT – BIG – ENOUGH'.

If the person on the other end of the phone had been within grabbing distance I would have pulled their fucking tongue out.

'Who do I complain to?' I said after counting to ten.

'The Postmaster General,' said the twat.

I had an idea.

'Have you got their number please?' I was politeness itself now.

'Yeah, all right then.'

As soon as I'd taken down the Postmaster General's number I made a sign saying: NO MORE PARCELS BEING ACCEPTED AT THIS POST OFFICE UNTIL I GET DIGITAL SCALES. ANY COMPLAINTS, PLEASE CONTACT THE POSTMASTER GENERAL ON . . .

Fuck me, did the shit hit the fan.

Incidentally, I'd already incurred the wrath of the Postmaster General by painting a smiley face on the crown on the front of our post box. To be fair, the box had been in a hell of a state when we arrived and, after repainting it, I'd simply made a small addition. It was a joke, for fuck's sake, but instead of simply asking me to repaint it the postmen and postwomen of Devon had threatened to go on strike. Seriously! Something about defacing the crown?

Within a day of me putting my sign up the Postmaster General had received the best part of a hundred calls and apparently he'd been spitting feathers. Instead of calling me up and trying to come to an agreement this dickhead decided to send a couple of heavies round.

'The Postmaster General's sent us to talk to you,' one of them said.

'Well, fucking talk then,' I said. 'You've got one minute.'

'It's about your sign,' said the other one. 'It's got to come down.'

'It'll come down when you lot get me some digital scales, and not before.'

'But you don't qualify for them.'

'Then I'm not taking fucking parcels!'

The two twits looked at each other.

'We'll close you down if you do that,' one of them said.

'You can fucking try, pal,' I snarled. Unfortunately the red mist was starting to appear now. 'Go on,' I continued. 'I fucking dare you.'

'Hold on,' said the first one. 'I think we can sort this amicably.'

'We can if you get me some fucking scales.'

'But as I said, you don't qualify.'

As he said that I could feel my blood pressure going

through the roof and had it been left another few seconds it would have been till-gate all over again.

'Don't listen to him,' said the other one quickly. 'Look, we'll get you some digital scales. I promise!'

The look of panic on this man's face as he saw Mount Edwards start to erupt was classic. I knew that I'd turned bright red, but what I didn't realise was that I was clutching a tin of beans that had been left on the counter. This had obviously been a contributing factor to him capitulating and when I finally took my hand off the tin he looked like somebody who'd just had a massive shit. Pure relief.

Our next-door neighbours when we lived in Otterton were a retired judge and his wife and although they were quite sweet, the wife, who was called Margaret, thought shopkeepers were just staff. Actually, let's not beat about the bush. She was a right stuck up cow and one day I decided to have some fun with her.

It was a Saturday morning and after enjoying my usual four hours sleep I'd dragged myself down to the shop at the usual time, and I mean dragged. Subsequently, I was found lacking in the sartorial department and was donning an old T-shirt, some tracksuit bottoms and a pair of flip-flops. At about 9 a.m. Margaret walked in and the first thing she did was look me up and down before letting out a sigh. I didn't have the strength to throw the till at her so, after bidding her a good morning, I asked her what she wanted.

'I'm holding a dinner party next week and I'd like some cheese.'

We actually specialised a bit in cheeses, so she'd come to the right place.

'Anything in mind, Margaret?'

'Do you have anything unusual? I'd like to offer my guests something they've never tasted before.'

'Have you ever heard of Foskin?' I asked.

'Foskin, you say?' said Margaret, thoughtfully. 'No, I don't think I have.'

'I dare say you'll have tasted some over the years, Margaret.'

'Really?' she said. 'Is it popular?'

'It can be,' I replied. 'It's very rare though, as it only comes in very small amounts.'

'It sounds lovely. Tell me, are you able to procure some Foskin for me?'

It was almost time for the big reveal.

'I actually make it myself,' I said to her, with almost a straight face. 'Would you like me to show you how?'

Fortunately for Margaret, Theresa was in the shop at the time and just as I was pulling my tracksuit bottoms down a cry of, 'MARTIN!' came from the post office.

To be fair to the old girl, Margaret cottoned on immediately (she'd have been a right goer in her day!) and after going very red she said, 'Ooh, you naughty man,' before making her exit.

SEVENTEEN

As taxing as it was running the shop and the post office, we were determined to make a go of it. Not because we wanted to make a load of money, there was obviously a ceiling as to how much if that we could make, but I was determined to do the best I possibly could with the tools at my disposal and accept whatever that brought. More than anything, we wanted to make our business the hub of the village and if that meant opening 365 days a year, so be it.

There were a lot of old people living in Otterton at the time and on Christmas Day morning we used to open up and lay on some Buck's Fizz and sherry. Quite a few of these people were on their own and although we couldn't offer them lunch at least we could get them all a bit merry. None of them had freezers and so we used to allocate them a space each in ours and whenever they wanted a burger or some fish fingers or whatever, they'd simply pop in and help themselves.

By the time we'd been there about a year I'd become

like a warden in a sheltered accommodation building. If ever there was an emergency involving an old age pensioner they'd call the emergency services first, and then me. One year, for Children in Need, I dressed up as prostitute all day and, fuck me, did I look good. I had stockings, suspenders, a skirt that looked like a belt, the lot. The bloke who delivered the papers got the shock of his life that morning. As did most of our customers.

By mid-afternoon my knickers were starting to chafe a bit and just as I was trying to alter things down below the telephone went. It was a neighbour of a lady who was our oldest customer and apparently she'd had a fall.

Without even stopping to sort out the chafing I asked Theresa to look after the shop, took off my high heels and ran to the old lady's house. None of the emergency services had arrived yet and, with the house being completely locked downstairs, I managed to find a ladder and then put it under an open window at the front. By now a small crowd had gathered and as I started climbing I heard a couple of wolf whistles.

I'd forgotten I was dressed as a prostitute.

'Whoever that was, fuck off!'

Just then I heard an ambulance approaching. I was still facing the wall at the time, but just as it sounded like the ambulance was outside I heard a loud bang. The ambulance had crashed into a car parked outside the house! After finding the old girl, who was fine, fortunately, I grabbed the keys and opened the front door.

'You stupid bastard,' said one of the paramedics who was waiting on the other side. 'That crash was your fault.'

'How the hell was it my fault?' I protested.

'You distracted me,' said the paramedic. He wasn't at all happy.

'Admit it,' I said, finally sorting out my chafe. 'You fancy me.'

'Do I heck,' he said, barging past.

As well as a lot of pensioners we also had our fair share of young families in Otterton and quite a few of those were living on the breadline. Plenty of people used to ask for tick at the shop and the majority used to get it but there were still one or two who were too embarrassed to ask. They were the ones I felt most sorry for and they were the ones I wanted to help. I could spot them a mile away. They'd spend about half an hour looking through the shelves and were obviously trying to find something they could afford.

'What are you after?' I'd ask.

'Oh, erm, I'm not sure really. I'm looking for something for tea.'

'You were looking at burgers.'

'I can't afford them.'

'Yes you can. Take a pack.'

'I can't do that.'

'Take them, or you're fucking well barred!'

That always worked.

I could tell which ones were genuine and which ones were taking the piss. It's easy in a village as everyone knows everyone else's business so if somebody had a reputation for being a dodgy bastard it would undoubtedly get discussed in the shop. That was one of the benefits of having so many old ladies coming in. I knew everyone's business.

One of the biggest falling outs I had in Otterton – and there were one or two – was with the landlord of the local pub. I was looking at using a cleaning company that he'd been using and for some reason he became all funny about giving me their details. He was a dodgy twat this bloke – and annoying – so God knows what the reason was. One day I got word through the old ladies that the person who ran the cleaning company was at the pub so I rang him up and asked him if he'd send them up afterwards.

'I don't think so,' he said. 'He's not interested in working for you.'

It wasn't what he said that brought the mist up, it was the way he said it. He was being cocky, and I don't like that. After hanging up on him I went to the log shed and found my axe. I'd only had it a few days and it was sharper than a serpent's tooth, and, in the right hands, just as deadly. After picking it up I walked into the road and marched down to the pub. It was about 10 a.m. and all I could see out of the corner of my eye were net curtains twitching. I won't lie. I love playing up to an audience, but the red face and the steam coming out of my ears and nostrils were completely genuine. The reaction of the crowd merely fuelled my anger.

By the time I got to the pub, which was about 200 yards away, I was ready to kill the fucker and to herald my arrival I decided to kick his door in. After doing just that, I walked into the bar where he and the cleaner bloke were sitting at a table. The two men were shitting themselves, I could tell, so in order to build on this I strolled up to the table without saying a word, pulled the axe over my head with both hands, and then proceeded to chop the table completely in two. I'm sure they thought they were goners.

God, that was satisfying!

After that I bid them both good day, threw the axe over my shoulder and marched back to the shop. Job done.

Fuck knows how but in 1990, after we'd been in Otterton for two years, I was voted onto the parish council. Given what you've just read it's astonishing, but their motivation for inviting me must have had something to do with keeping your friends close to you and your enemies even closer. Being a Marmite sort of person I was probably considered to be both, depending on who you asked, so it made sense. More importantly, though, I cared about the village and the parish council knew that full well. What's even more surprising, though, is that I lasted for over a year in the position. It all went tits up, of course, and it ended with me attacking a table again. But not with an axe.

Before that happened we managed to win the title of Devon's Best Kept Village and I flatter myself that this was more than partly down to Theresa and me.

We'd started selling hanging baskets for a fiver each, which was another good earner, and because they made the outside of the shop look quite attractive the entire bloody village started buying them. As a result, somebody suggested we enter this competition and after installing a few flowerbeds around the village and sprucing up the public areas a bit, we bloody won.

Another little battle I had before resigning from the parish council involved the local vicar. The husband of one of my elderly customers had died and she'd wanted to include his nickname – which was Chummy – on the gravestone. The vicar refused her request outright, claiming it was the kind of name you'd give to a dog. After trying to reason with the pious prick on her behalf – and failing, unfortunately – I went to the papers and the local television station. The following day we had reporters from the local rags down here and from Television South, but the horrible old bastard still refused to budge. Given that congregations were dropping like a pair of lead knickers at the time you'd have thought he might have granted this but not a bit if it. Even the Synod backed up the old fart so I had to concede defeat. I did think about going around there with my axe and chopping his pews in half, but in the end thought better of it.

In hindsight I wish I had done. Or at least set fire to his cassock. I had form in that department!

One day the parish council held a meeting about what we were going to do with the local playground. It was absolutely fucked and with the child population growing we had to do something about it. After a bit of research I came up with an idea. I still had some mates in the Marines and I asked if they could build us a child-friendly playground. We'd pay for the materials via fundraising, but they'd design and build it. They thought it was a fabulous idea and were going to use it as a PR exercise, so I wrote up a formal proposal with their help and put it to the council.

Every member of the parish council thought it was an absolutely brilliant idea, except one. There's always one! She was a right sour-faced old bat and she said that without a maintenance contract in place she wouldn't give it the go ahead. She also had other complaints, which were something to do with health and safety, and I could tell by her manner that she was going to do everything in her power to prevent it being built.

As soon she started talking I could feel the red mist start to engulf me and as soon as she finished talking I stood up, took hold of the rim of the table, which every member of the council was sitting around, and flipped it over. 'As far as I'm concerned, you can go and fuck yourselves!' I said. 'I resign.' And with that, I walked out. In hindsight I should have ripped off her head and shat down her wizened old neck. I hate people like that.

Despite us making a go of the business and taking a genuine interest in the village, Theresa had never settled in Otterton and after four years she'd finally had enough. We'd already toyed with the idea of leaving and put the business on the market about a year before that, but we'd had no takers. I suppose that was another reason for building the business up: to make it as attractive as possible to potential buyers.

The fact that Theresa lasted as long as she did is a minor miracle. Because of the hours I was working, she had no help with the children whatsoever and to all intents and purposes she spent four years virtually on her own. Had I had more time I'd have been able to help out more, but even after four years I was still only having four hours sleep a night and my eyes were literally burning. We never argued about our situation. We didn't have time. We just got on with it – separately. Theresa deciding to go was exactly what we needed. All five of us. I'd been a part-time dad for four years and moving back to Essex, which was the only place Theresa wanted to be and was still where most of our friends were, would, providing I could find a job with normal hours, allow me to become a full-time dad instead.

We finally agreed that Theresa and the kids would return to Essex while I sold the business and, because we'd managed to save a few bob, we were able to rent a house for them to live in. The day before they were due to leave, Bryn ran headlong into a radiator and after taking him to the doctors it was advised that he stay put for a few days. 'I can't do it Martin,' Theresa said to me. 'I've got to go tomorrow.'

I still don't know how she did it but the following day Theresa set off from Otterton to Brentwood, which was a mere seven hours by train, with three children, aged eleven, six and five, two dogs, and fuck knows how many suitcases. Such was her determination to get there you could have added the same again and she'd still have made it. Never underestimate the power of a determined woman.

It took me another three months to sell the business, which I sold to a man who ended up going to prison for five years for defrauding the Post Office of over £1 million. I suppose you could blame that on me in a way, as I was the one who sold it to him. I think I had an idea he was a dodgy bastard, but I was desperate. I remember him coming to try out for a few days before signing on the line. I didn't want him to realise how difficult it was to run the place so I did as much preparation as I could prior to him coming and then tried to make it look easy. I must have got away with it as he eventually signed but when the money came through it was £800 short. By that time I was in a similar position to Theresa mentally – as in, I just didn't want to be there anymore – so I just packed up and pissed off.

There are three things I'd do differently in Devon, if I had my time again. First, I'd have a full survey done on the post office. We couldn't really afford one at the time but had we had one done we'd have saved ourselves a fortune and there's no way we would have moved there. That's the one that Theresa kicks herself about the most, so I won't labour the point. Next, I'd somehow find the money to hire a postmaster. That would have taken a huge amount of work off my shoulders and would have given me more time with Theresa and the kids. Like the survey, we convinced ourselves that we couldn't afford it – or maybe I did – but I'm sure we could have, at least for the last two years. Finally – and this is the one I regret not doing the most – I'd find something out about the vicar and then blackmail the old bastard into allowing pet names and nicknames on the graves, and if that didn't work, I'd bury him alive in half a ton of horseshit.

Go in peace.

*****

Ultimate Survivor

Whether it was a reaction to the uncertainties we'd experienced in Devon, I'm not sure, but the first thing I did when I got back to Essex – apart from appreciating the incredible difference in Theresa and the kids, who seemed to be happier than they'd ever been – was to take a job with a security company I'd worked for previously. I needed to start earning money but what I also needed – or thought I needed – was some familiarity and some security. This backfired on me bigtime as I ended up doing more hours in that job than I'd done in the post office, if that were possible. What it did do, however, was give me the impetus I needed to start up on my own again and it reignited my determination to succeed. There was no long-term plan. No cries of *This time next year I'll be a millionaire, Rodders.* I just wanted to earn enough money to look after my family and be able to take some time off – occasionally. The post office may have been punishing in many ways (that's a fucking understatement) but Theresa and I had made a success of that business and once I'd got over my initial post-Devon frame of mind, which was, *never-a-fucking-gain*, I was ready to re-group and give it another go. We both were. This wasn't going to happen immediately, however, and the only thing I really knew at the time was if I ever did go ahead and start a new business it would be in security.

The next company I worked for was owned by an ex-major from the SAS and the man he had running it for him was a former sergeant major. My position was regional manager and the region I managed was the City of London. Bearing in mind there are probably more security guards in the City than there are in the rest of London put together, this was an ideal place to, a) make a few contacts, and b) find out how best to run a successful and ethical modern security company. I didn't know it when I started but unfortunately I wasn't working for one of those. In fact, they were the antithesis of that description. In a way, though, that was perfect as once I'd cottoned on to their ineptitude they gave me a valuable lesson in how not to do it. One of the most memorable instances – this was on top of me discovering that some of the guards were doing 16-hour shifts, which was illegal – happened when I was in the City one day.

Part of my remit with this firm was to create some new business, so I'd been visiting some of our old clients with a view to getting them back on board. I might not be everybody's cup of tea (or anyone's, if you listen to Theresa after I've incurred her wrath!), but if I get on well with somebody I'll stick with them for life and I've always applied exactly the same philosophy in business, whether that be with a client, a supplier or an employee. Show me loyalty and I'll move heaven and earth for you. It's as simple as that. Do the dirty on me though, and I'll cut you off. And possibly your balls. If you have any. That was basically my sales pitch when I was regional manager and a lot of the time it worked. I never over-promised and the first thing I always did was to try and instil some trust.

One day I received a telephone call just after a pitch. It was my boss.

'Where are you and what are you doing?'

From his tone he sounded like he thought I was tossing it off and that immediately rubbed me up the wrong way. 'I'm in the City trying to win you some business,' I snapped. 'What did you think I was doing?'

'Get back here now,' he snapped back. 'We've got an inspection.'

What they wanted me to do because of this inspection was falsify a load of records to make it look like our guards had all passed the vetting procedure, which they evidently hadn't. They were also amending the payroll for some reason and in order to do this they were resurrecting dead people and retired people. The whole thing was as dodgy as fuck and the moment I found out what they were up to I told the boss exactly where he could stick it. He went off his rocker but I couldn't have given a fuck. Had I lifted a finger to assist them I'd have been as guilty as they were. I may be many things but I'm not a crook. Unhinged? Definitely. Unpredictable? Undoubtedly! Dodgy? No way.

Despite me going to work for yet another security company straight after this – one that did things by the book, I hasten to add – I was already more than halfway towards starting up on my own and had a couple of contacts who had said that when I did go it alone they'd be my first clients.

Literally the day before I'd walked out on the dodgy outfit, Theresa and I had taken out a loan for an extension on our bungalow and when that came through as being accepted I decided to go for it. Instead of building the extension straight away I put the loan money in a business account and fitted out the garage as an office. The company was called Ultimate Security.

One of the contacts who'd promised to come with me, who was called Una, ran a research company that did a lot of work for the government. This meant all their security guards had to be cleared by the Home Office. I'd forgotten about this and when my contact reminded me, having given notice on their current security contract, I did my best to act like I'd remembered. I hadn't, of course, and spent the next three weeks desperately trying to source some appropriate guards. Fortunately, I managed to find two: Martin White and David Pongen, and so they were my first two guards.

I did all the relief work, such as weekends and sick cover (although they very rarely were sick), and the rest of the time I spent looking for new business. One of the biggest problems you'll face when starting your own security business, although it's probably the same in most industries, is cashflow, and with two full-time guards on my books I was always chasing my tail. I started doing some painting and decorating for our next-door neighbour and with Theresa now nursing full-time, which is something she'd always dreamed about doing, we were just about getting by.

Incidentally, the initial uniforms my guards wore when I started out were supplied by Primark and cost a total of about £40 each. What sort of shoes you were supplied with was down to how long your patrol was, so if you had a long patrol, say two to three hours, you'd get Clarks shoes, and if it was any shorter, you'd get something cheaper.

The third guard I hired was a retired policeman called Dougie. He's one of the nicest people you could ever meet and the reason I took him on in the first place was because I'd managed to win a contract guarding some offices in the West End. Dougie's patrol was three hours, three times a night, so his shoes had to be like fucking mattresses. There were about forty buildings in all and each was six storeys. I did a relief shift for him once and it almost killed me!

One night, at about three in the morning, Dougie called me up.

'Mr Edwards,' he said. (Dougie always insisted on calling me Mr Edwards), 'I'm afraid I'm stuck in the lift.'

'But you're not supposed to take the fucking lift,' I replied. 'You're supposed to take the stairs.'

'A momentary lapse of reason?' suggested Dougie.

'An attack of fucking laziness more like. Hold on. I'll be there in an hour.'

The company vehicle was a snot-green Peugeot 107 and the reason I bought it was because nobody else would.

Ultimate Survivor

Seriously. It was so horrible to look at that I got it for next to nothing and when my eldest daughter, Sian, came to work for the company many years later, it was her company car. My youngest daughter, Rhian, always hated being driven in it and on the few occasions I had to drive her to school she'd asked to be dropped about a mile away. Looking back, it was a perfect fucking deterrent really. If you ever want to push somebody away, buy yourself a snot-green Peugeot.

After we'd been going about a year, in which time we'd managed to build up a nice little client list but were still being plagued by cashflow issues, I received a telephone call from the security manager of a massive IT services company called Computacenter. Seamus O'Doherty was his name, which has to be one of the most Irish names of all time, and the reason I knew him was because I'd been based at Computacenter in between leaving those dodgy bastards and setting up on my own company, and he and I had got on well together.

What's ironic here is the reason I'd been put at Computacenter in the first place is because the company I was employed by didn't want me working in the City, and the reason they didn't want me working in the City is because they were aware of my intentions to go it alone and were worried about me pinching business. Had they sat down and thought about it for a second, they'd have realised that in order to operate in the City of London you have to be a certain size, otherwise nobody will take you seriously. Putting me at Computacenter was madness as I was spending the vast majority of my time with the man who gave the contracts.

'They've been fucking shite since you left,' said Seamus. 'Now do you want this contract or don't you?'

'It all depends,' I said.

'On what?' said Seamus.

'On how much the contract is worth.'

'It's worth £1.8 million a year.'

'In that case,' I said. 'I'm afraid I can't take it.'

At least 80 per cent of my expenditure was payroll and I'd have to pay my guards before getting the money back, so the outlay on a contract that size was too big. I simply couldn't do it.

'I'll tell you what,' said Seamus. 'I think you should meet Alan Pottinger, the company secretary. I can't promise anything but he might be able to come up with a solution.'

Seamus must have given me a glowing reference because no sooner had I sat down with Mr Pottinger, who was a lovely man, he offered to pay me half up front and half in arrears.

'I still can't do it,' I said, slightly embarrassed.

'What do you mean?' said Alan. 'That's half.'

'Yes,' I replied. 'But it's 80 per cent payroll.'

He wasn't going to let this go and in hindsight I owe Alan Pottinger a very big drink.

'How much equity do you have in your house?' he asked.

'About £100,000.'

'Then I suggest you take a mortgage out on it,' he said.

'Can you give me five minutes?' I asked.

'Of course.'

After having a quick fag and a think I called Theresa and told her what was happening.

'What should I tell them?' I asked her.

'It's up to you,' she said. 'But if you think you can make it work, just do it.'

After having another quick fag I went back in and

told them that I'd mortgage the house and so providing I could sort that out we had a deal.

By the time I got home the enormity of what I was about to do had hit home with Theresa and the first thing she said to me when I walked through the door was, 'What if it doesn't work?'

'Then we lose the house,' I said honestly.

'Then what?'

'Then we'll rent a flat. I'll find a job, you'll carry on nursing and we'll all live unhappily ever after.'

Given what Theresa had been through in Devon that last bit wasn't funny, but the fact remained that even if it did go tits up and we did lose everything, we'd still be OK. Despite what we've been through that has never really been in doubt.

Inevitably there were setbacks when we were building up the business and they ranged from the embarrassing, such as a guard getting pissed on site during a shift and me being informed by the client, to the downright annoying, such as when the council gave us three weeks' notice on using the garage as an office, the twats. That particular one really pissed me off and we ended up having to rent an office behind a pub down the road. The office measured about 10 foot by 10 foot and my desk consisted of a flap of wood that attached to the wall and an old stool. I didn't use a computer (still don't), so it didn't bother me.

One of the most interesting 'challenges' I ever faced as the owner of a security company was many years later, when my regional director headbutted a member of the public.

I have to admit I was slightly surprised when I found out, but as somebody who himself had been known to lose his temper occasionally I decided not to jump to conclusions. He was in tears when he came to see me, so the first thing I did was try and put him at ease. He'd been with me for donkey's years and, guilty or not, I didn't want to see him cry.

'Stop blubbing, you wimp,' I said. 'Nobody's died. Yet!'

'Sorry, boss.'

'Right then,' I continued, 'is it true that you headbutted a member of the public in Covent Garden?'

'Yes, boss.'

'And would you like to tell me why you thought that was necessary?'

'He was hitting his wife. I had to do something. Are you going to sack me, boss?'

He obviously didn't know me.

'Sack you?! What the hell are you talking about? I'd have fucking killed the bastard! Consider yourself reprimanded and congratulated. Now fuck off.'

The contract for the Computacenter job was eventually signed in a pub I knew and afterwards the three signatories – me, Alan and Seamus – decided to stay for a celebratory pint or twelve. At this point, the only thing that was still bothering me about the job, apart from the fact that we'd lose our home if it went tits up, was that the security staff who were already in place there were very heavily unionised, and that had been a contributing factor when it came to making the decision. What had swung me on this was the hope that I'd manage to find somebody to put in there who'd keep the bastards happy and in check without having to make too many concessions. I'd only been at the site for a month as an employee, but that had been long enough for me to realise that the people already *in situ* at Computacenter were far more bothered about their rights than they were about doing a good job. I knew for a fact that they were going to be my biggest headache.

While I'm not a religious man I'm a big believer in fate

and literally a minute after signing the contract I looked over at the bar and saw Tony, the landlord. He happened to be the uncle of a guard who was already working for me. More importantly, he was a retired sergeant major from the Scottish Regiment who, as well as being somebody you'd think twice about messing with, absolutely hated his job. One of the first things he'd ever said to me was that he was on the point of killing his regional manager. And, I believed him. As I sat there staring at Tony – who was probably whingeing to somebody about his job – I thought, *He's our man.* Five minutes later I'd offered him the job and fortunately for me (but not the unionised guards, who were about to be well and truly put in their place) he accepted. He was a guard when he started but many years later Tony ended up becoming my MD of operations. He and a man called Steve Hall, who also joined me early on, started a long line of staff who remained loyal to me and in those early days that was incredibly important as it allowed me to concentrate on growing the business.

One of the next big contracts we went up for was 8 The Strand in London: a huge building near Trafalgar Square that's just a stone's throw from the City. The contract was given to us by a lady called Alison McDonald who was a client of mine from a past company. We were still too small to be taken seriously in the City, but we were definitely getting closer, both financially and geographically. Steve Hall had to do the walkaround for this one, which is when you visit the site and collate all the information that will allow you to tender. I took him through it on a mobile phone while I was standing in the Dordogne River with the kids. The only thing that I found stranger than this was the realisation that we'd managed to get away on holiday, something that was still about as rare as rocking-horse shit.

Shortly after winning the contract for 8 The Strand we

found out that the company who'd been offering it, a South African organisation, had been holding back 10 per cent of their guards' money in lieu of them behaving themselves and doing a good job. The guards had been brought in from South Africa and the money was supposed to be returned to them after two years. As well as being illegal, this was just plain wrong. The first thing we did when we started there, as well as getting rid of the security manager who was a twat of the highest order, was to have this money returned to the guards and for it never to happen again. Had the South African company not agreed to this, we'd have told them where to shove it, but they did.

A few months and a few more new clients later, we finally won our first contract in the City of London. There was no ultimate goal with regards to building the business – not at the start, anyway – but infiltrating the City of London had been the closest I'd come to having an ambition, save for keeping our heads above water day to day. When it happened, it was like cocking a snook at all the people who'd either slagged me off or doubted me. And there'd been a few! The security industry was extremely incestuous, and the amount of politics and jealousy washing around it at this time was incredible. Incredible, and very unhealthy. Far be it from me to blow mine and Theresa's trumpet but we'd managed to achieve what hundreds had failed to do, and that put a lot of people's noses out of joint. How did that make me feel? Absolutely fucking brilliant, that's how. It was a vindication of our efforts – of sticking at something and, dare I say it, doing it by the book.

The property in question was Tower 42, a skyscraper on Old Broad Street that had once been the tallest building in the United Kingdom. My contact there was a lovely man named Terry Marsh and, after being dicked around by his current supplier for God knows how long, he decided to have a changing of the guard, so to speak. Soon after signing the contract, I decided to do a bit of corporate hospitality and asked Terry if there was anything he'd like to go to.

'The previous company used to take me to Wimbledon,' he said. 'That was good.'

'Wimbledon it is then,' I said.

'One of the finals,' said Terry.

'Obviously,' I replied. 'You leave it to me.'

'Make sure you get tickets for you and Theresa,' he said. 'I'd like you to join us.'

'Will do.'

About two days later I handed over a cheque for £28,000 for four tickets to the ladies Wimbledon final. It was 2002, the year Venus and Serena Williams were playing, and although the other three enjoyed themselves I bloody hated it. The tennis itself was quite good, but the event was all a little bit up its own arse for my liking and I can't be doing with that. Tennis? Absolutely. Twats? No thank you.

After that, we got another City of London skyscraper called City Point, which came courtesy of a very good friend of mine called Paul Hanrahan. I'd worked for Paul many times over the years as an employee of various other companies and we trusted each other implicitly. You see, in an age when corporatism seemed to be taking over every industry going, including security, we still operated, in many ways, like a small local business. By 2004 we were employing over 300 people but the irony was that we'd achieved that by acting small. One of the best examples of this happened when Paul Hanrahan introduced me to a company on Marylebone Road who were having problems with their security company. After meeting the chairwoman and the security manager of this company I tried to ascertain what the issues were.

'How much are you paying them?' I asked.

'Oh, we can't tell you that I'm afraid.'

'Look,' I said, in what was probably quite an irritated manner, 'I'm not being funny but unless you two tell me exactly what you're paying and exactly what you're getting for your money, I can't help you. Now, do you want some advice or don't you?'

This was a big organisation and the chairwoman had started spitting fucking feathers!

'I am *not* used to being spoken to like that by . . . contractors,' she said disparagingly.

Fortunately, Paul stepped in at this point, as if he hadn't, I might well have pushed her chair up her arse.

'The reason I asked Martin to speak to you is because he's *not* a contractor,' he said. 'He's a partner. That's how he treats his customers and as long as you do the same, you'll get exactly what you need.'

This woman obviously trusted Paul as much as I did so she sat back in her chair and tapped her security manager on the shoulder.

'Tell Martin everything he needs to know,' she said.

The security manager gawped at her, as if to say, *Really! Him? He's a fucking moron!*

To return the favour I shot him a glance that said in no uncertain terms that if he didn't pipe down and do as he was told, I'd kill him.

About twenty minutes later, having quizzed the security manager about their current arrangement, I sat back in my chair and prepared to summarise, à la Lord Sugar in *The Apprentice*.

'You're being done over,' I said sagely.

'Really?' replied the boss.

'Well and fucking truly,' I confirmed.

'So what the hell should we do about it ?' she asked.

'Give them a month's notice,' I said.

The manager almost shat himself there and then.

'What?' he squeaked. 'We can't do that.'

As opposed to leaping over the desk and slapping the useless twat, which is what I might have done twenty years ago, I bit my tongue – literally – took a deep breath, and then proceeded to explain myself.

'Oh, I see,' said the manager after I'd finished.

'So do I,' said his boss. 'You're right, Martin. We are being ripped off.'

By George, I think they'd got it!

'What should we do after giving them notice,' she asked.

'Let me run the site for a month or so,' I suggested, 'and then put it out to tender.'

I could easily have got the contract there and then but I wanted to do things completely by the book. As it turned out that was a good move because as well as them receiving no value for money it was a political fucking quagmire in that place and there was a hell of a lot to sort out. Let's just say that there were one or two bad eggs who had to be chucked out – and they were. When the contract was eventually put out for tender we pitched and were successful. On our first official day running the place I personally escorted two guards onto the premises. This was at six o'clock in the morning and who happened to be there when I marched them all in? The chairwoman.

'What on earth are you doing here?' she asked.

'I'm starting everybody off,' I said.

'What, you? But you're the owner.'

'I made you a promise that I'd sort out your security. Not the company – me – and that's exactly what I'm doing.'

Another pitch was for the Shard, which is the tallest building in the UK. I can't go into too much detail (it's security, for fuck's sake!), but my methods and procedures were as unorthodox as ever and the people managing the building – and one of the owners – got the shock of their bloody lives.

Once again, the man who got the pitch was my old mate Paul Hanrahan and the night before he called me up.

'Whatever you do,' he said, 'Don't mention the bloke's hair, ok?'

'Which bloke?' I asked.

'The bloke who's going to be leading the negotiations. He only owns five per cent of the building but he's still the man in charge. Anyway, as you'll find out when you see him. His hair, which may or may not be his own, bears a striking resemblance to Elvis Presley's, so I just thought I'd warn you.'

Given my propensity to say the wrong thing this was probably a good move. Then again, I often said the wrong thing on purpose, so whether or not I mentioned it would depend on whether I liked him. We'd see. I found out the same day that the other person pitching was a mate of this bloke's. What's more, he was also somebody I didn't really care for very much so the chances of me mentioning the hair – real or not – appeared to be growing by the minute.

The following day I arrived at Graceland (or this bloke's head office) and, as the other bloke was pitching first, I decided to go and get myself a coffee and a bacon sandwich. As I was siting there I received a text from Steve Hall which said, 'Don't look at the wig. Give my love to Elvis.' I thought, you absolute bastard! I'd never be able to keep a straight face now.

Fortunately for me, Paul Hanrahan was also in the meeting and after showing the first bloke out he whispered to me, 'You're in. The rest of them fucking hate him!' Brilliant, I thought.

After sitting myself down, I was introduced to everyone there and after that was done the King finally spoke.

'The Shard,' he began. 'How many of your men will it take to guard it?'

'Well,' I began. 'That all depends on...'

'Never mind that,' he interrupted. 'I'll ask again. How many men of your men will it take guard The Shard.'

'Two hundred,' I said.

'Dogs?'

'Two border terriers,' I replied. 'I take them for a walk every morning.'

I thought I'd throw in a sense of humour test.

'Oh yes, very droll,' said the King. He then shot me a knowing glance.

'You're ex-forces, aren't you,' he said. 'Special forces?'

'Might have been. Not telling.'

'I've got friends who were special forces,' said the King.

'Have you now,' I replied. I think I had him.

'How would you guard my Bentley?' he said suddenly.

'I'd park my Bentley in front of it so nobody would nick it, that's how.'

'Very goooood,' said the man who was about to award me our biggest ever contract.

'Would you like to know anything else?' I asked.

'I think that'll be it for now,' he said. 'We'll be in touch.'

I went straight over to the pub after that and half an hour later he called me and confirmed that we'd got the contract. Get in there!

EIGHTEEN

They say that money doesn't buy you happiness and, on the whole, I'd agree with that. Over the years, I've met hundreds of people who've come into a few quid and many have become either miserable, greedy, or both. Actually, let's add have also become a complete and utter tosser to that list.

What money does buy you, however, is the opportunity to do a bit of good every now and then. In 2005 I was asked to get involved in something that has changed my life forever. Something that, save for the birth of my grandchildren, has provided me with more pleasure and pride than anything else on earth. Don't get me wrong. I'm proud of the fact that Theresa and I managed to create a successful business and I'm grateful for the life it's given us. None of it holds a torch to this, though.

The offer came about through a dear friend of ours called Emma, who was the deputy headmistress of a special needs school called Corbets Tey in Upminster. One day Emma asked me if I'd like to come and have a shufti. No offence to anyone who knows me, but I've always preferred dogs and children to adults and because of that – and because she'd told me so much about the place – I said I'd come along.

Like all special needs schools the work they do at Corbets Tey is incredibly important and my enthusiasm must have been obvious to Emma because after my visit she asked if I'd like to volunteer. I think they were also a bit short of male staff at the time, so the idea ticked more than a box.

Although I still owned Ultimate Security I was no longer involved day-to-day and had been made chairman. As well as being absolutely fucking knackered it had all become a bit corporate for my liking and that wasn't my cup of tea. I was ostensibly a small business owner who had created a monster and despite the success (we must have been turning over about £70 million at the time) I'd lost interest. Subsequently, I had rather a lot of time on my hands so the offer to spend some of it at Corbets Tey was a godsend.

At the end of my first day at the school I received my first official warning. Surprised? Of course not. I'd spotted some bullying in the playground and ended up saying to the three lads responsible that not only were they a bunch of fucking bullies but they were also cowards. Because of the language I'd used this had got back to the parents and at the end of the day Emma called me in for a quick word.

'You can't swear at the children, Martin,' she said.

'Even if they swear at me first?'

'Even if they swear at you first. We have to set an example.'

It was like being back at school!

I ended up staying at Corbets Tey for ten years and Rhian, my daughter, even went there as a teaching assistant. Rhian and I are similar in many ways (I often refer to her as me with tits) and she too fell in love with the place.

After a couple of years I was asked if I'd like to sit on the board of governors at the school and I agreed. The first image that came into my mind when they asked was me losing my temper as a parish councillor and pushing over that table. Then again, the only reason I'd lost my temper was because one of them had been obstructive, so providing they did as they were told there shouldn't be blood. Fortunately, we were all fairly like-minded so apart from the odd cross word – which usually began with the letter F – it was all tickety-boo.

One day at one of our meetings Emma suggested that we stage an opera at the school.

'OK,' I said. 'If we're going to do it, let's do it properly. Let's get a professional opera company in to help us stage it.'

After my fellow governors and I decided that this idea was a goer we ended up speaking to a company called English Touring Opera and they suggested putting it on at the Queen's Theatre, in Hornchurch. All the kids would be involved some way or another, but instead of it being done at the school or in a village hall it would be staged at a professional theatre.

The total cost for producing the opera was £28,000 and the body we hoped would fund it was the Parent–Teacher Association. Not a fucking chance! Despite the fact that it was going to be self-funding they still came back to us with a massive list of negatives. And, an emphatic no, of course.

After ripping up the list of negatives I wrote out a cheque for £38,000 there and then and told my fellow governors that if we didn't make the money back, they could keep it. As far as I was concerned staging an opera was a brilliant idea and I wasn't going to let anybody spoil it.

In the end that production made a total of £54,000, so instead of losing money or simply wiping its face like we'd hoped, it made a £16,000 profit. More importantly though, every single kid in that school had an absolute whale of a time. As well as working with English Touring Opera, a tremendous bunch of people, we asked some theatre and opera students to come in and mentor the pupils. One of these students, a young lady called Joanna Marie Skillett, has gone on to become a major recording artist and Theresa and I went to see her perform at the Royal Albert Hall. Joanna has since become a patron at Corbets Tey and has also gone into education.

This wasn't the aim of the exercise, but the performance of the opera, which was a complete sell-out, was probably the best night of my entire life. Every pupil who was able to do so took to the stage at some point during the performance and those who couldn't did something integral to the show. That was the only stipulation when I wrote out the cheque: that every pupil should be involved as much as possible. The pupils also wrote the lyrics to the opera, while English Touring Opera wrote the music. How amazing is that?

Had I known it was going to happen I'd have left five minutes early, but at the very end of the performance Emma invited me onto the stage. Then, in front of everybody, she thanked me for all my help. I don't mind admitting that I was in floods of fucking tears when she did that and as well as it being the best night of my life I'd also put it down as being my biggest achievement. In fact, if I had to be remembered for anything, apart from eating spiders or stapling my forehead or my lip to a desk, it would be working with those kids and helping that school to put on an opera.

The reason I eventually left Corbets Tey as a volunteer is because it was all getting a little bit physical for me. It's hard enough looking after my grandchildren these days, so the prospect of me handling a classroom of kids as I approached my sixties started to become quite daunting.

A few months before I left I was asked to volunteer in the sixth form for a while and, after ascertaining that the pupils were all a little bit overweight, I decided I was going to knock them into shape. In hindsight this was probably a bad idea. After all, me and a load of special needs kids out on the road – what could possibly go wrong? Even so, the school thought it was great so, after kitting them all out at a sports shop, I approached my local gym and asked them how they'd feel about having a few special needs kids coming in for a session once a week. Fortunately, they were fine with it and, as well as giving me a good rate, they also got some of their instructors involved, which meant that in some ways it was like the opera.

And in some ways it wasn't.

Unfortunately, only a very small minority of customers at the gym seemed to be comfortable training around the kids, but as opposed to simply avoiding them or even voicing their concerns to the management, many of them were just downright rude. If anything's going to summon up my red mist it's a fitness freak wearing a fake tan and a fake personality being cruel to a special needs kid. How I didn't commit mass murder in that fucking gym is beyond me. After spotting one of these bastards doing an impression of one of the kids one day – and not in a nice way – I decided that enough was enough. After waiting until this twat finished his workout I followed him into the changing rooms and, after asking the only other customer in there to fuck off, I set about teaching this arsehole a very important lesson in humility and compassion.

He was a bit taller than me, about 6 feet, and must have been about thirty years old. He also had a face that only a mother could possibly love and after walking to the toilets I saw him standing in front of a mirror. He'd obviously heard me telling the other Muscle Mary to fuck off and I could tell he was shitting himself.

'I saw what you did behind that kid's back,' I growled, blocking the exit.

'I don't know what you're talking about,' he said in a panic.

Because he was obviously as soft as fucking shit I decided to have some fun. I've often been described as being quite scary so after contorting my face a bit and then growling a couple of times I walked towards him as slowly and as menacingly as I possibly could. It may have been slightly theatrical – over the top, even – but it had the desired effect and by the time I reached this perma-tanned prick he was literally begging for mercy. I'd never had as much fun in a gym in my entire life and after hearing the changing-room door go I issued him a very quick but very earnest warning.

'If I ever see you being cruel to anybody ever again,' I said standing over him, 'I will break your fucking neck. Do you understand?'

'Yes,' whimpered the prick. 'I promise!'

Job done.

While I was working at the school a client of ours called Barry Rushmore asked if we'd give his daughter some work experience. Evie is her name and she has something called Chromosome 8p Deletion Syndrome, which is a rare disease that affects different parts of the body.

Had Barry asked prior to me working at the school I'd undoubtedly have said yes, but for different reasons. The whole experience of working with young people meant that I knew what the benefits might be to Evie joining us, so I was doing it because I wanted to, not because I thought I should. It's the difference between sympathy and empathy, I suppose. Although Evie didn't need my sympathy. Far from it.

During her initial three months with the company, Evie was made an ambassador for the charity that supports people with Chromosome 8p Deletion Syndrome and as part of her ambassadorship she organised a big fundraising bash in London. Without her knowing, Theresa and I organised a table at the event and invited all our family. Evie was flabbergasted when she saw us all and she made a brilliant speech. Later that evening, I got talking to Evie and she let slip that in addition to doing some work experience for us she was also working in a pub part-time.

'What the hell are you doing that for?' I asked her.

'I've only got three months' work experience with Ultimate, and that'll finish soon. I've got to do something.'

Because I wasn't at the company day-to-day I'd lost touch with things like that, but by the end of the evening I'd promised Evie that I would sort her out a year's contract.

'But you're not my boss,' she said.

'I am the owner though,' I countered, 'and if I say you've got a year's contract, you've got a year's contract.'

In truth, this could have got me into all kinds of trouble with the staff at Ultimate, as despite me being the owner I had no jurisdiction over who they hired and fired. Evie's a great girl, though, and I thought, *Balls to it*. If I ruffle a few feathers, so be it. Fortunately, the people running Ultimate were fine with what I'd done and I'm happy to report that, five years on, Evie's still at the company.

Speaking of which.

In 2015, I decided to sell Ultimate Security. Actually, I'd wanted to sell up about ten years before but after being completely dicked around by somebody I'd almost given up hope, of everything! This was actually the last time I thought about committing suicide. I'd thought about it before, like the time I was at school, the intention was far more real this time.

Ultimate Survivor

I won't go into detail but somebody had made an enquiry about buying by the company and a year later we were no nearer completing. Had it just been me and him involved it would have been fine, as in I'd have killed him, but it wasn't. There were dozens of people involved in the acquisition and, ultimately, and understandably, everybody had their own interests at heart. It got to a point where I couldn't take it anymore and so I decided I was going to drive my Range Rover into a wall. It almost sounds like I'm trivialising suicide but I promise you, I'm not. I talked earlier about all the different voices in my head and at this point in time there was just one, and that voice was saying, 'Die. Just fucking die.' I remember getting into the Range Rover and starting the engine and at that moment Sian called me. 'Are you alright Dad?' she asked. As much as I love her, and Theresa and Bryn and Rhian, the only reason I didn't go through with it is the effect it would have had on my granddaughter, Sophia. As somebody who was very badly abused as a child I'm more than aware of the confusion you experience when somebody who you think is supposed to love and protect you hurts you very badly and taking my own life would have made me no different to my father. I'm now lucky enough to have three grandchildren, Sophia, Jack and Maggie, which to me are three very good reasons to carry on living.

By 2015, we were the largest independent security company in Britain and were starting to get some serious acquisition enquiries.

People often ask me how the company became so successful and apart from my natural charm and ability, which is legendary throughout the security industry, and parts of Devon, the only thing I can think of is the way we treated our staff. Every other company seemed to adhere to the industry standards when it came to looking after their employees, which were always based on giving them the bare fucking minimum. It didn't take much to be different then.

On Christmas Day, for instance, either myself or my daughter, Sian, who was a director at Ultimate and who was in charge of our compliance, would visit every single site to wish our guards a Happy Christmas. And to hand out a few presents, of course. I can guarantee that none of our competitors did that. Absolutely no chance.

But as well as it simply being the right thing to do, I was sure that all the perks and extras we gave our members of staff – and the better wages – were worth more to us financially than recruiting and training new ones. It's simple when you think about it.

Something else that made us different was that, apart from Sian, my entire board of directors were second-chancers. What I mean by that is over the years they'd messed up in some way and had to work their way back up the company. I told you about the regional director who head-butted that bastard in Covent Garden? Well, he was one of them.

This certainly wasn't done by design, but I came to have what I believe to be the most loyal and proficient board of directors I could ever have wished for, and part of that was to do with how they got there. Without them the company would never have become as successful as it did, so I owe them all a big thank you.

I ended up selling Ultimate Security in 2016 to a South African company called Bidvest. My valuation, which was eight figures, was met, and, after wading through all the usual paperwork and what have you, the sale finally went through. Theresa and I kept three quarters of it, and the other quarter went to the members of staff who'd helped us make the company a success.

Since then Theresa and I have been dividing our time

between our home in Essex, which we bought about ten years ago, and our house in North Yorkshire, which we go to about once a month. Each morning I do the two-hour dog walk regardless of where we are (I don't even need a dog!), and if we're in Essex we'll usually spend some of our day with our granddaughter. I don't mind admitting that when she came along I was going through hell mentally and there were times when I could quite happily have ended it all. My brother, Tony, ended up committing suicide about thirty-five years ago and, although we were very different people, we obviously had certain things in common. Had Sophia not turned up when she did, I very much doubt I'd still be here, and that's no exaggeration. Male mental health is very topical at the moment and although I think that's a good thing, I'm far too long in the tooth to start lying on a couch, and unless they're keeping my ticker going or lowering my cholesterol, I'm not interested in pills.

The enquiring mind of a child has been the best therapy I could wish for. A child who calls me Grumps instead of Martin, has no interest in my past, and who bosses me around mercilessly.

Why is it the best therapy?

Well, that's easy.

First of all, I don't think I've ever really stopped being a child myself. Not at heart, at least, which is why I always gravitate towards children – and them to me. It's also a massive contrast to the life I've led and to the things I've been exposed to. It's pure, I suppose, and that's something that was always lacking in my own childhood and is something that fascinates me.

Yes, that little girl and Jack and Maggie are what keep me going these days.

That and the odd drink.

ACKNOWLEDGEMENTS

First of all I must praise Jamie Hogg, not only for having the skills to unearth secrets I had buried for over half a century, but for being there for me as a true friend. Thanks Jamie.

I would also like to thank my brother-in-law Ronnie, for help with the photos, and oldest friend, Dai. For as long as I've known Dai he has never judged me and for that – and for his unfaltering friendship – I will always be truly grateful.

As for many people, lockdown was a struggle at times, but it was made a lot easier and more enjoyable by our neighbours, the Caruthers family. The 'patio pub' we set up was an absolute life-saver! I am also grateful to Rhona, for our daily 'psychologicals' debate.

For many years Theresa and I have had a house in North Yorkshire and over the years we've met some amazing people. Most notably, Bruce and Rachel Tunstall and the Lambert family. You could not wish for better friends and they make a very special place even more so.

Moving overseas, I'd like to say thank you to

Ultimate Survivor

Pasquale and Jenny for introducing us to Sant'Agata on the Amalfi Coast. Sant'Agata and North Yorkshire are the only two places on earth where I get a good night's sleep and, just like Yorkshire, the people have been amazing. They are, Don Alfonso and the team at Don Alfonso's (I'm proud to call you family), Nino and his beautiful family who make our stay at Sant'Agata so wonderful and stress-free, Orlando and family at The Smoking Cat, who specialise in cheap cocktails and fantastic company, Peppe Il Buco (The Bear), Lucio, for looking after us from start to finish, and Ivan, Francesca, Georgia and Aldo at La Conca.

Mille Grazie one and all xx

Apologies to the dog for blowing his cover

Investigate all our other titles and
stay up to date with our latest releases at
www.scratchingshedpublishing.co.uk